NATIONAL ACADEMIES *Sciences Engineering Medicine*

NATIONAL ACADEMIES PRESS
Washington, DC

Artificial Intelligence and the Future of Work

Committee on Automation and the
U.S. Workforce: An Update

Computer Science and
Telecommunications Board

Division on Engineering and
Physical Sciences

Board on Human-Systems Integration

Division of Behavioral and
Social Sciences and Education

Consensus Study Report

NATIONAL ACADEMIES PRESS 500 Fifth Street, NW Washington, DC 20001

This activity was supported by grant number CNS-1937181 to the National Academy of Sciences from the National Science Foundation. Any opinions, findings, conclusions, or recommendations expressed in this publication do not necessarily reflect the views of any organization or agency that provided support for the project.

International Standard Book Number-13: 978-0-309-71714-4
International Standard Book Number-10: 0-309-71714-0
Digital Object Identifier: https://doi.org/10.17226/27644

This publication is available from the National Academies Press, 500 Fifth Street, NW, Keck 360, Washington, DC 20001; (800) 624-6242 or (202) 334-3313; http://www.nap.edu.

Copyright 2025 by the National Academy of Sciences. National Academies of Sciences, Engineering, and Medicine and National Academies Press and the graphical logos for each are all trademarks of the National Academy of Sciences. All rights reserved.

Printed in the United States of America.

Suggested citation: National Academies of Sciences, Engineering, and Medicine. 2025. *Artificial Intelligence and the Future of Work*. Washington, DC: National Academies Press. https://doi.org/10.17226/27644.

The **National Academy of Sciences** was established in 1863 by an Act of Congress, signed by President Lincoln, as a private, nongovernmental institution to advise the nation on issues related to science and technology. Members are elected by their peers for outstanding contributions to research. Dr. Marcia McNutt is president.

The **National Academy of Engineering** was established in 1964 under the charter of the National Academy of Sciences to bring the practices of engineering to advising the nation. Members are elected by their peers for extraordinary contributions to engineering. Dr. John L. Anderson is president.

The **National Academy of Medicine** (formerly the Institute of Medicine) was established in 1970 under the charter of the National Academy of Sciences to advise the nation on medical and health issues. Members are elected by their peers for distinguished contributions to medicine and health. Dr. Victor J. Dzau is president.

The three Academies work together as the **National Academies of Sciences, Engineering, and Medicine** to provide independent, objective analysis and advice to the nation and conduct other activities to solve complex problems and inform public policy decisions. The National Academies also encourage education and research, recognize outstanding contributions to knowledge, and increase public understanding in matters of science, engineering, and medicine.

Learn more about the National Academies of Sciences, Engineering, and Medicine at **www.nationalacademies.org**.

Consensus Study Reports published by the National Academies of Sciences, Engineering, and Medicine document the evidence-based consensus on the study's statement of task by an authoring committee of experts. Reports typically include findings, conclusions, and recommendations based on information gathered by the committee and the committee's deliberations. Each report has been subjected to a rigorous and independent peer-review process and it represents the position of the National Academies on the statement of task.

Proceedings published by the National Academies of Sciences, Engineering, and Medicine chronicle the presentations and discussions at a workshop, symposium, or other event convened by the National Academies. The statements and opinions contained in proceedings are those of the participants and are not endorsed by other participants, the planning committee, or the National Academies.

Rapid Expert Consultations published by the National Academies of Sciences, Engineering, and Medicine are authored by subject-matter experts on narrowly focused topics that can be supported by a body of evidence. The discussions contained in rapid expert consultations are considered those of the authors and do not contain policy recommendations. Rapid expert consultations are reviewed by the institution before release.

For information about other products and activities of the National Academies, please visit www.nationalacademies.org/about/whatwedo.

COMMITTEE ON AUTOMATION AND THE U.S. WORKFORCE: AN UPDATE

ERIK BRYNJOLFSSON, Stanford University, *Co-Chair*
TOM M. MITCHELL (NAE), Carnegie Mellon University, *Co-Chair*
DAVID H. AUTOR, Massachusetts Institute of Technology
JOHN C. HALTIWANGER, University of Maryland, College Park
ERIC HORVITZ (NAE), Microsoft Corporation
LAWRENCE F. KATZ (NAS), Harvard University
NELA RICHARDSON, ADP, Inc.
MICHAEL R. STRAIN, American Enterprise Institute
LAURA D. TYSON, University of California, Berkeley
MANUELA VELOSO (NAE), J.P. Morgan Chase AI Research

Study Staff

BRENDAN ROACH, Program Officer, Computer Science and Telecommunications Board (CSTB) (through December 31, 2023)
JON EISENBERG, Senior Board Director, CSTB
SHENAE BRADLEY, Administrative Coordinator, CSTB

NOTE: See Appendix D, Disclosure of Unavoidable Conflict of Interest.

COMPUTER SCIENCE AND TELECOMMUNICATIONS BOARD

LAURA M. HAAS (NAE), University of Massachusetts Amherst, *Chair*
DAVID DANKS, University of California, San Diego
CHARLES ISBELL, University of Wisconsin–Madison
ECE KAMAR, Microsoft Research Redmond
JAMES F. KUROSE (NAE), University of Massachusetts Amherst
DAVID LUEBKE, NVIDIA Corporation
DAWN C. MEYERRIECKS, The MITRE Corporation
WILLIAM L. SCHERLIS, Carnegie Mellon University
HENNING SCHULZRINNE, Columbia University
NAMBIRAJAN SESHADRI (NAE), University of California, San Diego
KENNETH E. WASHINGTON (NAE), Medtronic, Inc.

Staff

JON K. EISENBERG, Senior Board Director
SHENAE A. BRADLEY, Administrative Assistant
RENEE HAWKINS, Finance Business Partner (through May 8, 2024)
THƠ H. NGUYỄN, Senior Program Officer
GABRIELLE M. RISICA, Program Officer
AARYA SHRESTHA, Senior Financial Business Partner
NNEKA UDEAGBALA, Associate Program Officer

Reviewers

This Consensus Study Report was reviewed in draft form by individuals chosen for their diverse perspectives and technical expertise. The purpose of this independent review is to provide candid and critical comments that will assist the National Academies of Sciences, Engineering, and Medicine in making each published report as sound as possible and to ensure that it meets the institutional standards for quality, objectivity, evidence, and responsiveness to the study charge. The review comments and draft manuscript remain confidential to protect the integrity of the deliberative process.

We thank the following individuals for their review of this report:

KATHARINE G. ABRAHAM (NAS), University of Maryland, College Park
JACK CLARK, Anthropic PBC
ERICA R.H. FUCHS, Carnegie Mellon University
AVI GOLDFARB, University of Toronto
FARNAM JAHANIAN, Carnegie Mellon University
ANTON KORINEK, University of Virginia
ARVIND NARAYANAN, Princeton University
FRED OSWALD, Rice University
NIKOLAS ZOLAS, U.S. Census Bureau

Although the reviewers listed above provided many constructive comments and suggestions, they were not asked to endorse the conclusions or recommendations of this report nor did they see the final draft before its release. The review of this report was overseen by **DARON ACEMOGLU (NAS)**, Massachusetts Institute of Technology, and **ELSA M. GARMIRE (NAE)**, Dartmouth University. They were responsible for making certain that an independent examination of this report was carried out in accordance with the standards of the National Academies and that all review comments were carefully considered. Responsibility for the final content rests entirely with the authoring committee and the National Academies.

Contents

PREFACE — xi

SUMMARY — 1

1 INTRODUCTION — 15
Goals for This Report, 15
Why Is This Topic Important Now?, 16
How to Think About Artificial Intelligence and Its Impact on the Workforce, 18

2 ARTIFICIAL INTELLIGENCE — 21
Technical Progress in Artificial Intelligence, 25
Drivers of Technical Progress in Artificial Intelligence, 36
Final Observations, 39

3 ARTIFICIAL INTELLIGENCE AND PRODUCTIVITY — 41
Artificial Intelligence: A General-Purpose Technology, 44
Historical Changes in Productivity Growth, 45
Explanations for the Slowdown in Productivity Growth, 49
Effects of Artificial Intelligence on Productivity, 56
Productivity, Labor Markets, and Inequality, 80
Drivers, Barriers, and Risks of Artificial Intelligence Adoption, 82

4 ARTIFICIAL INTELLIGENCE AND THE WORKFORCE   **86**

    The Role of Technology in Eroding and Augmenting Demand for Expertise, 92

    Demand for Expertise in the Industrial Revolution, 98

    Demand for Expertise in the Computer Era Before Artificial Intelligence, 101

    Demand for Expertise in the Artificial Intelligence Era, 107

    Evidence on Artificial Intelligence and Expertise, 125

    How Feasible Will It Be for Workers to Acquire Newly Valuable Expertise?, 127

    Workforce Risks, 128

    Directions for Further Research, 131

5 ARTIFICIAL INTELLIGENCE AND EDUCATION   **133**

    Artificial Intelligence as an Input for Education, 135

    Implications of Likely Artificial Intelligence Impacts on the Labor Market for Education, 142

    Future Opportunities and Research Needs, 146

6 MEASUREMENT   **147**

    New Data Sources, 150

    Knowledge Gaps and Challenges, 156

    Addressing Knowledge Gaps, 158

7 CONCLUSION   **162**

    Findings, 162

    Opportunities to Influence How Artificial Intelligence Will Impact the Workforce, 169

    The Road Ahead, 176

APPENDIXES

A	Statement of Task	181
B	Presentations to the Committee	182
C	Committee Member Biographical Information	184

Preface

In 2017, the National Academies of Sciences, Engineering, and Medicine released the report *Information Technology and the U.S. Workforce: Where Are We and Where Do We Go from Here?* That report looked at the impacts of emerging information technologies, including artificial intelligence (AI), on the U.S. workforce and set forth a research agenda for better understanding these impacts. Since the report's publication, rapid developments in AI, including the emergence of large language models, have renewed interest from policy makers and the public alike in the implications of AI for the future of work.

The present study, requested in Section 5105 of the 2021 National Defense Authorization Act, builds on the 2017 report to provide an updated view of AI's implications for work and the workforce. The study reviews current knowledge about the workforce implications of AI and related technologies, including for economic productivity and growth, job stability, equity, and income inequality; identifies key open questions; and describes salient research opportunities and data needs. The full statement of task for the committee is provided in Appendix A.

The National Academies established the Committee on Automation and the U.S. Workforce: An Update (see Appendix C) to conduct the study. The committee met in person in March 2023 and met virtually nine times to receive briefings from experts and stakeholders (see

Appendix B), review relevant reports and technical literature, deliberate, and develop this report.

The committee would like to thank the National Science Foundation for its support of this study. Last, the committee would like to acknowledge the excellent assistance throughout the study of the following National Academies' staff: Brendan Roach, Shenae Bradley, and Jon Eisenberg.

Erik Brynjolfsson, *Co-Chair*
Tom M. Mitchell, *Co-Chair*
Committee on Automation and the U.S. Workforce: An Update

Summary

Interest in how advances in artificial intelligence (AI) will affect workers has been growing in recent years, especially with the rapid increase in capabilities and adoption of large language model (LLM)-based chatbots and other generative AI.

This report, requested in Section 5105 of the 2021 National Defense Authorization Act,[1] builds on a 2017 National Academies of Sciences, Engineering, and Medicine study[2] that examined the impacts of information technology on the workforce. It reviews current knowledge about the workforce implications of AI and related technologies, identifies key open questions, and describes salient research opportunities and data needs. The key findings are as follows:

Finding 1: AI is a general-purpose technology[3] that has recently undergone significant rapid progress. Still, there is a great deal of uncertainty about its future course, suggesting that wide error bands and a range of contingencies should be considered.

Finding 2: AI systems today remain imperfect in multiple ways. For example, LLMs can "hallucinate" incorrect answers to questions, exhibit biased behavior, and fail to reason correctly to reach conclusions from given facts.

---

[1] Public Law (P.L.) 116-283.
[2] National Academies of Sciences, Engineering, and Medicine, 2017, *Information Technology and the U.S. Workforce: Where Are We and Where Do We Go from Here?* The National Academies Press, https://doi.org/10.17226/24649.
[3] General-purpose technologies like the steam engine and electricity have widespread applications and were thus key drivers of economic growth. As discussed in more detail later, AI is advancing exceptionally rapidly, reflecting several key technical breakthroughs.

Finding 3: Significant further advances in AI technology are highly likely, but experts do not agree on the exact details and timing of likely advances.

Finding 4: The substantial and ongoing improvements in AI's capabilities, combined with its broad applicability to a large fraction of the cognitive tasks in the economy and its ability to spur complementary innovations, offer the promise of significant improvements in productivity.

Finding 5: As was the case with earlier general-purpose technologies, achieving the full benefits of AI will likely require complementary investments in new skills and new organizational processes and structures.

Finding 6: The labor market consequences of widespread AI deployment will depend both on the rate at which AI's capabilities evolve and on demographic, social, institutional, and political forces that are not technologically determined.

Finding 7: AI can be used to improve worker outcomes or to displace workers. Too often an exclusive focus on worker displacement neglects two other potentially positive labor market consequences of AI—new forms of work that demand valuable new expertise and AI systems that work jointly with workers to enable them to use their expertise more effectively to accomplish a broader variety of valuable tasks, perhaps with less formal training.

Finding 8: History suggests that even if AI yields significantly higher worker productivity, the productivity gains might fall unevenly across the workforce and might not be reflected in broad-based wage growth.

Finding 9: AI will have significant implications for education at all levels, from primary education, through college, through continuing education of the workforce. It will drive the demand for education in response to shifting job requirements, and the supply of education as AI provides opportunities to deliver education in new ways. It may also shift what is taught to the next generation to prepare them to take full advantage of future AI tools and advances.

Finding 10: Better measurement of how and when AI advancements affect the workforce is needed. To help workers adapt to a changing world, improving the ability to observe and communicate these changes—such as the impact of LLMs on knowledge work and robotics on physical work—as they occur is crucial.

Finding 11: Responses to concerns that AI poses potentially serious risks in areas such as fairness, bias, privacy, safety, national security, and civil discourse will modulate the rate and extent of impact on the workforce. It will take deep technical knowledge and may require new institutional forms for governments to stay abreast of and address these issues, given the rapidly changing technology.

ARTIFICIAL INTELLIGENCE

The year following ChatGPT's introduction in November 2022 marked a major inflection point for AI with the emergence of and widespread public access to generative AI, especially LLMs. These LLMs exhibit major new AI capabilities compared to earlier AI systems, including the ability to hold meaningful conversations about diverse topics in dozens of languages, summarize the key points discussed in large text documents, perform a variety of problem-solving tasks, and write computer programs.

This rapid rate of AI progress is likely to continue for some years, owing to expected large commercial and government investments to develop bigger and better models, the availability of increasingly diverse and ever larger data sets to train AI systems, progress in open-source efforts to develop more shareable and portable models, and a burst of effort by both start-ups and mature corporations to apply this technology to a wide range of applications. There are also forces that work to slow the rate of advance, such as the need to address shortcomings of this imperfect technology, the need for the technology to be socially acceptable and trusted by the public (e.g., to avoid implicit social biases or to avoid helping bad actors achieve harmful goals), potential government regulation, and decisions by companies to limit access to AI capabilities in light of these and other challenges, including privacy concerns.

Other areas of AI—including speech recognition; computer vision and other forms of computer perception; the application of machine learning to large, structured data sets; autonomous vehicles and robotics—are experiencing slower but continued technical progress. There is some possibility that future advances in LLMs and extensions such as multimodal foundation models trained on a combination of text, images, videos, voices, and sounds may spill over to accelerate progress in these areas as well, although this is not guaranteed.

There is great uncertainty regarding which specific AI capabilities will appear in the coming years and when. As a result, decision makers need to create policies that will be robust to a variety of possible future technology advances and timetables. Moreover, the capabilities developed and, more importantly, whether and how they are implemented will depend on society's collective choices.

ARTIFICIAL INTELLIGENCE AND PRODUCTIVITY

Productivity growth—growth in the amount of output per unit input—is crucial for improving long-term living standards. Advances in general-purpose technologies are key to enhancing productivity. Although AI is a general-purpose technology—that is, one that is pervasive, improves over time, and spawns complementary innovations—offering substantial productivity improvements in specific tasks and with the potential for impact in every economic sector, its overall impact on aggregate productivity remains minimal, potentially reflecting its low adoption rate across the economy thus far. However, given AI's wide applicability and the rate of its technical development, significant impacts on productivity are likely in the coming decade.

Improvements in productivity stem from finding more effective ways to use labor and other inputs. Technological progress, especially in the form of general-purpose technologies like AI, is the primary driver of long-term economic growth, influencing investment in physical capital and improving productivity. The productivity effects of AI, which can substitute and complement labor, depend on how AI affects different sectors and tasks.

Generative AI has already been found to increase productivity in specific applications including contact centers, software development, and writing. Of course, many other tasks are not suitable for AI, at least in its current form. Considering the set of tasks potentially affected and the factors on which productivity effects depend, AI has the potential to increase aggregate productivity growth substantially for the broader economy in the coming decade. Although it is notoriously difficult to predict the details of future impact, some estimates suggest as much as a doubling of the rate of growth in the U.S. gross domestic product (GDP) from about 1.4 percent currently to 3 percent. Moreover, generative AI's potential to accelerate scientific discovery and innovation could further compound productivity gains. However, tremendous uncertainty remains about the exact magnitude and timing of any productivity gains, and productivity could be hurt in some cases by increased fraud, misinformation, or other dangers.

Even if the productivity gains are large, there is no guarantee that these benefits will be distributed equitably. Without institutional and policy changes, the benefits might not be shared widely, potentially leading to job losses and wage disparities, increased inequality, and adverse effects on job quality and worker satisfaction. As productivity is not the only measure of human well-being, it is important to consider how AI might affect other aspects of human well-being, such as social progress and happiness as well as societal risks associated with AI. The latter includes threats to privacy, the potential for discrimination and bias, risks to democracy and political stability, and national security concerns—all of which will require attention by business leaders and policy makers.

ARTIFICIAL INTELLIGENCE AND THE WORKFORCE

Although there is widespread concern about the impacts of AI on jobs, at the time of this writing U.S. unemployment rates are very low compared to historical levels; apart from a spike in unemployment owing to the COVID-19 pandemic, they have been extremely low for the past several years. In addition, population and labor force growth rates in the United States and across the industrialized world are expected to decelerate. Against this backdrop of structurally strong demand for labor and structural headwinds impeding increases in labor supply, it is difficult to predict whether adoption of new AI will result in a decline in aggregate labor demand, manifesting in either fewer jobs (relative to working-age population) or, more likely, lower pay for existing work.[4] Additionally, adoption of recent AI advances in the workplace is still nascent and—despite recent improvements—measurement of AI's impacts is still limited, precluding a definitive assessment of the current impacts of AI on the workforce.

What is easier to predict is that adoption of AI will alter the nature of jobs—the set of tasks that define the job, and the share of these tasks that will be done by AI or in collaboration between human workers and AI tools. As a result, the key question is how AI will alter the demand for different types of worker expertise. ("Expertise" here refers to a specific body of knowledge or competency required to accomplish a particular objective—for example, baking bread, taking vital signs, or coding an app.)

New technology can erode the value of existing types of expertise (e.g., tax preparation software erodes the value of tax expertise) or create opportunities for jobs that require new kinds of expertise (e.g., computers create new jobs that require software engineering expertise). The creation of demand for new expertise is a critical force that counterbalances the tendency of new technology to erode the value of old expertise.

The future impact of AI on the demand for expertise is uncertain, but three plausible scenarios emerge. First, AI could accelerate occupational polarization, automating more nonroutine tasks and increasing the demand for elite expertise while displacing middle-skill workers. Second, AI might advance to outcompete humans across nearly all domains, greatly reducing the value of human labor and creating significant income distribution challenges. However, the committee believes that this scenario is unlikely in the near future owing to the limitations of AI, demographic trends, and the potential for new forms of work to emerge.

---

[4] Because most people are dependent on labor income for their livelihoods, a fall in earnings does not unambiguously imply a fall in employment; it is possible that more workers will work more hours to meet economic needs. Thus, earnings rather than employment are likely to be a better summary measure of labor demand.

Third, a more speculative scenario envisions a future in which the demand for expertise borrows attributes from both elite and mass expertise, leading to a reinstatement of the value of mass expertise in new domains. The creation of demand for novel human expertise that possesses market value and augments labor demand is a central attribute of the process of technological change but often is underemphasized compared to the countervailing force of automation. In the two major technological transitions preceding the AI revolution (from the artisanal era to the industrial era, and from the industrial era to the computer era), important categories of previously valuable human expertise were stranded—that is, made economically redundant—by new machines and novel forms of work organization. The value of artisanal skills was eroded by the rise of the factory system, and the value of skills in repetitive clerical and production tasks was eroded by computerization. Over the longer run, new forms of expertise gained value and catalyzed job creation, although often benefiting different workers from those who were displaced. Indeed, recent research estimates that more than 60 percent of current employment is found in occupational specialties that were not present in 1940. There is, however, substantial uncertainty about what types of new work will follow from the widespread use of AI, what skills it will require, what it will pay, how much of it there will be, and who will do it. But there is no question that AI will both strand some forms of human expertise and create demands for others.

The following questions are thus key to assessing the impact of AI advances on jobs:

- *What expertise will be substituted with or made obsolete by AI?* AI tools may soon equal or exceed human capabilities in a variety of tasks requiring elite expertise, such as digesting and summarizing large document collections; proofreading; writing certain business and legal documents; producing presentations and marketing materials, including charts, slides, and illustrations; and helping to manage complex systems such as computer networks and perhaps air traffic control systems. In such cases, AI is likely to substitute for human expertise, eroding the value of such expertise. Note that these types of expertise reflect knowledge work rather than physical work involving manipulating objects in the external world. At present, progress in robotics is slower than progress in AI that impacts the preceding types of knowledge work, but continued progress in robotics is anticipated in the longer term, over time substituting for routine and widely available physical expertise such as package delivery and food preparation in high-volume restaurants. The application of LLMs and other modern AI techniques may help speed up this progress.
- *What expertise will be augmented or newly demanded as a result of AI adoption?* The answer to this is even more uncertain than the answer to the previous

question. However, it appears likely that AI will be used in many (not all) cases to assist humans in performing tasks, thereby augmenting and complementing their expertise rather than substituting for it. For example, doctors are not expected to be replaced by medical diagnosis systems but rather to be assisted by them, resulting in an increase in the quality of decisions that will ultimately be made by the human doctor. Similarly, in many occupations AI tools will enable an increase in the quality of outcomes and the breadth of tasks human workers can undertake. For example, architects assisted by AI may be able to develop and evaluate a wider range of novel building designs. It is important to note that society has a choice in whether and where AI is used to augment human expertise versus substitute for it. Beyond augmenting existing types of human expertise, AI may lead to demand for new expertise as well. One broad possibility is that because AI will progress more rapidly in cognitive than physical applications, AI may raise the value of human dexterity and flexibility relative to cognitive capabilities. In this case, AI could prove more complementary to hands-on expertise, as seen in care work (including health care), the skilled trades, construction, and maintenance and repair. But this prediction presumes that AI capabilities in the cognitive realm substitute rather than complement labor in the cognitive domain and that the application of generative AI to robotics does not yield equally rapid progress.

- *How feasible will it be for workers to acquire newly valuable expertise?* Fortunately, this is a question over whose answer society has some control—one can choose whether to enrich the educational opportunities made available to the workforce and the degree to which governments subsidize the cost to workers of that retraining. Of course, the feasibility will depend on what types of expertise are newly required and the time and effort needed to acquire that expertise. Nevertheless, for many types of expertise, new training and certificate programs may provide a significant opportunity for governments to assist workers in adapting to the job disruptions likely to be produced from adoption of AI, while at the same time speeding its successful adoption and the attendant improvements to productivity and the GDP.

- *How will the organization of work and employer power dynamics evolve?* The consequences of previous technological transitions for the welfare of workers and the strength of the middle class have depended not only on the nature and application of technologies but also on the frameworks and legal institutions that have shaped their design, adoption, and use and the distribution of economic surplus among owners, managers, and line workers. The middle-class prosperity that accompanied the second industrial revolution is owed in part to the success of labor unions and supporting legislation in negotiating for higher pay, reasonable hours, safe working conditions, and employment security. In more recent decades, U.S. worker bargaining power has eroded as labor union representation has shrunk, employers have mobilized against worker organizing efforts, and labor markets have "fissured" as companies outsourced tasks and responsibilities.[5] Many rights and norms are increasingly contestable in the era of AI, including the definition and ownership of intellectual property, the right to privacy, and expectations about surveillance and coercive monitoring. The outcome for worker and societal welfare necessarily depends on the legal, regulatory, and bargaining regimes in place. Absent well-functioning institutions, the committee does not presume that market outcomes will be socially desirable ones.[6] AI can also have other types of impacts on workers' quality of life. For example, AI may be used to monitor worker activity and productivity: a potential tool to better link individual worker performance and compensation but also an enabler of surveillance that workers may find objectionable. For creative artists, AI raises a different set of issues. For example, if an AI system produces a song or movie in the voice, image, and style of a singer or actor, what compensation is that artist due? In short, AI adoption is likely to raise a variety of new questions about worker rights, privacy and surveillance, intellectual property, and more. Its impact is already far wider than simply shifting supply and demand for workers' expertise.

ARTIFICIAL INTELLIGENCE AND EDUCATION

Rising educational attainment in the workforce has played a key role in U.S. economic growth over the past 150 years, although large socioeconomic gaps in access to high-quality education over the past 50 years have contributed to rising income inequality. Access to high-quality primary and secondary education and to continuing education opportunities is likely to be a strong determinant of future U.S. economic growth.

Rapid advances in AI alter both the demand for and the supply of educational opportunities. As AI advances result in shifting skill demands for workers, access to

---

[5] D. Weil, 2014, *The Fissured Workplace: Why Work Became So Bad for So Many and What Can Be Done to Improve It*, Harvard University Press.

[6] This is a simple Coasean observation, not an indictment of markets per se: when the ownership of a property right (including the right to take or not take an action) is ill-defined, the market equilibrium set of actions involving the property right is likely to be inefficient because externalities in the exercise of this right will not be internalized. See R.H. Coase, 1960, "The Problem of Social Cost," *Journal of Law and Economics* 3(October):1–44.

continuing education will be key to enabling the workforce to adapt. At the same time, AI may play a key role in providing new online learning environments for primary, secondary, and continuing education, especially environments that can customize to the differing learning needs and learning styles of each individual student. Indeed, multiple AI-enhanced online learning systems are already in widespread use.

Recent advances in LLMs offer the potential to design much more flexible, natural, and adaptive computer-based teaching environments than those currently in use, largely owing to their natural language and reasoning capabilities. Although there is not yet proof that these new LLM-driven methods lead to better student learning outcomes, they exemplify the explosion of creative new work going into designing and experimenting with this new generation of AI teaching tools.

Although the impacts of AI on the labor market remain uncertain, AI is likely to shift the demand significantly for different types of worker expertise and to result in a large increase in demand for continuing education and retraining programs to help workers acquire the expertise needed to adapt to the changing jobs environment. Furthermore, online tools that can help workers understand which job advances are within reach given their current skills and existing courseware can be instrumental in giving agency to workers as they try to adapt. The use of AI to build systems to fulfill these needs holds significant promise.

MEASUREMENT

Given the great uncertainties in predicting exactly what technical advances in AI might occur in the near future and how these advances will impact demand for various types of expertise and workers, it is imperative to improve the observation and tracking of technical progress in AI, its adoption in practice, and its impacts on the workforce in near real time—and to share this information with the workforce.

Compared to 2017, when the prior National Academies' report was published, much more and better data are available to answer important questions about the impact of AI on the workforce. For example, the Census Bureau has created a new Annual Business Survey that includes questions about adoption of AI at the firm level, and this has been integrated with worker-level data housed by the Census Bureau. Furthermore, patent data from the U.S. Patent and Trademark Office have now been integrated into employer–employee data at the Census Bureau.

Private-sector data hold the potential to provide a much more real-time and large-scale picture of the state of job demand, skill supply, and salaries paid for different skill mixes, complementing the data collected by government agencies. For example,

LinkedIn holds a large real-time data set of résumés, ADP a large real-time data set of salaries paid, and Indeed.com a large real-time data set of job postings and salary offerings. Although companies such as LinkedIn and Lightcast make some statistical summaries of data available, challenges remain. Organizations are reluctant to share their detailed data owing to competitive concerns and privacy issues. Realizing the potential benefits of private-sector data will require new models for public–private data sharing, although the payoff in the ability to track and communicate changing skill demands to the workforce could be immense.

Many challenges remain in collecting and accessing the private data needed to ensure a clear picture of the state of AI adoption and of the corresponding changes in demand and supply of different worker skills. One challenge is to measure the complementary intangible capital investments and organizational restructuring that firms may undertake when adopting new technologies and that directly influence the workforce. Another is to modernize measures of productivity growth that were originally devised for goods-producing sectors such as manufacturing, to cover diverse productivity impacts of software tools. Yet another is to manage the different data schemas and formats used by different data sources.

A variety of steps can be taken to improve society's ability to track and respond in a timely fashion to the impacts of advanced technologies on the workforce. New legislation could allow government statistical agencies to share their business data more widely. Steps can be taken to create shared data schemas across different government agencies, enabling greater integration of data from different government sources. Privacy-enhancing technologies such as multiparty secure computation can be adopted to enable greater data sharing while preserving privacy and confidentiality. New approaches that tap into the vast real-time data sets held by private organizations, while protecting commercial and privacy interests, could produce a major improvement in the ability of workers and decision makers to observe the current state and direction of demand for different skills and to react appropriately.

FURTHER DATA COLLECTION AND RESEARCH INITIATIVES AND OTHER OPPORTUNITIES

As AI technology advances and is broadly adopted, there are numerous opportunities for industry, nonprofit institutions, worker organizations, academia, civil society, and government to influence the direction of this development.

Opportunities to Influence the Rates and Direction of the Development of Artificial Intelligence

1. Support basic research in AI, including explainability, alignment, and safety research. Basic research is likely to have social returns that exceed the private returns, and thus markets will tend to underinvest in it.

2. Support research into standards and guardrails that could promote the adoption of AI in business environments.

3. Incentivize and establish enabling standards and regulations to encourage sharing and transparency regarding the data used to train advanced AI models, enabling a level playing field where new companies can enter the market and contribute to progress.

4. Fund AI research toward specific applications deemed to be of high priority to society, such as education and training, health care, climate change, and national security, where there are large positive externalities. Markets measure private benefits, not positive externalities experienced by parties who are not part of the transaction, even when such benefits are large. There is a strong economic rationale for government policies to promote research and activities in sectors with large positive externalities.

5. Support initiatives such as the National AI Research Resource and the Microelectronics Commons that can provide hubs for evolving research models and provide computational resources and foster talent needed to keep U.S. universities vital players in the development of frontier AI methods. Universities play critical roles both in educating the next generation of AI and other talent and in driving frontier research in AI and its applications across many fields.

Opportunities to Speed and Share the Productivity Benefits of Artificial Intelligence

1. Invest in efforts by national statistical agencies and in public–private partnerships to collect and disseminate better data on AI adoption, AI's contribution to productivity growth, and the factors that contribute to variation in this contribution across sectors and firms.

2. Support research into the effectiveness of policies that could enable labor mobility among occupations, firms, and geographical locations and help workers take better advantage of new job opportunities.

3. Support research into areas that contribute to regulatory uncertainty—such as product liability, copyright, privacy, and bias—and that complicate efforts of decision makers to assess benefits and risks, speed adoption and implementation, and drive productivity gains.

4. Support research to identify and assess the potential for AI technologies to create new harms either inadvertently or through abuse and help policy makers understand and consider the associated trade-offs and work with the private sector to develop sensible guardrails.
5. Support research to understand the implications for market concentration in AI, such as winner-take-most dynamics, and options for maintaining a competitive marketplace while still enabling the benefits of scale and scope.
6. Increase efforts to identify which specific occupational tasks are affected by AI as well as which old and new skills and expertise will therefore be in greater or less demand.
7. Support AI research that speeds scientific discovery, which is a key contributor to productivity growth.

Opportunities to Influence the Balance Among Worker Augmentation, New Work Creation, and Labor-Displacing Automation

1. Support research on human-complementary AI and prioritize AI research that emphasizes improving quality through human–AI teaming.
2. Support research into best practices for fostering inclusive AI adoption within firms and organizations, including workers' representative organizations and other ways to strengthen worker voice in business decisions.
3. Support research into how the cost of capital and the cost of labor affect business decisions about AI adoption for automation and for augmentation.
4. Support research to explore how workers might be protected by the establishment of new norms or legal protections for the rights of individuals to control and be compensated for the use of their likenesses, their other personal attributes, and their creative works.
5. Increase AI expertise within the federal government to support effective investment, oversight, and regulation across all mission areas, including transportation, labor, health care, education, environmental protection, public safety, and national security.
6. Evaluate and certify the quality of purported human-complementary technology before adopting it for publicly funded programs in such areas as education and health care.

Opportunities to Understand the Implications of Artificial Intelligence for Education and Assist Workers with Retraining and Continuing Education

1. Support research on effective continuing education approaches, especially short-term programs that teach specific skills in high and growing demand—thereby helping foster workforce flexibility.
2. Support research on how AI, augmented reality, and other technologies can be used to improve education—in particular, the types of continuing education and retraining programs identified in the preceding item.
3. Support research into how standards and certification for training programs can help community colleges and other educational institutions more effectively signal graduates' skills to employers and improve the match of new graduates to in-demand job opportunities.
4. Support an appropriate organization to develop, maintain, and disseminate a "career roadmap" that would enable workers to understand the shifting demand for different types of skills and workers as well as the continuing education opportunities available to them to acquire high-demand skills that will advance their careers.
5. Support research into new education objectives for all levels of education, including K–12, in order to provide the current and next generation with the knowledge and skills needed to take full advantage of future AI capabilities.

Opportunities for More Exact and Timely Tracking of Artificial Intelligence's Impacts on the Workforce

1. Improve and expand existing data collection efforts by government agencies, including high-frequency, real-time tracking of the use of AI by businesses and workers and the impact on the workforce.
2. Create new public–private data partnerships in which privately held data about skills supply and demand and wages currently paid for these positions are shared, and in which data about continuing education opportunities and their link to getting a better job are collected—with current summaries of both made available to the workforce, supporting workers' efforts to improve their livelihoods.
3. Measure and mitigate disparate impact of new technologies on underrepresented groups or communities as well as the global impact of differences in AI adoption between high-income and low-income countries.
4. Measure and characterize the heterogeneity in patterns of AI adoption across economic sectors, across firms within sectors, and across geographical regions, along with heterogeneous impacts on productivity and the workforce.

5. Undertake scenario planning to allow workers, businesses, and policy makers to gain a better understanding of the wide range of plausible scenarios for future advances in AI, including radical improvements.

* * *

It is impossible to predict exactly the nature of the coming changes in AI and all of their effects on the economy and society. Accordingly, it makes sense to build in the ability for rapid data gathering and analysis to track these changes, and to build as flexible an approach as possible for reacting to the changes observed. In practice, this means increased capacity for research not only in AI but also in the social and behavioral sciences so that AI's implications can be better understood. It also means that rather than trying to predict any specific future path, society needs the flexibility to rapidly sense and respond to opportunities and challenges—and to be prepared for a variety of scenarios and possibilities. Most importantly, as AI becomes more capable, policy makers, business leaders, AI researchers, employers, and workers all have an opportunity to shape the future of the workplace and workforce in ways that are consistent with societal values and goals.

1

Introduction

GOALS FOR THIS REPORT

In 2017, the National Academies of Sciences, Engineering, and Medicine published a comprehensive report exploring the landscape of artificial intelligence (AI) and its implications for work and the workforce.[1] Since then, the effects of AI have expanded at an unprecedented rate, permeating various facets of daily life and significantly altering the workforce terrain. In light of this rapid evolution, the mandate for this follow-on report is clear: to assess the "current and future impact of artificial intelligence on the workforce of the United States across sectors."[2] This undertaking is not just an update but a reconceptualization, accounting for the leaps in technology and the consequent ripples throughout the labor market and wider economy.

The charge to the study committee was to focus specifically on the economic, productivity, and workforce dimensions of AI. It is important to acknowledge that AI's effects are by no means limited to these areas—it has profound implications for democracy, geopolitics, national security, scientific progress, and mental health, among others. Although these spheres are undoubtedly significant, they fall outside the scope of this report. Consequently, this report will concentrate on changes in the technology and capabilities of AI, its adoption and productivity effects, interactions between AI and the

---

[1] National Academies of Sciences, Engineering, and Medicine, 2017, *Information Technology and the U.S. Workforce: Where Are We and Where Do We Go from Here?* The National Academies Press, https://doi.org/10.17226/24649.

[2] 2021 National Defense Authorization Act, P.L. 116-283, section 5101.

workforce, the implications for education and skill requirements, and the measurement challenges and opportunities in various economic sectors.

WHY IS THIS TOPIC IMPORTANT NOW?

Today, the speed of technological progress is reshaping not just the tools but also the fabric of the workforce and societal structures. AI has emerged as a general-purpose technology with sweeping implications that demand immediate attention and thoughtful analysis. AI stands out among general-purpose technologies owing to its core attribute—a focus on intelligence. This arguably makes it the most general of all general-purpose technologies.

The progression of AI has reached an inflection point with the rise of foundation models such as large language models (LLMs) and multimodal systems, which have begun to be integrated rapidly with a multitude of other technological tools, augmenting their capabilities and applications across industries. The capabilities of these systems have sparked not just excitement but also genuine surprise, leading to their emergent and swift adoption across various sectors.

Although AI has garnered more than its share of hype, the enthusiasm surrounding AI is not misplaced, nor is it purely conjectural. Policy makers, executives, and industry leaders are rightfully eager to understand these advances, as the implications are multifaceted, impacting productivity, the workforce, education, and society at large. The transformative effects can be seen in multiple domains: software development has already witnessed dramatic productivity gains, and the work of paralegals, customer service agents, and others who summarize documents is already being reshaped by AI. Textual monologues are evolving into interactive dialogues; for example, a book might soon serve as a conversational tutor powered by a sophisticated LLM, providing a new avenue to just-in-time, personalized training for the workforce. Entertainment, finance, health care, education, retail, manufacturing, transportation, and many other industries are poised for transformation. These are but a few instances in the litany of ongoing changes propelled by AI.

In contemplating what the future holds, one must approach predictions with humility, acknowledging the lessons of the recent past. The 2017 report did not grasp the full trajectory of AI's progress—for instance, emergence and adoption of LLMs outpaced expectations, while the road to fully autonomous vehicles has proved lengthier than anticipated. Although it is easy to overestimate the impact of new technologies in the short term and underestimate it in the long term,[3] AI is sure to continue to advance and catalyze change; what remains uncertain is the precise nature and timing of these capabilities.

The magnitude of AI's impact should be distinguished from the immediacy of that impact. Most general-purpose technologies have historically taken considerable time to integrate fully into society, often owing to the need for intangible complements such as new skills, altered business processes, and co-invention. AI, however, is displaying characteristics that suggest a more accelerated trajectory. The uptake of products like ChatGPT, which soared to reach 100 million users in mere months,[4] suggests an appetite and readiness for rapid adoption comparable to or greater than that for smartphones, which now connect more than two-thirds of the global population.

This swift integration of AI is facilitated by its connectivity to platforms, application programming interfaces, and the cloud, alongside plugins that incorporate capabilities of complementary software and overarching software architectures such as LangChain and AutoGPT that employ LLMs as subroutines. It is becoming increasingly clear that AI, much like the Internet, is not simply a tool but also a platform upon which numerous other innovations can be built, adopted, and diffused at a remarkable pace.

The trajectories that AI-enabled futures might take can lead to outcomes of profound benefit or significant disruption. The goal of this report is thus twofold: to responsibly inform about the current state and capabilities of AI as they relate to the workforce and to offer insights that prepare us for the challenges ahead and opportunities that will arise. It also considers how AI is likely to augment human labor, reshape job markets, and influence workforce dynamics.

The future is not preordained; individuals, businesses, nonprofits, colleges and universities, civil society institutions, and government influence it by the choices they make every day, large and small. This moment presents the opportunity to ensure that the awakening of AI augments collective capabilities, enhances human well-being, and constructs a future workforce that is resilient, adaptive, and equipped to meet the challenges of the 21st century.

---

[3] This observation is often attributed to Roy Amara. See S. Ratcliffe, ed., 2016, "Roy Amara 1925–2007, American Futurologist," *Oxford Essential Quotations*, Vol. 1 (4th ed.), Oxford University Press, https://doi.org/10.1093/acref/9780191826719.001.0001.

[4] J. Porter, 2023, "ChatGPT Continues to Be One of the Fastest-Growing Services Ever," *The Verge*, November 6, https://www.theverge.com/2023/11/6/23948386/chatgpt-active-user-count-openai-developer-conference.

HOW TO THINK ABOUT ARTIFICIAL INTELLIGENCE AND ITS IMPACT ON THE WORKFORCE

It is helpful to begin by considering the question of how to think about AI and its future impact on the workforce. Drawing on presentations to the committee (see Appendix B), the study committee formed a set of key assumptions for how to think about AI and the workforce. These assumptions, which also help motivate the committee's formulation of the topics examined in this report, are as follows:

- *AI technology is at an inflection point where recent advances promise to have significant impacts on many parts of the workforce.* Technical progress in AI is currently largely driven by recent progress in LLMs such as those that underlie ChatGPT, which was introduced in November 2022. Unlike earlier AI systems, LLMs show novel abilities—for example, to write useful computer software, to pass a variety of graduate exams, and to communicate fluently in many languages. Although today's AI systems still remain imperfect in many ways (e.g., they can "hallucinate" incorrect answers to factual questions, and they can exhibit biases), many AI experts expect this accelerated rate of progress to continue for some time. Chapter 2 examines the current state of AI, including LLMs; where AI might be headed; and factors that could accelerate and decelerate the current rate of progress.
- *Productivity growth is mainly driven by improved technology.* Productivity growth, the increase in the amount of output per unit input, is the key to higher living standards. It is mainly a function of improved technologies, especially general-purpose technologies, that affect many sections of the economy, improve rapidly, and catalyze complementary innovations. AI, which seeks to augment intelligence itself, has all the characteristics of an important general-purpose technology.
- *Jobs can be thought of as bundles of tasks.* One way AI will tend to impact jobs is through its impacts on individual tasks. For example, the job of a physician includes tasks such as (a) diagnosing the patient, (b) generating potential therapies given the diagnosis, and (c) having a conversation with the patient to explain therapy options and jointly choose the way forward. Any given AI system might impact one of these tasks without an equally significant impact on other tasks—for example, an AI system to suggest likely diagnoses might primarily impact the first of these tasks. The impact of AI will not be limited, however, solely to replacement or augmentation of tasks within existing occupations. Widespread adoption of AI may, for example, catalyze fundamental

changes in the structure of jobs and industries, as occurred during the transition from the artisanal to the industrial eras, when many forms of home-based production were ultimately displaced by the factory system. Major transitions of this sort are disruptive to careers and livelihoods. Even if the longer-term consequences are favorable, the transition is likely to be economically (and perhaps societally) destabilizing. Evidence suggests that it took at least five decades for working-class wages to begin rising again after the advent of the Industrial Revolution.[5]

- *AI can affect a work task either by automating it to replace a worker or by assisting the worker in performing the task.* Which of these occurs is at least partly a design choice, not a preordained outcome. For example, an AI system to analyze medical radiological images might be used to replace a human at this task; alternatively, it might be used to provide a second opinion to the human who remains responsible for the final decision. Businesses and governments can make choices that will influence which of these future outcomes occurs.

- *AI improvements to productivity can result in either a decrease or an increase in total employment, depending on economic factors.* As worker productivity increases, certainly fewer workers will be needed to produce the same total output, regardless of whether the improved productivity comes from replacing or assisting workers. However, this does not imply that employment will decrease. It is also possible that improved productivity will lead businesses to decrease prices, resulting in increased demand, which may be large enough to require hiring additional employees despite the increase in productivity per unit output. For example, when jet engines replaced propellers in airplanes, pilot productivity (passenger miles flown per hour of pilot work) increased significantly. However, the result was an overall increase in the number of pilots employed, owing to the resulting increase in demand for airline flights. What is more, AI can lead to the creation of new products and services, which in turn increase overall employment. In general, the impact of AI productivity improvements on overall demand for workers involves a complex interaction among a variety of supply, demand, and price elasticities. Chapter 3 examines the relationships among productivity, AI, and economic growth.

- *Because AI involves automating and augmenting expertise, it is useful to analyze its impact in terms of what types of human expertise it makes more and less valuable.* For example, the adoption of computers over the past decades for

---

[5] J. Mokyr, C. Vickers, and N.L. Ziebarth, 2015, "The History of Technological Anxiety and the Future of Economic Growth: Is This Time Different?" *Journal of Economic Perspectives* 29(3):31–50. Mokyr was, in turn, drawing on D. Bythell, 1969, *The Handloom Weavers: A Study in the English Cotton Industry During the Industrial Revolution*, Cambridge University Press.

non-AI tasks such as e-mail and office work has led to devaluing expertise at carrying out many middle-skilled, routine-intensive office tasks, while increasing the value of the types of expertise associated with advanced graduate degrees. Given the very different profile of recently developed AI capabilities (e.g., the ability to pass the verbal and quantitative reasoning sections of the Graduate Record Examination used for graduate school admissions), what will be AI's influence on future demand and supply for various types of human expertise? Chapter 4 examines potential AI impacts on the workforce in terms of the types of human expertise that might become in greater or lesser demand.

- *Given the shifting nature of jobs created by the impact of AI, it is important to consider how to adapt approaches to education.* During this time of great change, many workers will find continuing education and just-in-time training to be useful in improving their job prospects. A new generation of K–12 students and post-secondary students graduating into the workforce may require a different set of skills and training. This raises the questions of what content should be taught, when in a person's career to teach it (i.e., K–12, college, continuing education), and how to teach (e.g., how can AI lead to improved educational services). Chapter 5 considers what should be taught to whom as well as the potential of AI systems to provide new modes of personally customized education.

- *Given the great uncertainties, both about exactly what AI technical advances might occur in the near future and about how they will impact demand for various types of expertise and workers, it is imperative to improve the tracking of technical progress in AI, its adoption in practice, and its workforce impacts in near real time—and to share this information with the workforce.* AI technology is undergoing rapid and difficult-to-predict changes, but these changes are very likely to impact the workforce. A conclusion is that it is possible to help the workforce adapt by better understanding and sharing the changes that are actually occurring in real time over the coming months and years. Chapter 6 considers how to measure AI's progress and impacts, what kinds of data are already being collected, and the opportunities to collect additional data (including from public–private partnerships) to produce a much more informed picture of the evolving state of AI, jobs, and the workforce.

2

Artificial Intelligence

This chapter describes the technical field of artificial intelligence (AI), including significant recent progress that is likely to impact the workforce. AI is the part of computer science that focuses on producing computer capabilities similar to those usually associated with human intelligence, such as computer vision, speech recognition, natural language understanding, commonsense reasoning, and robots capable of autonomous operation in the physical world. The term "artificial intelligence" was first used 1955, and research in AI has produced steady progress for decades. In early years, researchers attempted to write computer programs manually to perform tasks such as computer vision, speech recognition, and several types of problem solving. In recent decades, the paradigm for developing AI systems has shifted from one of manual programming to machine learning in which programs are instead *trained* to perform tasks.[1] For example, it is extremely difficult to program a computer manually to recognize different types of animals in photos, but with today's technology it is relatively easy to use machine learning to train such a program by showing it images of different animals, each labeled with the type of animal present. Between 2005 and 2018, this paradigm shift toward training AI programs rather than manually developing them resulted in major advances and new commercial applications with near-human abilities in fields from image classification to speech recognition.

More than a decade ago, machine learning capabilities began to accelerate dramatically with a discovery of the power of methods based on neural networks when

---

[1] E. Brynjolfsson and T. Mitchell, 2017, "What Can Machine Learning Do? Workforce Implications," *Science* 358:1530–1534, https://doi.org/10.1126/science.aap8062.

supplied with sufficient data and computational resources. Machine learning models referred to as deep neural networks were first applied to numerous pattern recognition and prediction tasks such as speech recognition and medical diagnosis from imagery in dermatology and radiology. The methods showed remarkable abilities and began to show human parity on numerous benchmarks.

Over the past 5 years, between 2018 and 2023, AI has experienced a major new surge of progress resulting in AI systems with truly remarkable capabilities in comparison to what existed in 2018. This advance was due in large part to new innovations in neural networks (e.g., the adoption of a family of neural networks known as "transformers"), and a shift from training AI systems using *human-labeled* data to instead using *unlabeled* text, often from the web, allowing vastly larger sets of training data.[2] As a result, the development of AI technology, and its impact on the economy and the workforce, is approaching an inflection point. Much of this recent AI progress is owing to the development of large language models (LLMs) such as OpenAI's ChatGPT, which exhibits abilities to generate text responses to human prompts significantly beyond those of earlier AI systems. For example, ChatGPT can hold conversations in multiple languages about diverse topics, automatically summarize the key points discussed in large text documents, perform a variety of problem-solving tasks, write computer programs, and pass the Advanced Placement (AP) exams in statistics and in biology with scores above the 80th percentile compared to advanced high school students who take these tests. LLMs are one type of generative AI—that is, AI systems capable of generating text, images, or other content based on input user requests.

In parallel with the development of LLMs, AI programs that can generate realistic images from input text descriptions (e.g., "a falcon landing on a camel in an oasis"), realistic sounding voices speaking messages that are input as text, and computer programs that implement some tasks described by text input have also emerged and demonstrated significant progress in recent years. Together, these generative AI models trained on very large data sets and then used to support a variety of tasks are often referred to as "foundation models," owing to their ability to repurpose and focus on numerous specialized tasks through methods for shaping them to perform better in specific domains with modest amounts of additional engineering investment. For example, methods have been developed, referred to as fine-tuning, that apply domain-specific data to boost the performance of a foundation model for tasks within a target domain.

---

[2] Producing large training data sets with human-labeled examples is very costly, whereas unlabeled text is freely available on the Internet. For example, creating the ImageNet training data containing 1 million hand-labeled images was a very significant undertaking and led to major advances in computer vision in the early 2010s. In contrast, recent LLMs such as ChatGPT have been trained on roughly 1 trillion sequences of text from the Internet—a data set roughly 1 million times the size of the human-labeled ImageNet data set.

These dramatic advances in generative AI come along with continuing solid progress in other subareas of AI, such as robotics, where, for example, self-driving vehicles are now being tested in multiple U.S. cities, and in the application of machine learning to very large nontextual data sets, leading to advances, for example, in molecular biology and protein folding.

This rapid rate of technical progress in AI is likely to continue in the near term, as companies and governments direct increasing resources into AI research and development, although AI technical experts agree that there is considerable uncertainty about precisely which new capabilities are likely to emerge over the coming years and exactly when they might occur. Already there is much new research directed toward building more powerful LLMs (e.g., systems that will work with video streams in addition to text) and finding new ways of using them (e.g., connecting LLMs to computer programs such as search engines, math calculators, and route planners). The latter includes rich multi-step analyses that enable arbitrary files, such as spreadsheets and technical papers, to be input as context, and that assist users with multiple scientific analyses and visualizations. Signs of the economic impact are already visible—for example, Microsoft's GitHub Copilot is a system that improves productivity of computer programmers by acting as a programming assistant, automatically generating software from text descriptions of what the code should do. In one test, programmers who used Copilot developed software in about half the time required by programmers who did not.[3] Beyond productivity, qualitative studies of job satisfaction have demonstrated that tools for assisting engineers are boosting job satisfaction.

Note that Copilot is an example of how AI tools can *assist* human workers rather than *replace* them. Of course, if programmers were to become twice as productive and the volume of programming work were to remain constant, only half as many programmers would be needed. However, as discussed in Chapter 1, the situation is more complex than such a simple replacement model would suggest. The total demand for programming work may well increase if increased productivity leads to lower costs per unit of software produced. Whether increased programmer productivity will result in a need for more or fewer programmers depends also on the elasticity in the demand for software. As in many cases, it is easier to predict which tasks AI might assist or automate than it is to predict AI's final impact on the total demand for labor.

As will be discussed in Chapter 4, although broad forecasts of AI's effects on total labor demand are eagerly sought by both the public and the press, they are highly speculative, with a generally poor historical track record. One might have anticipated, for example, that the advent of accounting, bookkeeping, payroll, and tax preparation

---

[3] S. Peng, E. Kalliamvakou, P. Cihon, and M. Demirer, 2023, "The Impact of AI on Developer Productivity: Evidence from GitHub Copilot," arXiv preprint, arXiv:2302.06590.

software over the past several decades would have eroded employment in accounting, bookkeeping, payroll, and tax preparation services. Indeed, this erosion was confidently predicted by a highly impactful academic study.[4] Instead, U.S. employment in this occupational category doubled from 0.6 million to 1.2 million between 1990 and 2024, which is more than twice the growth rate of overall nonfarm employment.[5] The most relevant concern for present and future workers is not whether AI will eliminate jobs in net but how it will shape the labor market value of expertise—specifically, whether it will augment the value of the skills and expertise that workers possess (or will acquire) or will instead erode that value by providing cheaper machine substitutes. The answers to such questions are rarely self-evident.

Beyond this point, it might well turn out that the very definition of the job of programming might be changed by systems such as Copilot. Perhaps future programmers working with systems such as Copilot will spend less time writing low-level code and more time designing the higher-level software architecture and functionality, resulting in a shift in required skills for the job and an advancement in the sophistication of artifacts programmers produce.

One interesting property of the new LLM generation of AI is that in contrast to robotics, which involves work in the physical world, LLMs operate in the cognitive world of knowledge work. Furthermore, because LLMs are able to process and then summarize large volumes of text, one of their uses involves advising human decision makers by summarizing information in relevant documents that the decision maker might not have time to read fully. Likewise, the summarization abilities, coupled with now common powers of meeting transcription, enable people to absorb the content from meetings that they cannot attend, freeing them to develop and create. In this role of summarizing and advising, LLMs might operate as assistants to improve the quality of human decision making, although there may well be other cases where LLMs become sufficiently capable that one can trust them to make some decisions themselves. The threshold for entrusting AI to make the decisions in different use cases, as well as the evolving competence of AI systems, will play a key role in determining where AI replaces, versus assists, human decision makers.

Although recent AI progress has been impressive, it is important to note that these new AI systems are still far from perfect. Technical advancements are needed along multiple dimensions. For example, generative models may generate inaccurate yet persuasive output without warning—a problem with reliability sometimes referred to as "hallucination." The incorrect statements can come amid multiple accurate statements

---

[4] C.B. Frey and M.A. Osborne, 2017, "The Future of Employment: How Susceptible Are Jobs to Computerisation?" *Technological Forecasting and Social Change* 114:254–280.

[5] On employment in accounting, tax preparation, bookkeeping, and payroll services, see https://fred.stlouisfed.org/graph/?g=1oMKn. On nonfarm employment, see https://fred.stlouisfed.org/graph/?g=1oMKB.

and be offered in a highly confident manner. This problem with reliable output and difficulties with detection of inaccuracies limit the general use of LLM systems in high-stakes decision making such as direct uses in clinical decision support in health care. Furthermore, LLMs' reasoning and problem-solving abilities are incomplete, and they sometimes fail to draw correct logical conclusions given a collection of input facts. Acceptance of these systems in the workforce will require in many cases that the systems be endowed with the ability to provide well-calibrated confidences and be able to justify or explain their conclusions more correctly. Other challenges limiting their uses include concerns about bias and fairness; caution and testing are required before introducing these systems into society. It is clear that these issues will be critical to widespread adoption. Several AI researchers have published papers documenting these and other shortcomings of today's AI systems,[6] and some have pointed out flaws in benchmark data sets used to evaluate AI system capabilities (e.g., questions used to test AI capabilities might occur nearly verbatim in the vast collection of web text that forms their training data, casting doubt on the use of these questions to measure AI capabilities to reason about novel situations). Despite these real shortcomings in today's AI systems, recent technical progress does in fact constitute a very significant qualitative advance in AI capabilities. Shortcomings such as hallucinations and biases are being addressed and reduced (although not eliminated) in more recent systems, and additional technical advances over the coming years appear likely to reduce these shortcomings further while adding significant new capabilities.

TECHNICAL PROGRESS IN ARTIFICIAL INTELLIGENCE

This section provides a summary of recent advances in AI across multiple areas. Parts of this section are based on the 2023 paper by Bubeck and colleagues, titled "Sparks of Artificial General Intelligence: Early Experiments with GPT-4."[7]

Large Language Models

The greatest advances in AI over the past decade have come from advances in neural networks, and the greatest advances in neural networks over the past few years have come from LLMs, such as OpenAI's GPT-4, Google's PaLM, and Meta's LLaMA.

---

[6] M. Mitchell, 2023, "How Do We Know How Smart AI Systems Are," *Science* 381(6654), https://doi.org/10.1126/science.adj5957.

[7] S. Bubeck, V. Chandrasekaran, R. Eldan, et al., 2023, "Sparks of Artificial General Intelligence: Early Experiments with GPT-4," arXiv preprint, arXiv:2303.12712.

A neural network is a network of interconnected computational units, each of whose exact operation is determined by a number of learned numerical parameter values. These learned parameter values are determined by training the neural network on a set of examples, each of which provides an input to the network, and the desired output for that input. For example, to classify images of different skin blemishes as cancerous or noncancerous, a neural network was trained on more than 100,000 images of blemishes, each labeled as cancerous or noncancerous (and if cancerous, the type of cancer).[8] During this training process, the numerical parameter values of each computational unit throughout the network are chosen by attempting to best fit these training data (e.g., attempting to produce the desired network output for each input image). Many practical neural networks contain millions of such numerical parameters. In general, training neural networks is very costly, as it requires iteratively tuning and retuning these parameter values. However, once the network is trained, it is much less costly to apply it to a new input example to calculate the corresponding output.

An LLM is a neural network trained to take as input a sequence of text tokens (words, numbers, punctuation) and to predict the next text token. Nearly all of today's state-of-the-art LLMs use a particular neural network graph structure called the "transformer architecture," which was first introduced in 2017 by researchers at Google.[9] Following the introduction of the transformer architecture, progress in building increasingly capable LLMs has been rapid. Such LLMs are then used as the basis for systems such as ChatGPT (itself based on an LLM called GPT-4), which can conduct conversations with human users by applying next-word prediction repeatedly in order to generate the software's portion of the conversation.

Although it sounds relatively uninteresting to train a computer to predict the next word in a sentence, LLMs trained with this objective have been found to exhibit surprising capabilities, including capabilities that had not been achieved previously by AI systems. For example, these systems can perform tasks such as

- Produce highly grammatical sentences as output;
- Operate across hundreds of different natural languages;
- Given multipage input documents, summarize these documents, and answer questions about their content;
- Write working computer programs in several computer languages;
- Solve many math word problems;

---

[8] A. Esteva, B. Kuprel, R. Novoa, et al., 2017, "Dermatologist-Level Classification of Skin Cancer with Deep Neural Networks," *Nature* 542:115–118, https://doi.org/10.1038/nature21056.

[9] A. Vaswani, N. Shazeer, N. Parmar, et al., 2017, "Attention Is All You Need," *Advances in Neural Information Processing Systems* 30.

- Write poetry; and
- Suggest plans to achieve the user's input goals.

To appreciate the kinds of capabilities of LLMs, consider one of the most capable LLMs as of July 2023, GPT-4, drawing on examples from Bubeck and colleagues.[10] Figure 2-1 illustrates some of the diverse tasks that GPT-4 is capable of performing. Notice in the top left of the figure that GPT-4 responds to the prompt "Can you write a proof that there are infinitely many primes, with every line that rhymes?" by writing the proof as a poem. This kind of behavior far outstrips the state of AI from 5 years earlier. One caveat here is that it is likely that a proof of this theorem was included somewhere in the vast set of Internet data used to train GPT-4, although it is highly unlikely that it included the proof written as a poem. The top right of this figure illustrates GPT-4's ability to draw crude illustrations by writing code in the popular text-formatting language LaTeX. The third example in the figure demonstrates that GPT-4 can create computer code in the popular Python programming language, following complex natural language instructions specifying precisely what the code should do. (In this case, it must display data in a desired form.) At the bottom of this figure, the final example shows the ability of GPT-4 to perform mathematical reasoning, both generating the correct answer and explaining its reasoning steps.

Figure 2-2 provides a further example of the abilities of GPT-4—in this case, reasoning about the physical world. Here, GPT-4 is given the challenging task of determining how to create a stable stack from an unusual collection of objects. As its response illustrates, it answers correctly and somewhat creatively. It is interesting that here it is able to answer correctly about how to assemble this physical structure despite the fact that it has been trained only on data from the Internet and has no direct experience stacking items.

How can such capabilities arise from a system trained simply to predict the next word? Although researchers are still trying to understand the full answer, it is in part owing to the scale of training data used and the form of the neural network trained. These models have been trained on hundreds of billions of words of text taken from the Internet and use transformer networks that contain hundreds of billions of numerical parameters whose values are learned, or tuned, during training to fit these large-scale text data. Specifically, the LLM is trained, for each text snippet, to predict the next token in the sequence. It appears that by forcing the learned network parameters to perform this next-word prediction very well, for hundreds of billions of examples, the network is also forced to learn how to represent the meaning of the input text very well, so that the correct next word can be predicted across a diverse range of possible input sequences.

---

[10] S. Bubeck, V. Chandrasekaran, R. Eldan, et al., 2023, "Sparks of Artificial General Intelligence: Early Experiments with GPT-4," arXiv preprint, arXiv:2303.12712.

GPT-4

Prompt: Can you write a proof that there are infinitely many primes, with every line that rhymes?

GPT-4:

```
Yes, I think I can,
Though it might take a clever plan.
I'll start by noting Euclid's proof,
Which shows that primes aren't just aloof.
Assume we have a finite list,
Of primes, and that none have been missed.
Multiply them all together,
And add one, just to be clever.
The result will be a number,
That has no prime factors, oh wonder!
But every number has a prime,
That divides it, it's just a matter of time.
So we've found a contradiction,
And our finite list needs eviction.
There must be infinitely many primes,
And that's the end of my rhyming lines.s
```

Prompt: Draw a unicorn in TiKZ.

GPT-4: [Produces LaTeX compiling to following picture.]

Prompt: Can you generate a pyplot for the following data: $x = [1, 3, 5, 6, 8], y1 = [2, 3, 5, 18, 1], y2 = [3, 5, 6, 8, 1], y3 = [5, 1, 2, 3, 4], y4 = [9, 7, 2, 3, 1]$. I want $y1, y2$ to be in the same plot, but $y3$ is in another plot next to that plot, $y4$ is in below. I want the legend of $y1$ to be "bob", $y2$ to be "alice", $y3$ to be "bilbo", $y4$ to be "allie". I want the x-axis to be labeled with "time" and y axis to be labeled with "money". I want to add a 10 %-40% random error bar to each curve, through all times (including non-integers). I want smoothed curves to show the plot, and smoothed error bar. Do not use linear interpolation, use smooth interpolation! I want to also add some small zig-zag to the smoothed curve to make it look more real. I want to put a baseline as the mean of each line. I want to put a pie chart below indicating the fraction of the four people in each time step. I also want an animation to show how the fractions are changing in the pie chart in **continuous time**. Interpolate the missing fractions! I also want vertical line animation in other three plots to match the pie chart. I want the fanciest plot. Please add as many fancy things as possible.

Here is a possible code to generate a pyplot for the following data, with some comments to explain the steps:

GPT-4: [We give two snapshots from the animation resulting from the produced code]

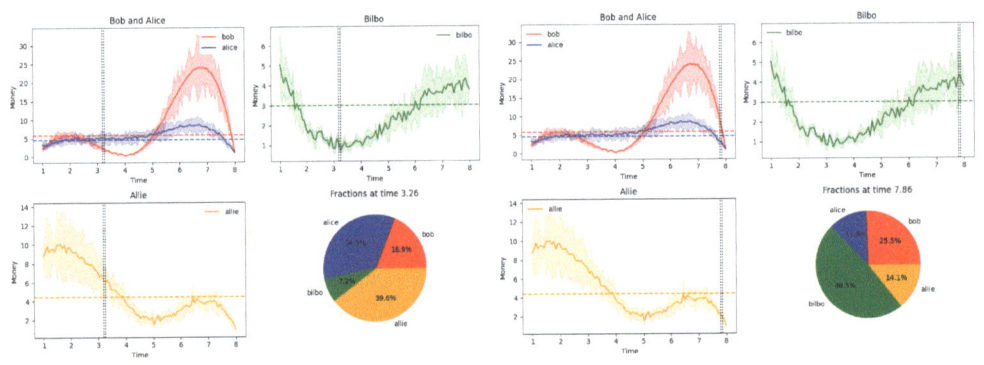

Prompt: Suppose $g(x) = f^{-1}(x), g(0) = 5, g(4) = 7, g(3) = 2, g(7) = 9, g(9) = 6$ what is $f(f(f(6)))$?

GPT-4: There are different ways to approach this problem, but one possible method is to use the fact that $g(x) = f^{-1}(x)$ implies that $f(g(x)) = x$ for any x in the domain of g. That is, applying f to both sides of the equation $g(x) = f^{-1}(x)$ gives $f(g(x)) = f(f^{-1}(x)) = x$. This means that we can undo the effect of f by applying g, and vice versa. Using this idea, we can try to find $f(6)$ by looking for the value of x such that $g(x) = 6$. From the given information, we see that $g(9) = 6$, so $f(6) = f(g(9)) = 9$. Similarly, we can find $f(9)$ by looking for the value of x such that $g(x) = 9$. We see that $g(7) = 9$, so $f(9) = f(g(7)) = 7$. Finally, we can find $f(7)$ by looking for the value of x such that $g(x) = 7$. We see that $g(4) = 7$, so $f(7) = f(g(4)) = 4$. Therefore, $f(f(f(6))) = f(f(9)) = f(7) = 4$.

FIGURE 2-1 Examples of GPT-4 capabilities.
SOURCE: S. Bubeck, V. Chandrasekaran, R. Eldan, et al., 2023, "Sparks of Artificial General Intelligence: Early Experiments with GPT-4," ArXiv preprint, arXiv:2303.12712. CC BY 4.0 DEED.

> **GPT-4 vs ChatGPT**
>
> **Prompt:** Here we have a book, 9 eggs, a laptop, a bottle and a nail. Please tell me how to stack them onto each other in a stable manner.
>
> **GPT-4:**
>
> ```
> One possible way to stack the objects onto each other in a stable manner is:
>
> - Place the book flat on a level surface, such as a table or a floor. The book will serve as the base of
> the stack and provide a large and sturdy support.
> - Arrange the 9 eggs in a 3 by 3 square on top of the book, leaving some space between them. The eggs
> will
> form a second layer and distribute the weight evenly. Make sure the eggs are not cracked or broken, and
> handle them gently to avoid dropping them.
> - Place the laptop on top of the eggs, with the screen facing down and the keyboard facing up. The
> laptop will fit snugly within the boundaries of the book and the eggs, and its flat and rigid surface
> will provide a stable platform for the next layer. Make sure the laptop is closed and turned off, and do
> not press any keys or buttons.
> - Place the bottle on top of the laptop, with the cap facing up and the bottom facing down. The bottle
> will add some height and balance to the stack, and its cylindrical shape will reduce the contact area
> with the laptop. Make sure the bottle is empty and closed, and do not shake or tilt it.
> - Place the nail on top of the bottle cap, with the pointy end facing up and the flat end facing down.
> The nail will be the final and smallest object in the stack, and its sharp tip will prevent it from
> rolling or sliding off the bottle. Make sure the nail is clean and straight, and do not touch or move
> it.
> ```

FIGURE 2-2 Example of GPT-4 answering a question about the physical world.
SOURCE: S. Bubeck, V. Chandrasekaran, R. Eldan, et al., 2023, "Sparks of Artificial General Intelligence: Early Experiments with GPT-4," ArXiv preprint, arXiv:2303.12712. CC BY 4.0 DEED.

As a simple example, consider the input sequence "I parked my car in the…." In order to predict that "garage" is a highly probable next word, the network will have to have learned a representation of text that incorporates the "common sense" that cars are typically parked in garages. Trained LLMs are found to implicitly have much of this kind of commonsense knowledge and, as illustrated in the preceding examples, much more.

To be precise, one technical caveat must be mentioned here: Although the core transformer on which GPT-4 is based has been trained as described earlier (to predict the next word in a sequence), GPT-4 was subsequently extended by fine-tuning it with human-provided feedback. In particular, after initial training to predict the next word, GPT-4 was given a set of inputs, and it was then applied to produce multiple distinct probable outputs (e.g., "I parked my car in the ..." "road." or "garage." or "lawn."). Human labelers then provided feedback regarding which of these outputs was most useful and for "trust and safety" to reduce the likelihood of producing undesirable outputs. These human-labeled data were then used to learn a separate "reward function" that outputs a numerical score characterizing the desirability of any output, and this reward function was then used by a machine learning algorithm known as "reinforcement learning" to learn a final policy for producing output responses. Details are available in the GPT-4 technical report.[11] The significance of this use of human feedback is that it provides a mechanism to guide the LLM to produce outputs according to certain human preferences. For example, this can be used to steer the LLM away from biased or offensive outputs and toward outputs that human users find most helpful. Despite this use of human-labeled training data to augment the vastly larger number of unlabeled predict-the-next-word examples, the authors of GPT-4 report that the ability of GPT-4 to pass a variety of exams (e.g., AP exams in chemistry, macroeconomics, and statistics) appears to stem from training on the unlabeled data and that additional training using these human-labeled data does not significantly affect its scores on these and other tests.[12]

These and other capabilities of GPT-4 and other LLMs have inspired an enormous amount of follow-on research and development. A partial list of recent developments includes the following:

- *Multimodal models*. Although the first LLMs applied only to text, current efforts involve training on a combination of modalities including text, video, and sound. GPT-4, for example, is already capable of working with images. Google has announced that it is developing a new model, Gemini, which will be trained from the ground up to handle multimodal input/output.
- *Plugins*. As noted earlier, LLMs make a variety of errors, including factual errors and errors in various types of reasoning such as multiplying large numbers. One way to reduce factual errors is to interface LLMs to search engines, as when Microsoft interfaced GPT-4 to its Bing search engine. This allows the combined system to answer questions more accurately by first searching for relevant web documents and then allowing GPT-4 to read the document before answering the question. Similarly, other plugin software utilities have

---
[11] OpenAI, 2023, "GPT-4 Technical Report," arXiv preprint, arXiv:2303.08774.
[12] H. Nori, N. King, S. Mayer McKinney, D. Carignan, and E. Horvitz, 2023, "Capabilities of GPT-4 on Medical Challenge Problems," arXiv preprint, arXiv:2303.13375.

now been connected to ChatGPT, including utilities such as a numerical calculator (which, assuming the LLM is able to invoke the tool correctly, eliminates mathematical errors) and Wolfram Alpha (which provides various types of factual knowledge and calculations). Significantly, this trend provides a pathway to boost the reliability, accuracy, and depth of knowledge of LLMs in specific domains by leveraging previously developed software. Thus far, correct tool invocation has proven to be a surprisingly hard technical problem.

- *Software architectures that use LLMs as submodules.* A variety of recent research has explored new types of software architectures for AI assistants that are based on calling LLMs as submodules, or subroutines. For example, LangChain is one popular example of open-source software that enables software developers to combine LLMs including GPT with internal data and internal software applications. AutoGPT is another open-source example that allows building agents that call GPT multiple times to perform different tasks, and that provides functions including file storage and memory, which are missing from bare LLMs. Systems that provide multistep engagements around tasks, such as GPT Code Interpreter, enable users to input technical papers and data files and engage in multiple-step analyses, with explanations of work undertaken by the system on its problem-solving steps along the way to a solution. This trend opens a way for the open-source research community, and other researchers outside the companies developing these large models, to participate in moving the field forward.

- *Smaller and/or more specialized LLMs.* Given the size of GPT-4 and similar LLMs, which typically have hundreds of billions of parameters and thus take months of supercomputer time to train and cannot be downloaded easily to standard-size computers, there is considerable interest in finding ways to build smaller models with similar capabilities or with strong capabilities in specific domains. For example, in March 2023 Bloomberg announced that it is building an LLM specifically trained on financial data and text, with the intent to use it for financial applications. In the open-source community, there has also been a great deal of activity exploring how to train smaller models. When Meta released its LLaMA LLM, a variety of research teams from various universities built on this by fine-tuning smaller versions of LLaMA using, for example, training data collected by querying Open AI's GPT LLM. This produced

13-billion-parameter models such as Alpaca,[13] Vicuna,[14] Koala,[15] and Orca,[16] each of which fine-tuned the 13-billion-parameter version of LLaMA using new data and resulting in stronger performance than the original 13-billion-parameter LLaMA LLM. These open-source efforts show that LLMs can now be trained to approach, although not yet match, the accuracy of the strongest available LLMs, despite being 10 to 100 times smaller, and that large models such as GPT-4 can be used to produce the training data for these smaller models.

The preceding list of ongoing research directions captures only a fraction of the efforts to extend the capabilities of LLMs and AI systems based on them. Technical experts generally agree that further advances should be expected in coming years, but great uncertainty remains about what specific new capabilities future LLMs will exhibit and in what timeframe.

Computer Vision

Computer vision is the branch of AI that deals with perceiving and manipulating image and video data. Research in this area has also advanced significantly over the past decade, in several directions. Computer vision tasks include object recognition (the ability to recognize objects and people in images), object tracking (the ability to track an object such as an individual person from frame to frame in a video stream), computational photography (the ability to improve image capture and preprocessing, such as auto-focus and red-eye removal), medical image analysis (e.g., automatic interpretation of X-ray images), and many other tasks.

One significant step forward in computer vision occurred in 2012, when the annual competition among computer vision systems for recognizing objects in images was suddenly won by a large margin by a new machine learning approach called "deep learning." In contrast to earlier approaches in which humans designed a set of low-level visual features to represent input images (e.g., features like edges and other local image properties), this new approach allowed the machine learning algorithm using multilayer neural networks to operate directly on the image pixels and discover its own features as part of the training process. Within a few years, the majority of research in computer

---

[13] R. Taori, I. Gulrajani, T. Zhang, et al., 2023, "Alpaca: A Strong, Replicable Instruction-Following Model," Stanford Center for Research on Foundation Models, https://crfm.stanford.edu/2023/03/13/alpaca.html.

[14] The Vicuna Team, 2023, "Vicuna: An Open-Source Chatbot Impressing GPT-4 with 90% ChatGPT Quality," March 30, https://lmsys.org/blog/2023-03-30-vicuna.

[15] X. Geng, A. Gudibande, H. Liu, et al., 2023, "Koala: A Dialogue Model for Academic Research," April 3, https://bair.berkeley.edu/blog/2023/04/03/koala.

[16] S. Mukherjee, A. Mitra, G. Jawahar, S. Agarwal, H. Palangi, and A. Awadallah, 2023, "Orca: Progressive Learning from Complex Explanation Traces of GPT-4," arXiv preprint, arXiv:2306.02707.

vision changed to adopt this deep neural network approach. Within a few more years, deep neural networks also led to rapid advances in speech recognition and many other sensory perception problems, and later in the analysis of text as well.

Recent years have produced steady progress in all of these areas of computer vision as well as the commercial adoption of computer vision in a variety of domains. Computer vision based on neural networks is now used to interpret a variety of radiological images, typically providing assistance to human radiologists. Object recognition is widely used to index image libraries (including personal photo libraries), enabling search over images based on the name of a person or object. Progress in self-driving vehicles relies heavily on computer vision and data from light detection and ranging (lidar) sensors to build a map of surrounding roads, pedestrians, obstacles, and vehicles, and to model their current and anticipated future directions of motion. In manufacturing, computer vision methods are widely employed to automate, or partly automate, the inspection of parts and processes.

One particularly active area of progress in computer vision stems from recent progress in generative AI models. Just as LLMs are able to generate text, researchers have now produced generative models that output images given only a text description of the content.

This ability to generate images automatically from text (and, in the other direction, to generate text captions from input images) signals a key technological advance in AI—namely, that the point has been reached where the semantics, or meaning of text, is represented inside the computer in sufficient detail to produce a visual illustration. This stepping-stone of developing amodal (i.e., shared across text and images) meaning representations suggests that future research in AI may be based on systems that handle both images and text simultaneously. The beginning of this trend is already visible, with OpenAI's GPT-4 accepting images as well as text as input and Google's Gemini system "created from the ground up" to be multimodal—that is, able to deal with images and videos as well as text.

What are the potential implications of computer vision for the future of work? Computer vision systems are already being used to perform tasks such as inspecting parts, analyzing radiological images, indexing video libraries, and modeling the external world for self-driving vehicles. In some cases, this can result in replacing human workers. For example, computer vision systems that capture license plate numbers as cars pass by, allowing owners to be billed automatically, have made it possible to largely automate the work of toll booth workers. Toll workers are thus being replaced, while some new U.S. jobs are being created by the design, manufacture, installation, and maintenance of computer vision systems. In other cases, computer vision can lead to higher quality or complete deployments of tasks previously performed by people alone—for example, the relatively low cost and high quality of computer vision for parts inspection leads in some cases to a more complete inspection of parts at multiple stages of manufacture. In yet other cases, the success of computer vision leads to completely new products or services—for example, to automobiles that visually track road lanes to alert drivers who drift out of lane. Predicting the exact impact of computer vision on the workforce is a complex problem, as different applications offer differing opportunities for computer vision to substitute for human labor, assist human labor, or create new products and services.

Robotics

The field of robotics continues to make steady progress as well. Unlike LLMs, which are purely software, or computer vision systems, which are software connected to cameras or similar sensors, robots are composed of complex mechanical systems (with motors, moving parts), various sensors (e.g., vision, touch, torque), and AI software to perform perception and control of the robot. Progress in robotics can therefore require progress in all of these component technologies—not just software.

Areas where robots are increasingly used in practice include the following:

- *Assembly and factory automation*. For decades, fixed-location, assembly-line robots have been used for machining and assembly. They are increasingly used in automotive and electronics assembly, as well as in industries that must manipulate liquids such as the food and beverage industry and the pharmaceutical industry.
- *Movement of warehouse inventory*. Unlike assembly-line robots, this application involves mobile robots that move around in engineered spaces such as warehouses. One notable example is the use of Kiva robots by Amazon. Kiva robots navigate Amazon warehouses with the help of barcode stickers on the floor and are used to retrieve items for orders placed through Amazon. These robots bring the items for an order to human workers, who then package them for delivery. Since its initial adoption of Kiva robots, Amazon has continued to add new robotic and computer vision support for its warehouse operations, in the direction of introducing more general-purpose robots that operate in the same space as people and introducing additional uses of computer perception to identify and select packages.
- *Self-driving vehicles*. This application is under development, and although AI-based driver assistance is in fielded use, fully autonomous driving in arbitrary environments has remained elusive owing to the broad variety of rare cases that must be handled in order to achieve 100 percent autonomous

driving. For example, Tesla's commercially available Full Self-Driving Beta is capable of driving autonomously most of the time when on standard U.S. interstate highways, which have few unpredictable moving obstacles such as pedestrians and dogs, but drivers must keep attentive and be prepared to take control. Alphabet's Waymo and General Motors' Cruise have already been testing autonomous taxis in limited areas, and in August 2023, California's Public Utilities Commission granted permission to both to operate autonomous taxis 24×7 throughout San Francisco. Despite difficulties to date in achieving fully autonomous driving, AI-based technology has already facilitated many auto safety features such as lane departure warning, adaptive cruise control, blind spot monitoring, and rear cross traffic alerting. These safety features, as with full self-driving technology, rely heavily on computer perception of surroundings, where great progress has been made. Current bottlenecks include planning and reasoning about how to respond to unanticipated events such as a ladder lying in the road or a construction site that temporarily blocks the view of oncoming traffic.

- *Drone delivery.* This application, also under development, seeks to provide airborne package deliveries via autonomous drones. In some ways, flying drones autonomously is an easier technical problem than driving cars autonomously, because there are fewer unexpected obstacles to avoid in the air. Several companies—including Amazon, Walmart, and UPS—are currently experimenting with autonomous drone delivery. Drone delivery company Zipline reported in March 2023 that it had completed more than 500,000 drone deliveries, many involving medical supplies in Africa.

Technical progress in robotics has been steady, although progress has not taken place at the rapid rate of progress in natural language processing driven by LLMs. However, there is a significant possibility that future advances in LLMs—especially the further development of multimodal visual-text-audio LLMs—may have a large impact on robotics by integrating the commonsense problem-solving abilities of LLMs with robotic perception and control. Although a burst of progress in robotics is not certain, the potential of future LLMs and other foundation models to accelerate progress in robotics is significant. Progress and widespread deployment in robotics will also require in many cases progress in the mechanical design and mechanical reliability of robots, and progress in sensor and effector technologies, in addition to progress in AI software to control the robot.

DRIVERS OF TECHNICAL PROGRESS IN ARTIFICIAL INTELLIGENCE

Several factors have driven and are likely to continue driving AI progress. These include the following:

- *Increasing volumes of online data available to train AI systems.* Over the past three decades, especially since the spread of the World Wide Web in the 1990s, the volume of online data has exploded. Such data are key to training accurate AI systems using machine learning. For example, hundreds of millions of historical credit card transactions are used to train the AI systems that routinely approve credit card transactions in real time based on their probability of being fraudulent. Importantly, the huge collection of online text found on the World Wide Web and social media platforms forms the backbone of text data used to train modern LLMs. Large collections of video data, such as YouTube, are likely to be key to training future multimodal LLMs.
- *Increasing computational power.* The past several decades of progress in integrated circuits have produced much faster parallel hardware necessary to support training LLMs and other large AI systems. One type of chip called a graphics processing unit, developed to support video graphics, has been found to provide the kind of parallel matrix computations central to training neural networks and is now widely used for this purpose. Specialized hardware designed specifically for AI is likely to continue this trend. In considering the computational needs for AI systems, it is important to note that training an AI system typically requires several orders of magnitude more computation than applying a trained AI system—one consequence of this fact is that while only a few organizations can afford the cost of training state-of-the-art LLMs, many organizations can afford utilizing these LLMs over the cloud. In the case of open-source models such as Meta's LLaMA models, it is also possible to download the already-trained models and execute them on local computers. Both Apple and Google are incorporating local execution of LLMs into their mobile phones.
- *Algorithmic innovations.* A variety of machine learning algorithmic innovations were central to recent AI advances. For example, the advent of deep neural network algorithms around 2010 led to major advances in computer vision and speech recognition over the subsequent decade. More recently, the development of the transformer architecture and the method of training these systems to predict the next word in a sequence was also an important step forward.

- *Increasing investments in AI technology.* Owing to AI's economic importance, private and government funding for AI research and development has increased significantly in recent years, especially over the past year or two. Competition among the major technology companies, international cooperation and competition in AI research and development, and investment in AI start-ups by venture capital firms are likely to keep this investment flowing for some time.

Factors that might limit the rate of future AI progress include the following:

- *Diminished engagement of universities in developing AI and a potential falloff in graduate training.* One important trend over the past decade has been a shift in where the largest AI research advances are being made. Although university researchers led AI development for many decades, openly publishing their most advanced algorithms, in recent years many of the greatest advances have come instead from large companies that have in some cases kept the details of their algorithms a secret. Importantly, the recent development of LLMs has been driven by a handful of large companies with little university involvement, and the AI algorithms that underlie major LLMs including GPT-4 and Gemini remain trade secrets, inhibiting the rate at which new advances can build on current approaches. Given that the development of a state-of-the-art LLM costs at least hundreds of millions of dollars, universities typically cannot participate in this kind of research. It is possible that if universities are unable to compete with research at the handful of well-resourced companies, the number of graduate students learning and developing the latest AI methods might suddenly decrease, thus decreasing the number of skilled researchers graduating as AI experts. Note that (1) it is not clear at present whether this shrinkage will occur, because some governments are considering new ways of providing computing resources to universities for AI research; and (2) it is not clear at this time whether future AI progress will stem solely from developing even bigger and more expensive models, or whether the open-source research community will find ways of building highly capable AI systems that are much smaller and less resource-intensive.
- *Equity of access.* Relatedly, much of the most advanced AI technology and the computing and data to develop it are primarily in the hands of a small number of large technology companies or smaller companies, many of which have ties to the large technology companies. Partially offsetting this has been the availability of open-source models, some of which were released by the technology companies.

- *Limits in access to ever-larger training data sets.* LLM development so far has followed a scaling curve, where each successive generation of increasingly capable LLMs is larger (i.e., has more trained parameters) and is based on a larger set of training data. It has been estimated that current state-of-the-art LLMs are based on roughly 1 trillion training examples of text snippets gathered from the Internet. If this scaling curve continues to hold, even larger data sets will be needed to make further advances. However, some relevant data sets, such as Google's YouTube collection of video data, are privately held and not widely accessible. Such limitations on access to large privately held data sets may reduce the number of organizations that can innovate at the frontier of the field. Furthermore, some Internet sources are now raising questions about how their data can be used. For example, Getty Images, which hosts and sells images over the Internet, has sued Stable Diffusion, one of the developers of generative AI software trained to generate images from text descriptions, for copyright infringement associated with the use of Getty's images for training.
- *Limits on access to sufficient computing capacity.* Training larger models requires more computing capacity, which in turn requires more high-end semiconductors, expanded or new data centers, and additional electrical power. All these are capital-intensive and push up against industrial capacity or regulatory constraints. Physical constraints on the smallest possible size for semiconductor transistors may in the future also constrain the ability to provide faster, more energy-efficient computation with each new generation of computing hardware.
- *Government regulations.* Governments in many countries are now considering potential regulations that would constrain the development or deployment of various types of AI systems. For example, Italy initially banned the use of ChatGPT shortly after its release because of concerns about ChatGPT's collection and use of user data as well as its failure to prevent underage users from accessing inappropriate content. More broadly, many governments are now taking a fresh look at AI, its potential impacts on society, and what types of norms are desired to guide its development and deployment. In most cases, it is likely that regulation of AI will occur at the level of individual applications (e.g., regulation of self-driving cars by the National Highway Traffic Safety Administration and state motor vehicle agencies or regulation of AI-based medical diagnosis systems by the Food and Drug Administration). However, there might also be regulations of more general AI technologies such as LLMs (e.g., to require that they report on their factual accuracy in various topics, or whether they can inadvertently output part of the text or images they were

trained on). The discussion of how governments should guide AI development is in early stages and is likely to continue for years, providing some uncertainty around commercial uses of AI.

- *Social acceptability*. To be socially acceptable, AI systems must align with the norms of society. For example, researchers and developers have worked over the past 5 years to reduce disparities in the accuracy of face recognition technology across different phenotypes that arose from biases in the demographic makeup of the training data sets. More broadly, bias, fairness, trust, and accountability of AI systems will need to be addressed as part of the process of introducing them into society. Note that the threshold on AI capabilities that result in social acceptability can vary widely across different applications, along with different costs of error: an error by ChatGPT might result in an incorrect answer, whereas an error by an AI-based delivery drone might result in crashing into a nearby pedestrian, and an error in an AI-based military system might have dramatically more costly impacts and corresponding public backlash.

FINAL OBSERVATIONS

AI technology appears to be at an inflection point, where rapid technical progress has occurred over the past few years and seems likely to continue for some time. Its impact on the workforce and on productivity is likely to be significant, with LLMs offering new opportunities for enhancing worker productivity across many industries, from health care to education to journalism to scientific research itself. Beyond LLMs, there is also substantial technical progress in other areas of AI, including robotics, perception, and machine learning applied to large, structured data sets. There is a significant chance that progress in these other AI areas may accelerate in the near future, as researchers explore how to use LLMs to impact these areas and if the anticipated generalization of LLMs to multimodal generative models occurs.

Exactly which work tasks and therefore which jobs will be most impacted remains to be seen. It is likely that AI will *assist* workers in some cases (e.g., assist doctors by providing a second opinion on medical diagnoses) and *replace* workers in other cases (e.g., just as computer vision algorithms have been instrumental in replacing toll booth operators with computers). Even in cases where AI assists and increases productivity of workers, it can be unclear whether demand for those workers will increase or decrease; improved productivity can lead to reduced prices and therefore increased demand, so that the final impacts depend also on elasticities in the demand for the goods that these workers produce. One must also be careful in extrapolating from the performance of recent AI systems on benchmark tests (e.g., passing the Law School Admission Test [LSAT]) predictions about which jobs an AI system might be able to perform (e.g., successful lawyers have many additional skills that are not tested by the LSAT).

Although current generative AI technology is imperfect—it can output "hallucinated" claims and can provide faulty solutions to problems it is asked to solve—it is already of clear use in providing assistance to programmers, authors, educators, and many other kinds of knowledge workers. There is much uncertainty about how the technology will develop further but little doubt that it will advance. There are already areas where it is significantly improving productivity (e.g., software development), and the burst of new venture capital in this area ensures that there will be a burst of new exploration into how to take advantage of this technology. The bottom line is that while substantial ongoing progress should be expected over the coming years, it is difficult to predict precisely which technical advances AI is likely to achieve next and on what timetable. To prepare, strategies and policies must be able to accommodate a variety of technology futures with differing timetables and technical advances.

3

Artificial Intelligence and Productivity

Productivity growth (see Box 3-1) is the most important determinant of higher long-run living standards. In turn, improvements in technology, especially general-purpose technology, are key to better productivity growth. The most promising general-purpose technology of the present era is artificial intelligence (AI). AI has increased productivity substantially for certain tasks, but thus far its impact on aggregate productivity has been minimal—which is to be expected because adoption is still relatively low. Because AI can apply to so many tasks in the economy and adoption is growing rapidly, however, its productivity impact this decade could be quite large. Harnessing the full potential of AI will take time and will require complementary investments and innovations in tangible and intangible capital, including human capital, organizational processes, and business models.

This chapter argues that AI is a *general-purpose technology*. It has the potential to influence every sector of the economy, it is rapidly improving, and it is fostering a vast array of applications. The chapter reviews some historical trends in productivity growth, including how it has varied over time and across sectors, industries, firms, and regions. It then explores AI's effects on productivity, noting its relatively low adoption rate so far but its rapid growth and high potential for productivity contributions. Because AI is ultimately about creating a new form of replicable and extensible intelligence, and because intelligence is so fundamental to solving many of the world's problems, AI may ultimately be viewed as the most general of all general-purpose technologies.

The chapter looks especially closely at *generative AI*, the most recent wave of AI, with some early case examples of its productivity effects and estimates of its broader

> **BOX 3-1 What Is Productivity Growth?**
>
> Productivity is defined as the amount of output produced per unit input. The greater the productivity, the greater the amount of goods and services that can be produced by an economy's labor, capital, and natural resources. Productivity makes it easier to address many challenges in areas as diverse as poverty reduction, better health care, improved environment, stronger national defense, and reduced budget deficits.[a] By definition, productivity growth does not come from working longer hours. Instead, it comes from using labor and other inputs more effectively.
>
> The most common productivity metric is labor productivity, typically defined as gross domestic product (GDP) per labor hour. Another useful metric is total factor productivity, which also includes capital as well as labor in the denominator. Adjustments in productivity metrics, although imperfect, can be made for capital quality, labor quality, capacity utilization, intangibles, and other factors.
>
> ---
>
> [a] For instance, the Congressional Budget Office projects that if productivity growth ends up being 0.5 percentage points higher than its baseline, the projected debt/GDP ratio for the United States would be about 40 percent lower by 2052. See Congressional Budget Office, 2022, "The 2022 Long-Term Budget Outlook," July 27, https://www.cbo.gov/publication/57971.

effects on the economy.[1] Because there are important differences in the exposure of different sectors and occupations to generative AI, aggregate productivity effects will depend on how generative AI affects the productivity of different sectors, different occupations, and different firms, and there is likely to be significant heterogeneity across all categories. Generative AI can complement labor, substitute for labor, or facilitate labor redeployment into new activities. All three of these effects can boost labor productivity over time, but they will have different effects on the distribution of benefits and on the lags, barriers, and costs.

This chapter develops a framework for predicting AI's productivity effects and identifies the following factors that will affect AI adoption and the size of these effects over time:

- The share of the economy where the technology can be applied,
- The size of the potential productivity effect in those applications,
- Complements and bottlenecks,

---

[1] There have been important advances in other areas of AI, but as discussed in Chapter 2, the progress in most of these areas, such as the fine motor skills necessary to deploy AI in smart robots and production systems, has significantly lagged the progress in generative AI.

- Time lags,
- Positive and negative economic spillovers and rent seeking,
- Heterogeneity of effects within and across businesses and sectors,
- Measurement issues, and
- Dynamic effects.

Most of these factors, such as the need for complementary investments, the issue of time lags, and the problem of measurement gaps, have also affected the adoption rate of previous technologies, impeding or slowing their productivity effects. But there are also possible differences in AI adoption and its aggregate productivity effects. One difference stems from the relatively greater breadth of AI's potential applications in so many parts of the economy, from agriculture to manufacturing to services.

A second and related difference stems from the fact that a very large percentage of tasks and occupations are exposed to AI, where exposure includes both AI as a substitute for human labor and AI as a complement to human labor. Rapid AI deployment could cause considerable disruption in the labor market as workers move between tasks and occupations. This disruption could weaken AI's productivity effects if labor reallocation does not occur rapidly and if displaced workers are not deployed into new tasks with productivity levels at least as high as those in their previous tasks.

A third difference is the fact that many of the complementary investments to use AI—for example, investments in data, in computing power, and in the cloud—are already in place, enabling businesses to deploy AI rapidly on top of their existing infrastructure and system. To many users, generative AI is just a new app or website, or even a new feature within an existing app.

A fourth difference is that generative AI is by its nature creative—it can accelerate the process of scientific discovery and boost innovation, leading to a faster rate of change in productivity. In the long run, the slope of change in productivity is more important than its level. Over time, even small changes in the rate of growth compound to become significant.

Although there is considerable uncertainty about the size and the timing of the increase in productivity resulting from AI, the chapter concludes that the increase is likely to be quite large over the coming decade. But it raises questions and concerns about how the benefits of greater productivity from AI will be shared. Will the benefits be inclusive, or will they result in more income and wealth inequality? Will significant job losses occur as AI is used primarily to automate existing jobs rather than to augment worker skills and create new job opportunities? Will wage growth continue to lag productivity growth as it has over the past 20–30 years during periods of both strong productivity growth and slow productivity growth?

Even if generative AI results in significantly higher productivity, history suggests that without institutional and policy changes, it is unlikely that the benefits will be shared widely. The benefits may be accompanied by significant disruption in the labor market, and many workers, including many highly paid cognitive workers with advanced educational credentials, may experience job loss, the need to develop new skills, and downward wage pressure. In addition, the use of AI to monitor and surveil worker performance to squeeze additional labor productivity may erode job quality, worker satisfaction, and worker commitment. Institutions and policies like labor market regulations, training policies, and tax policies can mitigate these effects.

Last, although the chapter focuses on AI's effects on productivity, it ends with a brief discussion of how AI may affect other measures of human well-being such as social progress and happiness as well as how it poses significant risks that could undermine human well-being, including risks to privacy, risks of discrimination and bias, risks to democracy and political stability, ethical risks, national security risks, risks of military arms races driven by new AI weapons, and even existential risks. In the words of Ian Bremmer and Mustafa Suleyman, "The decentralized nature of AI development and the core characteristics of the technology, such as open-source proliferation, increase the likelihood that it will be weaponized by cybercriminals, state-sponsored actors, and lone wolves."[2]

ARTIFICIAL INTELLIGENCE: A GENERAL-PURPOSE TECHNOLOGY

Although adoption of AI so far is limited, AI is a general-purpose technology, much like the steam engine and electricity. Historically, general-purpose technologies have been responsible for driving most economic growth and transformation. As defined by Bresnahan and Trajtenberg, general-purpose technologies have three essential characteristics: (1) they are pervasive, (2) they improve over time, and (3) they spawn complementary innovations.[3]

AI meets all three criteria:

1. *AI has the potential to influence nearly every sector of the economy.* AI can add intelligence to robots and production systems in manufacturing, transportation, and logistics. AI, especially large language models (LLMs) and

---

[2] I. Bremmer and M. Suleyman, 2023, "The AI Power Paradox," *Foreign Affairs*, August, https://www.foreignaffairs.com/world/artificial-intelligence-power-paradox.

[3] T.F. Bresnahan and M. Trajtenberg, 1992, "General Purpose Technologies 'Engines of Growth'?" NBER Working Paper No. w4148, August, https://ssrn.com/abstract=282685.

other generative AI, is expected to have an extensive impact on knowledge and information work: about 80 percent of jobs have at least 10 percent of their tasks suitable for LLMs.[4] In addition to LLMs, other types of foundation models[5] can work with graphics, audio, video, and other types of content.

2. *AI is rapidly improving.* As shown in Chapter 4, Figure 4-5, GPT-4 achieved 90 percent accuracy on the Uniform Bar Examination, while GPT-3 scored less than 20 percent. The 2023 AI Index[6] documents dozens of other areas of rapid improvement. In addition, LLMs display considerable capabilities overhang, giving rise to emergent properties such as code-writing and language translation abilities that were not anticipated when the models were created. Since the release of ChatGPT, there have been numerous additional breakthroughs in LLMs, including integration of traditional software tools such as calculators and search engines with LLMs, and a new generation of LLMs that manipulate sound and video in addition to text.

3. *AI is generating a vast array of complementary innovations.* One clear indicator of this is the vibrancy of the OpenAI plugin marketplace, which already boasts hundreds of applications. These plugins extend the capabilities of GPT and address many of its existing limitations. More generally, AI is a catalyst for improvements in many areas of science, engineering, health care, management, and even the arts.[7]

HISTORICAL CHANGES IN PRODUCTIVITY GROWTH

After a slowdown in 1973, labor productivity grew more rapidly in each business cycle but then slowed down substantially after 2007 (Figure 3-1).

This slowdown reflected mainly a decrease in the growth of total factor productivity (TFP) (Figure 3-2), which has persisted through 2023.

Part of the explanation of the slowdown in TFP growth is related to the business cycle, investment growth, and their interaction. Figure 3-3 shows that real gross private domestic investment in the United States grew strongly between 1990 and 2005, coincident with the introduction of the Internet and adoption of large enterprise

---

[4] T. Eloundou, S. Manning, P. Mishkin, and D. Rock, 2023, "GPTs Are GPTs: An Early Look at the Labor Market Impact Potential of Large Language Models," arXiv preprint, arXiv:2303.10130.

[5] Foundation models are vast systems based on deep neural networks that have been trained on massive data sets and can be adapted to perform a wide range of tasks. See R. Bommasani, D.A. Hudson, E. Adeli, et al., 2022, "On the Opportunities and Risks of Foundation Models," arXiv:2108.07258.

[6] N.N. Maslej, ed., 2023, "Artificial Intelligence Index Report 2023," Stanford University Human-Centered Artificial Intelligence, https://aiindex.stanford.edu/report.

[7] See, for instance, the array of applications discussed in the essays brought together in *Daedalus*, 2022, 151(2).

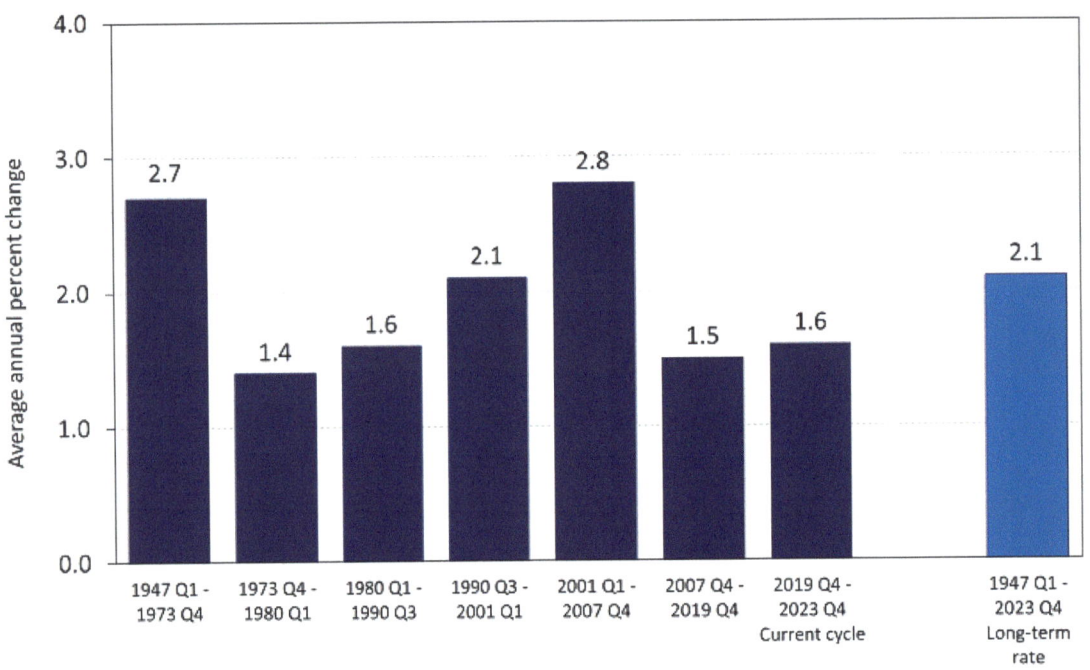

FIGURE 3-1 Labor productivity growth in the nonfarm business sector in the post-war period by business cycle.
SOURCE: U.S. Bureau of Labor Statistics, 2024, "Long Term Labor Productivity by Sector for Selected Periods: Productivity Change in the Nonfarm Business Sector, 1947 Q1–2024 Q1," last updated May 2, 2024, https://www.bls.gov/productivity/images/pfei.png.

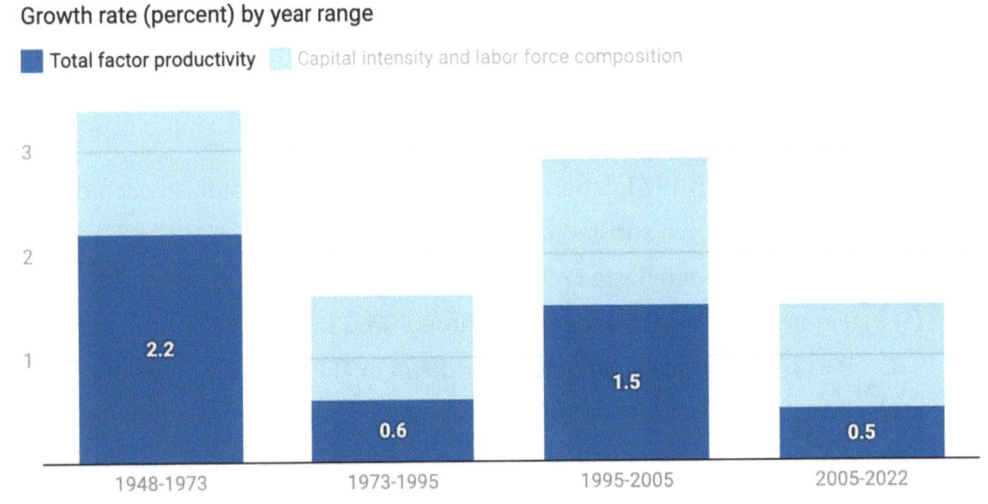

FIGURE 3-2 The slowdown in labor productivity primarily reflects slower total factor productivity growth.
SOURCE: Based on data from the Federal Reserve Bank of San Francisco, n.d., "Total Factor Productivity," https://www.frbsf.org/economic-research/indicators-data/total-factor-productivity-tfp, accessed August 1, 2024.

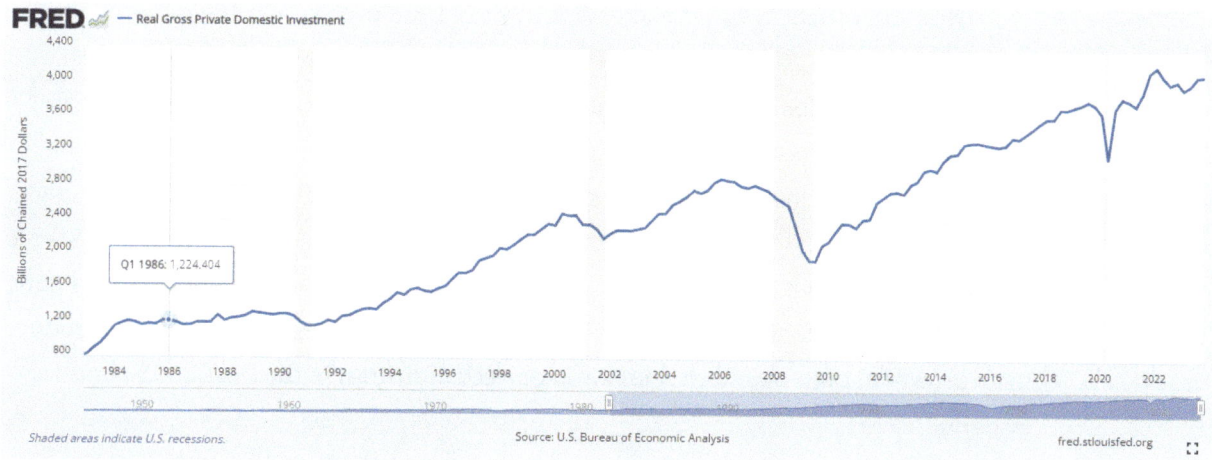

FIGURE 3-3 Real gross private domestic investment.
SOURCE: U.S. Bureau of Economic Analysis, 2024, "Real Gross Private Domestic Investment [GPDIC1]," retrieved from FRED, Federal Reserve Bank of St. Louis, https://fred.stlouisfed.org/series/GPDIC1.

information technology systems. It then fell during the 2007–2008 financial crisis and did not recover its 2006 peak until 2014.

Thereafter, real investment continued to rise, hitting a new peak in 2019, before declining sharply for a short time in 2020 as a result of the COVID-19 pandemic recession and recovering to a new peak in 2022. Overall, the macro environment affects not only business investment—the most procyclical component of spending—but also productivity growth. In particular, sluggish macroeconomic conditions, including the Great Recession of 2007–2009 and the COVID-19 pandemic recession of 2020–2021, slowed investment growth and capital deepening.

The anemic economic recovery after the Great Recession, with the macro economy operating below capacity and its potential for several years, also played a role in slower productivity growth. The Great Recession was sparked by a financial crisis that left many firms facing constraints on their investments in physical, intangible, and human capital. During the recovery, the decline in the growth of capital intensity per worker explains about one-third of the slowdown in labor productivity growth. But that slowdown actually began before the Great Recession, with labor productivity growth slowing each year from 2002 to 2006. TFP slowed precipitously across sectors and industries beginning in 2005–2006, which explains about 65 percent of the slowdown in labor productivity. In contrast, the composition of labor, a measure of the skills and experience of the workforce, was not a contributing factor to the productivity slowdown. Productivity growth from the composition of the workforce remained around 0.2–0.3 percentage points during the slowdown, similar to its long-run average.

How did productivity vary across industries? The slowdown in TFP growth in the United States in the 2005–2019 period was broad, affecting most sectors, industries, and geographies, albeit to differing extents.[8] Overall, information and communications technology (ICT) producing and using industries—"high-tech" sectors—accounted for the surge in productivity growth between 1995 and 2004, and they led the significant decline thereafter. Byrne and colleagues provide compelling evidence of the role of these industries.[9] Figure 3-4 shows patterns of growth rates of labor productivity in subperiods from 1990 to 2019 for high-tech and other industries. The widespread decline in productivity growth in both high-tech and non-high-tech industries in the post-2005 period is evident.

A 2023 study by McKinsey examines trends in productivity growth from 2005 through 2019. Mining, information, finance and insurance, and wholesale trade had the strongest productivity growth in the United States after 2005.[10] With the exception of mining, which benefited from technical progress in natural gas, these sectors are among the most digitized and ICT-intensive of all sectors. The star productivity performer was the information sector—including software, telecommunications and Internet services, and publishing—which is the most digitized of all sectors.

Productivity growth in manufacturing, real estate, and utilities slowed after 2005 but continued to outpace the average. There are important differences, however, within the manufacturing sector, with the share of more productive research and development (R&D)-intensive subsectors expanding and the share of less productive labor-intensive subsectors declining. Within manufacturing, almost all of the TFP growth during the entire 1987–2019 period came from one industry: computer and electronics products. Surprisingly, and driving the slowdown in productivity in the manufacturing sector, this subsector appears to have experienced negative TFP growth between 2014 and 2019.

There were also significant differences in productivity growth within services. Between 2005 and 2019, labor productivity grew and converged toward the average in several services, including professional services, arts and entertainment, retail trade, and administrative services. Increasing digitization (e.g., e-commerce in retail and streaming services in arts and entertainment) was a major factor behind productivity gains in these services. In contrast, several labor-intensive service sectors, including accommodation and food service, health care, transportation, construction, and government services,

---

[8] U.S. Bureau of Labor Statistics, 2021, "The U.S. Productivity Slowdown: An Economy-Wide and Industry-Level Analysis," *Monthly Labor Review*, April, https://www.bls.gov/opub/mlr/2021/article/the-us-productivity-slowdown-the-economy-wide-and-industry-level-analysis.htm.

[9] D.M. Byrne, J.G. Fernald, and M.B. Reinsdorf, 2016, "Does the United States Have a Productivity Slowdown or a Measurement Problem?" *Brookings Papers on Economic Activity* (1):109–182, https://doi.org/10.1353/eca.2016.0014.

[10] C. Atkins, O. White, A. Padhi, K. Ellingrud, A. Madgavkar, and M. Neary, 2023, "Rekindling US Productivity for a New Era," McKinsey Global Institute, February 16, https://www.mckinsey.com/mgi/our-research/rekindling-us-productivity-for-a-new-era#.

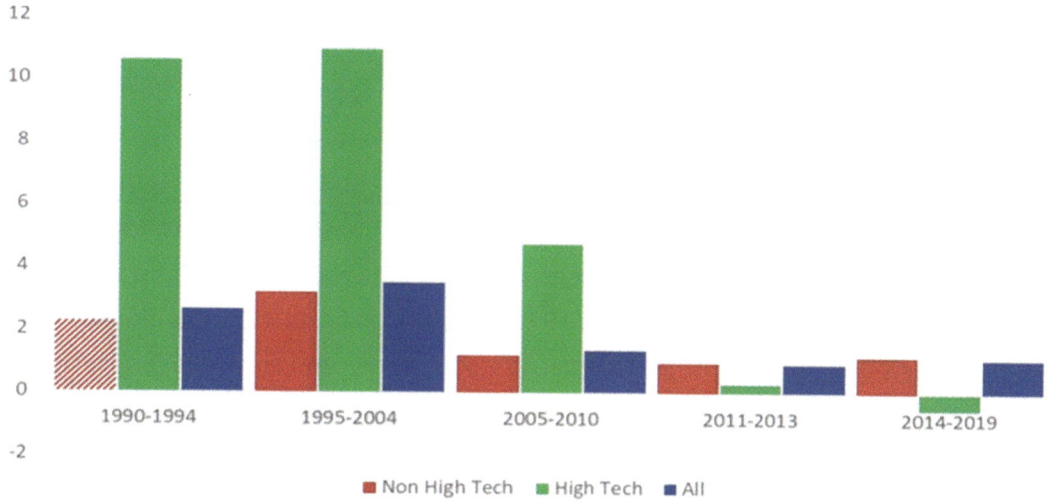

FIGURE 3-4 Growth in output per hour (average annual).
NOTE: "High tech" refers to the science, technology, engineering, and mathematics–intensive sectors (including information and communications technology and biotechnology) as defined in D.E. Hecker, 2005, "High-Technology Employment: A NAICS-Based Update," *Monthly Labor Review* 128:57.
SOURCE: Created based on data from the U.S. Bureau of Labor Statistics, Office of Productivity and Technology, "Industry Productivity Viewer," https://data.bls.gov/apps/industry-productivity-viewer/home.htm.

remained productivity laggards with below-average productivity growth rates. Together, these lagging productivity sectors accounted for nearly one-quarter of output, about 37 percent of hours worked, and two-thirds of employment growth, slowing aggregate productivity growth as workers shifted into less productive work.

EXPLANATIONS FOR THE SLOWDOWN IN PRODUCTIVITY GROWTH

Economists differ on explanations for the significant, unexpected, and persistent slowdown in labor productivity growth and TFP growth, which occurred not just in the United States but in the other advanced economies after 2006.

As noted in the preceding section, all of these economies were hit by the Great Recession and an anemic recovery that slowed investment and contributed to slower productivity growth. Small businesses, including many entrepreneurial start-ups, were hit the hardest; fewer new small businesses were started, and many were closed. Commercial bank lending to support and grow new businesses declined as did venture capital, which set higher bars for start-ups seeking funding. Business uncertainty about the future replaced the business euphoria of strong shared growth around the world that characterized the years leading up to the Great Recession. And investment is strongly negatively associated with higher uncertainty.[11] Overall, an adverse and uncertain macroeconomic environment was a major factor behind the productivity slowdown in the United States and other advanced industrial economies hit by the Great Recession, which had global repercussions for growth and investment.

Another explanation for the slowdown in productivity growth is that advances in innovation and technology fluctuate over time. Robert Gordon provides extensive evidence of the fluctuations in the pace of technological advances.[12] He argues that the ICT innovations of the 1980s and 1990s yielded significant gains in productivity, but the effects dissipated by the mid-2000s. Relatedly, Bloom and colleagues argue that research productivity has declined, as the inputs required to generate new advances have increased over time.[13]

Distinct but potentially related explanations are based on headwinds to productivity growth that have emerged over the past couple of decades. To provide guidance about these possible headwinds, it is instructive to review important structural changes in the economy since the 2000s. As the slowdown occurred, the productivity gaps among firms within sectors grew to unprecedented levels. The within-industry dispersion in TFP across establishments in the manufacturing sector has been rising, especially in the post-2000 period (Figure 3-5). While TFP is more difficult to measure at the firm level for other sectors, dispersion in labor productivity is rising across firms within industries in all sectors of the economy.[14] Andrews and colleagues provide evidence of rising productivity dispersion within industries in many Organisation for Economic Co-operation and Development (OECD) countries as well.[15]

Many factors appear to underlie the rising gaps in productivity performance across firms. The gap measures reflect rising dispersion of revenue per unit input and can reflect not only rising gaps in technical efficiency but also rising frictions and distortions that can be a drag on advances in productivity.[16,17] On the technical efficiency side, differences in the digitization of firms appear to be an important driver of differences in their

---

[11] N. Bloom, S.J. Davis, L.S. Foster, S.W. Ohlmacher, and I. Saporta-Eksten, 2022, "Investment and Subjective Uncertainty," National Bureau of Economic Research Working Paper Series, No. 30654, November, https://doi.org/10.3386/w30654.

[12] R. Gordon, 2017, "The Rise and Fall of American Growth: The US Standard of Living Since the Civil War," Princeton University Press.

[13] N. Bloom, C.I. Jones, J. Van Reenen, and M. Webb, 2020, "Are Ideas Getting Harder to Find?" *American Economic Review* 110(4):1104–1144, https://doi.org/10.1257/aer.20180338.

[14] R.A. Decker, J. Haltiwanger, R.S. Jarmin, and J. Miranda, 2020, "Changing Business Dynamism and Productivity: Shocks Versus Responsiveness," *American Economic Review* 110(12):3952–3990, https://doi.org/10.1257/aer.20190680.

[15] D. Andrews, C. Criscuolo, and P.N. Gal, 2016, "The Best Versus the Rest: The Global Productivity Slowdown, Divergence Across Firms and the Role of Public Policy," OECD Productivity Working Paper No. 05, November, https://www.oecd.org/global-forum-productivity/research/OECD%20Productivity%20Working%20Paper%20N°5.pdf.

[16] Rising frictions and distortions can yield increases in misallocation such that resources (e.g., capital and labor) are allocated less efficiently.

[17] C.-T. Hsieh and P.J. Klenow, 2009, "Misallocation and Manufacturing TFP in China and India," *Quarterly Journal of Economics* 124(4):1403–1448, http://www.jstor.org/stable/40506263.

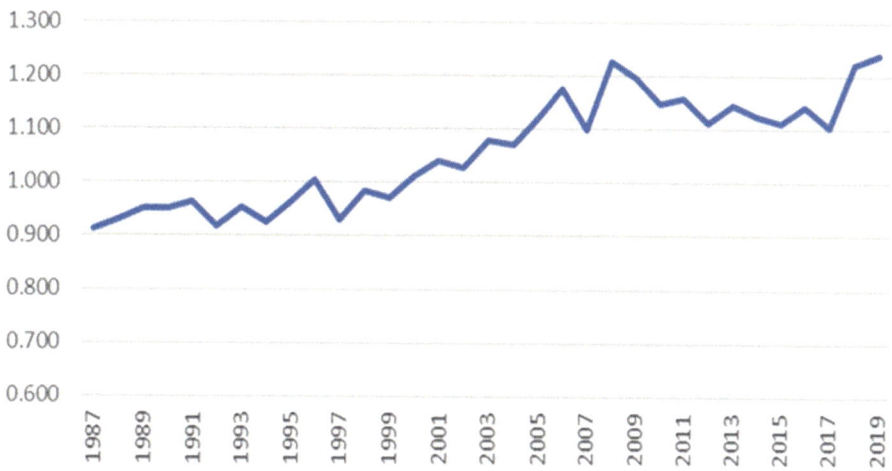

FIGURE 3-5 Rising within-industry productivity dispersion.
NOTE: Reported is the mean 90–10 within-industry differential of (log) total factor productivity across establishments across four-digit North American Industry Classification System industries in U.S. manufacturing.
SOURCE: Created based on data from U.S. Bureau of Labor Statistics and U.S. Census Bureau, 2023, "Dispersion Statistics on Productivity," https://www.census.gov/programs-surveys/ces/data/public-use-data/dispersion-statistics-on-productivity.html.

productivity. There was a 70 percent correlation between a sector's productivity growth and the level of its "digitization" during the past 30 years.[18] In the United States within manufacturing, which includes both ICT producing and many ICT using sectors and businesses, leading businesses (firms at the 90th percentile of productivity) operated at four times the productivity level of laggards (businesses at the 10th percentile of productivity) in 2019. The comparable number in the semiconductor industry was 14 times the productivity level.[19] Andrews and colleagues have suggested that an important factor underlying the rising productivity gaps among firms is slowing diffusion of technology as a result of rising frictions and distortions.[20]

The responsiveness of firms to changes in both their productivity performance and demand shocks appears to have slowed.[21] This may be the result of a number of factors including rising dispersion in markups (prices above costs) and increases in political and

---

[18] McKinsey Global Institute, 2023, "An Approach to Boosting US Labor Productivity," May 25, https://www.mckinsey.com/mgi/our-research/an-approach-to-boosting-us-labor-productivity.

[19] These statistics are drawn from the BLS/Census Dispersion Statistics on Productivity (DiSP) data product, https://www.bls.gov/productivity/articles-and-research/dispersion-statistics-on-productivity/home.htm. DiSP uses the Annual Survey of Manufactures and Census of Manufactures data.

[20] D. Andrews, C. Criscuolo, and P.N. Gal, 2016, "The Best Versus the Rest: The Global Productivity Slowdown, Divergence Across Firms and the Role of Public Policy," OECD Productivity Working Paper No. 05, November, https://www.oecd.org/global-forum-productivity/research/OECD%20Productivity%20Working%20Paper%20N°5.pdf.

[21] R.A. Decker, J. Haltiwanger, R.S. Jarmin, and J. Miranda, 2020, "Changing Business Dynamism and Productivity: Shocks Versus Responsiveness," *American Economic Review* 110(12):3952–3990, https://doi.org/10.1257/aer.20190680.

economic uncertainty.[22] These factors may have slowed the diffusion of new technologies across firms and increased the frictions associated with adjusting the scale and mix of operations at firms, including the adjustment of capital and labor.[23]

Accompanying the rising productivity gaps across firms has been a decline in measures of business dynamism and entrepreneurship. The rising frictions and distortions discussed above are potential mechanisms underlying this decline in dynamism. Figure 3-6 reports trends in a summary measure of business dynamism—the pace of job reallocation across establishments. Job reallocation is equal to the sum of the pace of job creation (expansions plus entering) and job destruction (contractions plus exiting). There has been a trend of decline in the pace of overall job reallocation since the late 1980s, but key innovative ("high-tech") industries have exhibited a decline only in the post-2000 period.[24] Preceding and accompanying the productivity surge from the high-tech industries in the 1990s, the pace of job reallocation rose in those industries from the 1980s through the early 2000s.

The share of employment at young firms exhibits broadly similar trends to the overall pace of job reallocation (Figure 3-7) with entrepreneurship surging in the high-tech industries in the 1990s through the early 2000s but declining thereafter. Detailed industry data show that the surge in entry preceded the surge in productivity in these innovation-intensive industries.[25] These patterns are consistent with waves of experimentation, innovation, dynamism, and productivity growth over the 20th century.[26]

---

[22] S.R. Baker, N. Bloom, and S.J. Davis, 2016, "Measuring Economic Policy Uncertainty," *Quarterly Journal of Economics* 131(4):1593–1636, https://doi.org/10.1093/qje/qjw024 and J. De Loecker, J. Eeckhout, and G. Unger, 2020, "The Rise of Market Power and the Macroeconomic Implications," *Quarterly Journal of Economics* 135(2):561–644, https://EconPapers.repec.org/RePEc:oup:qjecon:v:135:y:2020:i:2:p:561-644.

[23] J. De Loecker, T. Obermeier, and J. Van Reenen, 2022, "Firms and Inequality," CEP Discussion Paper No. 1838, London School of Economics and Political Science, Centre for Economic Performance, London, investigates the implications of rising dispersion in markups for declining dynamism and productivity. U. Akcigit and S. Ates, 2021, "Ten Facts on Declining Business Dynamism and Lessons from Endogenous Growth Theory," *American Economic Journal: Macroeconomics* 13(1):257–298, explores the contribution of slower diffusion for declining dynamism and productivity building in part on the evidence on declining diffusion in D. Andrews, C. Criscuolo, and P. Gal, 2016, "The Best Versus the Rest: The Global Productivity Slowdown, Divergence Across Firms and the Role of Public Policy," OECD Productivity Working Paper No. 5, OECD Publishing, Paris, https://doi.org/10.1787/63629cc9-en. The role of rising adjustment costs for declining dynamism and productivity is explored in R.A. Decker, J. Haltiwanger, R.S. Jarmin, and J. Miranda, 2020, "Changing Business Dynamism and Productivity: Shocks Versus Responsiveness," *American Economic Review* 110(12):3952–3990, https://doi.org/10.1257/aer.20190680.

[24] "High-tech" is the set of four-digit industries that are the most science, technology, engineering, and mathematics-intensive. See D.E. Hecker, 2005, "High-Technology Employment: A NAICS-Based Update," *Monthly Labor Review* 128:57. This includes the ICT industries in manufacturing and nonmanufacturing and the scientific development industries (new AI firms are often classified in the latter).

[25] C. Cunningham, L. Foster, C. Grim, et al., 2019, "Dispersion in Dispersion: Measuring Establishment-Level Differences in Productivity," NBER Conference on Research in Income and Wealth, July 15–16, https://www.nber.org/conferences/si-2019-conference-research-income-and-wealth.

[26] M. Gort and S. Klepper, 1982, "Time Paths in the Diffusion of Product Innovations," *Economic Journal* 92(367):630–653, https://doi.org/10.2307/2232554. Gort and Klepper document that innovation takes time and has distinct phases. The early innovation phase is dominated by entry and experimentation, including investments in changes in organization. During this time productivity growth may decline with a rise in experimentally oriented misallocation. A shakeout process ensues with successful innovators expanding while unsuccessful innovators contract and exit. The successful innovators grow rapidly (becoming the large, successful firms of that wave of innovation) with accompanying productivity growth. Historically, these dynamics can be stretched across many years.

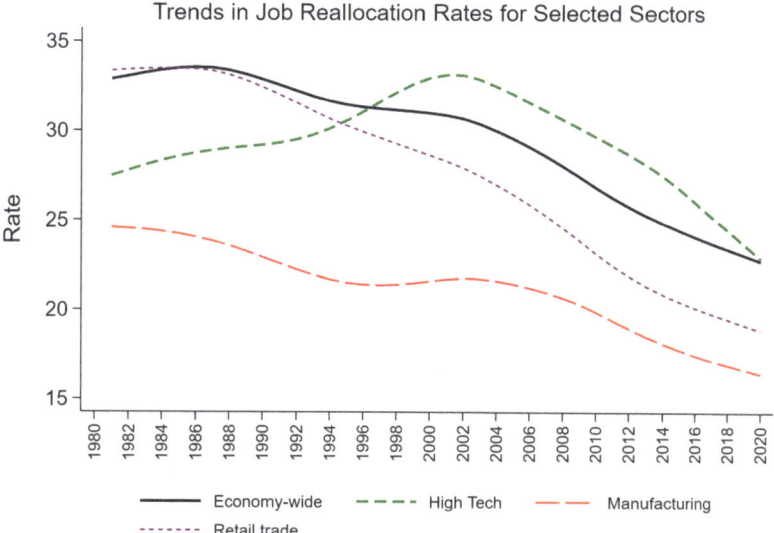

FIGURE 3-6 Declining pace of reallocation of jobs.
SOURCE: Created based on data from U.S. Census Bureau, Business Dynamic Statistics Datasets, https://www.census.gov/data/datasets/time-series/econ/bds/bds-datasets.html.

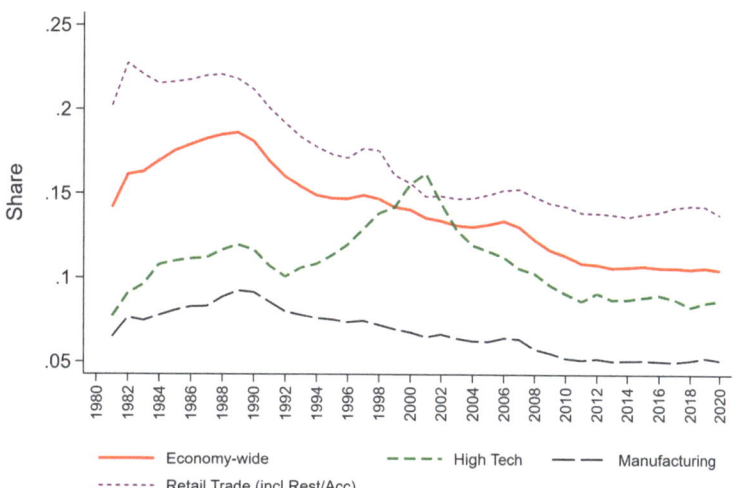

FIGURE 3-7 Declining entrepreneurship in the U.S. economy as shown by a declining share of employment at young (age ≤5) firms.
SOURCE: Created based on data from U.S. Census Bureau, Business Dynamics Statistics Datasets, https://www.census.gov/data/datasets/time-series/econ/bds/bds-datasets.html.

The flip side of the declining share of activity in young firms is the rising share of activity in large superstar firms.[27] One way of characterizing this pattern is to examine the share of activity in "mega firms" (firms with more than 10,000 employees). The rise in mega firms has been particularly pronounced in nonmanufacturing high-tech industries in the post-2000 period (Figure 3-8).

Overall, structural changes on many different dimensions have collectively spurred productivity growth. Economic theory suggests that over time, more productive firms grow while less productive firms are replaced or are driven by competition to improve their performance. Such productivity-enhancing reallocation has been an important contributor to productivity growth over time.[28] Relatedly, the innovative process itself is closely tied to the pace of reallocation, with young firms playing an outsized role in major innovations.[29,30] Unfortunately, as shown above, during the productivity slowdown there has been a decline in the pace of business dynamism and entrepreneurship in the United States. This has included a decline in the pace of entrepreneurship in the innovation-intensive sectors of the economy that played such an important role in the productivity surge in the 1990s.

The shift toward large mature firms likely reflects many factors. First, powerful network effects and economies of scale effects are likely behind the emergence of a handful of global high-tech producing and using firms such as Google, Apple, Meta, Microsoft, and Amazon. Related rises in concentration have occurred beyond the high-tech sector as globalization and information technologies have favored large incumbents. While rising concentration reflects the substantial innovations by superstar firms, the accompanying decline in competition is consistent with the rise in the level and dispersion of markups of price over cost. The rise in concentration and the accompanying rise in the dispersion of markups, possibly working together, might account for some or all of the decline in dynamism and productivity.[31]

Important changes in the allocation of talent across firms have accompanied these changes in the structure of firms. Sorting and segregation of workers across firms have increased—more highly educated workers are more likely to be at firms that offer higher wages and better working conditions, and less educated workers are more likely to be

---

[27] D. Autor, D. Dorn, L.F. Katz, C. Patterson, and J. Van Reenen, 2020, "The Fall of the Labor Share and the Rise of Superstar Firms," *Quarterly Journal of Economics* 135(2):645–709, https://doi.org/10.1093/qje/qjaa004.

[28] L. Foster, J.C. Haltiwanger, and C.J. Krizan, 2001, "Aggregate Productivity Growth: Lessons from Microeconomic Evidence," pp. 303–372 in *New Developments in Productivity Analysis*, C.R. Hulten, E.R. Dean, and M.J. Harper, eds., University of Chicago Press, http://www.nber.org/chapters/c10129.

[29] U. Akcigit and W. Kerr, 2018, "Growth Through Heterogeneous Innovations," *Journal of Political Economy* 126(4):1374–1443.

[30] D. Acemoglu, U. Akcigit, H. Alp, N. Bloom, and W. Kerr, 2018, "Innovation, Reallocation, and Growth," *American Economic Review* 108(11):3450–3491, https://doi.org/10.1257/aer.20130470.

[31] R. Cherif, F. Hasanov, and P. Aghion, 2023, "Fair and Inclusive Markets: Why Dynamism Matters," *Global Policy* 14(5):686–701, https://doi.org/10.1111/1758-5899.13250.

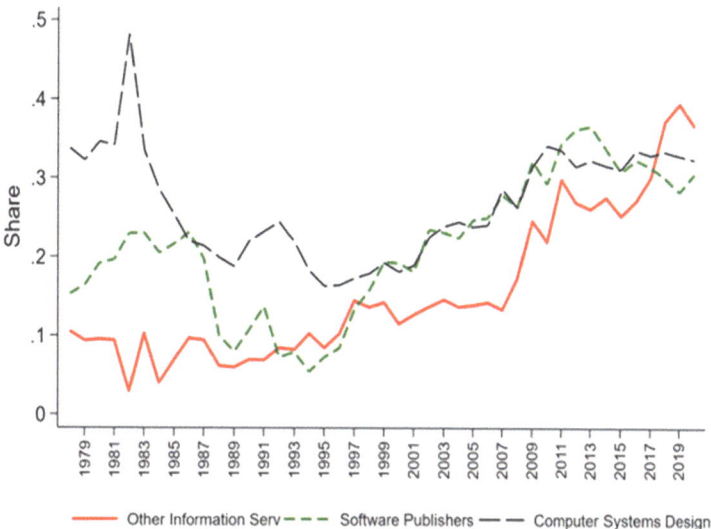

FIGURE 3-8 Rising share of employment in firms with more than 10,000 employees, selected high-tech industries. SOURCE: Created based on data from U.S. Census Bureau, Business Dynamics Statistics Datasets, https://www.census.gov/data/datasets/time-series/econ/bds/bds-datasets.html.

in low-wage firms and sectors.[32] These sorting and segregation effects have arguably reinforced the gaps between low- and high-productivity performers within sectors. Relatedly, Akcigit and Goldschlag find that over the post-2000 period, "inventors are increasingly concentrated in large incumbents, less likely to work for young firms, and less likely to become entrepreneurs."[33] Moreover, they find that an inventor's earnings increase and innovative output decreases when hired by an incumbent as compared to a young firm. They argue that these patterns are consistent with large incumbent firms having strategic reasons to slow innovation so as not to cannibalize their existing products and market shares. Their findings reinforce concerns about the potentially adverse implications for innovation and productivity growth of both increasing concentration of large incumbents in many sectors, especially mega firms in high-tech sectors, and decreasing entrepreneurship.

In spite of these structural headwinds to productivity growth, AI may yield a new and sustained surge in investment and productivity. Much of the remaining part of the chapter addresses this possibility. It remains to be seen whether AI yields this surge by disrupting the macroeconomic and structural changes discussed in this section and rekindling business dynamism. There is some evidence from the past few years that the

---

[32] J. Song, D.J. Price, F. Guvenen, N. Bloom, and T. von Wachter, 2019, "Firming Up Inequality," *Quarterly Journal of Economics* 134(1):1–50, https://doi.org/10.1093/qje/qjy025.

[33] U. Akcigit and N. Goldschlag, 2023, "Where Have All the 'Creative Talents' Gone? Employment Dynamics of US Inventors," Working Paper 23-17, Center for Economic Studies, U.S. Census Bureau.

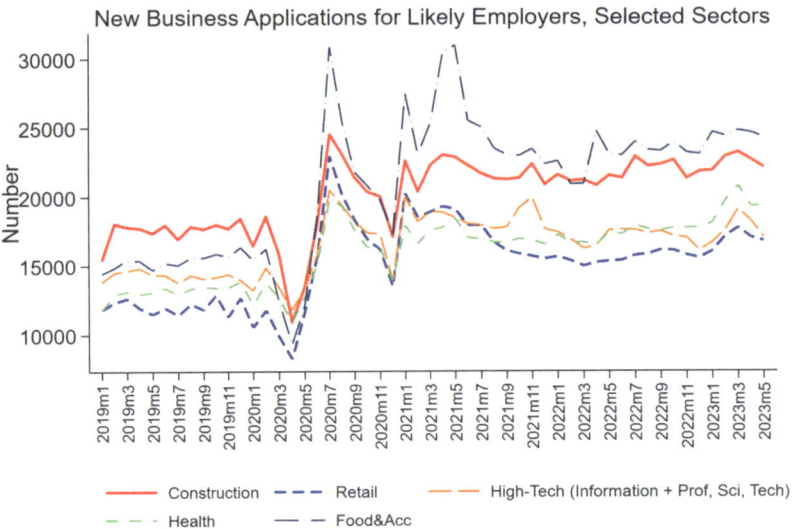

FIGURE 3-9 Surging business formation since 2020.
SOURCE: Created based on data from U.S. Bureau of the Census, Business Formation Statistics.

decline in business dynamism in the United States is being reversed. Business formation has been surging in the United States since 2020.[34] Some of this surge is undoubtedly associated with the structural changes induced by the COVID-19 pandemic in terms of changes in work and lifestyle (e.g., there has been a surge in business formation in e-commerce). This surge in business formation has continued through the present. As of May 2023, applications for new businesses that signal they are likely to be new employers remained more than 30 percent higher than in 2019. Moreover, this surge in business formation is occurring in key high-tech industries—the Information sector (NAICS 51) and the Professional, Scientific, and Technical Services sector (NAICS 54)—as shown in Figure 3-9. New AI firms are likely to be classified in one of these two industries.

EFFECTS OF ARTIFICIAL INTELLIGENCE ON PRODUCTIVITY

Overall Adoption Is Limited But Growing Rapidly

AI adoption in most firms is still low, but it has been gradually permeating economic activity over several years—for example, with the technology powering smartphones, in autonomous-driving features on cars, for digital retail sales via platforms like Amazon, for

---

[34] J.C. Haltiwanger, 2021, "Entrepreneurship During the COVID-19 Pandemic: Evidence from the Business Formation Statistics," pp. 9–42 in *Entrepreneurship and Innovation Policy and the Economy*, Vol. 1, National Bureau of Economic Research.

streaming services like Netflix, and in intelligent robots and intelligent systems in manufacturing. AI in the form of advanced analytics and machine learning algorithms has been effective at performing numerical optimization and predictive modeling in a wide range of industries.[35]

The adoption of AI tools has varied by firm characteristics and by sector. In the United States, larger, more highly digitized, and younger firms have been more likely to adopt AI.[36] In addition, adoption has been higher at firms with younger, more educated, and more experienced owners.[37] Overall, between 2016 and 2018, an estimated 13 percent of U.S. employees worked at firms using AI. Adoption rates also varied by industry; the largest percentages of firms with some AI adoption were found in information, financial services, management, and finance, and the largest percentages of workers with higher-than-average exposure rates to AI were found in these sectors as well as in retail trade, transportation, utilities, and manufacturing.[38,39]

According to results in the 2019 Annual Business Survey for U.S. companies, the main barriers to AI adoption by a firm are inapplicability to its business and cost. Among AI-adopting firms, 80 percent (employment-weighted) adopted AI to improve product or service quality, 65 percent adopted AI to upgrade existing processes, and 54 percent adopted AI to automate existing processes. Acemoglu and colleagues also report that firms adopting AI have higher productivity and lower labor shares than similar firms, a result that is consistent with automation being a major application for AI.[40] Of AI adopters, 15 percent reported an increase in employment and 6 percent reported a decrease, while 41 percent reported an increase in skill demand and none reported a decrease.

Although AI has affected specific applications and firms, to date the deployment of AI has been too small to have had a detectable effect on aggregate productivity growth or on productivity growth by industry. Indeed, the slowdown in TFP growth between 2005 and 2019 across sectors overlapped with the gradual roll-out of AI adoption.

---

[35] M. Chui, E. Hazan, R. Roberts, et al., 2023, "The Economic Potential of Generative AI: The Next Productivity Frontier," McKinsey & Company, June 14, https://www.mckinsey.com/capabilities/mckinsey-digital/our-insights/the-economic-potential-of-generative-ai-the-next-productivity-frontier.

[36] It can be challenging to define precisely what it means to "adopt AI." The following findings are drawn from the Annual Business Survey (ABS) of the U.S. Census, which targets owners and managers of about 850,000 U.S. firms of all sizes. The adoption question in the ABS starts with the following: "During the three years 2016 to 2018, to what extent did this business use the following technologies in production processes for goods or services?" Then for a series of technologies including AI, the responses possible are as follows: "Did not use; Tested but did not use in production or service; low use; moderate use; high use." A series of follow-up questions draws out how and why they are using the technologies.

[37] N. Zolas, Z. Kroff, E. Brynjolfsson, et al., 2020, "Advanced Technologies Adoption and Use by U.S. Firms: Evidence from the Annual Business Survey," *SSRN Electronic Journal*, https://doi.org/10.2139/ssrn.3759827.

[38] Ibid.

[39] European Commission and the U.S. Council of Economic Advisors, 2022, "The Impact of Artificial Intelligence on the Future of Workforces in the European Union and the United States of America," December 5, https://www.whitehouse.gov/wp-content/uploads/2022/12/TTC-EC-CEA-AI-Report-12052022-1.pdf.

[40] D. Acemoglu, G.W. Anderson, D.N. Beede, et al., 2022, "Automation and the Workforce: A Firm-Level View from the 2019 Annual Business Survey," NBER Working Paper No. 30659, November, National Bureau of Economic Research, https://doi.org/10.3386/w30659.

A few cases illustrate the various ways that AI has been affecting key industries. The information industry is the most digitized industry and has the highest share of both firms and employment with some AI adoption. AI is being applied in the financial services industry for a variety of purposes including risk assessment and capital allocation, stewardship in asset management, fraud detection, algorithmic trading, faster services (e.g., mortgage approvals), and core back-office support and compliance tasks. There have also been numerous AI applications in the auto industry including design and development, manufacturing and warehouse processes, analysis of road conditions, personalized vehicles and enhanced safety, auto insurance, and dealership experience.[41]

Yet, as noted above, the information sector experienced a sharp and unexplained deceleration in TFP growth after 2005. Information technology firms have been both the developers and the early adopters of AI technologies. Finance too has relatively high shares of firms and employment with some AI adoption, and it too experienced a significant deceleration in productivity growth. Indeed, in the area of securities and other financial investments, changes in productivity growth went from strongly positive in 1997–2005 to strongly negative in 2005–2019. The finance industry was hit hard by the 2007–2008 global financial crisis and the restructuring that followed, with negative consequences for its productivity growth.

A Framework for Thinking About the Effects of AI on Aggregate Productivity

How much will AI affect aggregate productivity? It is an important question but also one that is inherently difficult to answer. TFP has been called "a measure of our ignorance" because, by definition, it cannot be directly accounted for by any measured inputs.[42] Instead, it is the residual or unexplained additional output that is created after increases in capital and labor inputs are included.

Typically, this residual is interpreted as the result of technology broadly defined. This includes not only advances in equipment and machinery but also new production techniques and methods. Nonetheless, there are some key variables that will affect the magnitude of an increase in productivity growth that can be expected from a new technology such as AI. This section develops a framework for estimating the potential effects of AI on productivity and growth and for establishing bounds on how much additional growth to expect. The framework identifies eight key factors to consider.

A good place to start is with Hulten's theorem, which states that for efficient economies and under minimal assumptions, the first-order impact on aggregate output

---

[41] M. Singhal, S. Kadam, and S. Sahay, 2022, "29 AI Use Cases—Transforming the Automotive Industry," Birlasoft, CK Birla Group, https://www.birlasoft.com/articles/ai-use-cases-in-automotive-industry.

[42] M. Abramovitz, 1989, "Resource and Output Trends in the United States Since 1870," pp. 127–147 in *Thinking About Growth: And Other Essays on Economic Growth and Welfare, Studies in Economic History and Policy: USA in the Twentieth Century*, Cambridge University Press, https://doi.org/10.1017/CBO9780511664656.005.

of a TFP increase in an industry is proportional to that industry's sales as a share of aggregate output.[43] Hulten's theorem gives the first two factors to consider: (1) *the share of the economy that the technology affects* and (2) *the potential size of its productivity impact.* For instance, if LLMs affect 50 percent of the tasks in the economy and make those tasks 20 percent more productive on average, then a first-order estimate of the net effect of LLMs on aggregative productivity would be 50 percent of 20 percent, or 10 percent.

But that is only a start. A third factor is that most new technologies require *additional complementary investments* in workers, tangible capital, and intangible capital in order to be used effectively. For example, complementary investments to train workers to use the technology may be required. New business processes and organizational forms can also be important complements to new technologies.[44] Additional investment in physical capital may also be required. As an illustration, LLMs depend on training large neural networks that typically require significant investments in computing infrastructure. If such other investments are strict complements, meaning they are indispensable to using the new technology, then they can become bottlenecks. For instance, faster fiber-optic cables will generate no increase in bandwidth if they are not paired with suitable routers. Conceptually, if the production process in a manufacturing plant or industry consists of 1,000 steps that must be done in sequence, then speeding up 1 of them or even 999 of them will not increase throughput if at least one step remains a bottleneck.[45] Thus the need for complements, particularly when they become bottlenecks, can reduce the aggregate productivity effects of AI below what might be expected from Hulten's theorem.[46]

Over time, bottlenecks can be addressed. It's not uncommon for a bottleneck to become a focus of attention because the returns from alleviating it can be very high. One reason that Moore's law has advanced so consistently for more than 70 years is that whenever one aspect of the production process was not keeping up with the others, it

---

[43] C.R. Hulten, 1978, "Growth Accounting with Intermediate Inputs," *Review of Economic Studies* 45:511–518.

[44] E. Brynjolfsson and P. Milgrom, 2012, "Complementarity in Organizations," pp. 11–55 in *The Handbook of Organizational Economics*, R. Gibbons and J. Roberts, eds., Princeton University Press.

[45] A related phenomenon is sometimes called "Baumol's Cost Disease"; see W.D. Nordhaus, 2008, "Baumol's Diseases: A Macroeconomic Perspective," *B.E. Journal of Macroeconomics* 8(1):1–39. Even rapid productivity increases in one part of the economy will be dampened if other parts of the economy do not see an improvement. Over time, the productive sectors may require less labor and fall in cost. If demand does not grow commensurately, then the sectors with rapid productivity growth will shrink while the more stagnant sectors will become increasingly important.

[46] In particular, Hulten's theorem holds in a no frictions, no distortions, competitive (in output and factor markets) economy. The misallocation literature has emphasized that differences in productivity across countries, industries, and time depend critically on the frictions and distortions that inhibit the efficient allocation of resources. See C.-T. Hsieh and P.J. Klenow, 2009, "Misallocation and Manufacturing TFP in China and India," *Quarterly Journal of Economics* 124(4):1403–1448, https://doi.org/10.1162/qjec.2009.124.4.1403. These frictions and distortions can impact both the level and growth of productivity. In Hulten's economy, there is no dispersion in revenue productivity across firms because marginal revenue products are equalized instantaneously across firms (no markups, markdowns, other frictions, or distortions such as frictions in capital and labor markets). This perspective is not just that the productivity gains may take longer to be realized but also that they are dampened by the frictions and distortions inducing misallocation.

would draw attention, research, and investment. As bottlenecks are addressed, the long-run changes in output and productivity from a technology shock will tend to be larger in magnitude than the short-run changes.[47]

This highlights the role of *time lags* as a fourth factor. There are several reasons why the full impact of a new technology on productivity takes time. If the new technology changes tasks, jobs, and occupations—and the skills required for them—there could be considerable labor market disruption. The necessary labor market transitions could be substantial and costly. It also takes time to build and implement the new core technology as well as to implement complementary investments, which may include physical capital and infrastructure, human capital, and intangible assets. Furthermore, often the most effective combination of these assets is not well understood in advance and needs to be discovered by research or by experimentation. Overall, if a new technology can be expected ultimately to have a 10 percent effect on the level of productivity but it takes 10 years to fully implement, including time for the necessary redeployment of labor and time to create the necessary complements, then the technology's average annual effect on productivity will be only about 1 percent.

A fifth factor to consider is that private returns do not necessarily add up to equal social returns. In particular, a new technology may cause *positive or negative economic spillovers*—benefits or costs for businesses and individuals that are not directly involved in purchasing or using the technology. These externalities can have a positive or a negative effect on aggregate productivity. For instance, the introduction of LLMs may trigger a cascade of complementary innovations that create a great deal of value beyond the value created by the initial investment. The ChatGPT plugin marketplaces are examples of this. And, as discussed below, AI's tools for understanding protein folding are likely to create significant positive externalities in the pharmaceutical industry. With many general-purpose technologies like AI, complementary innovations ultimately do more to affect output and productivity than the initial innovation itself.

Spillovers can also be negative—for example, when AI is used for rent seeking or shifting market shares. For instance, a faster machine learning algorithm might make it possible to predict prices in a commodity market rapidly, allowing a trading firm to purchase or sell assets milliseconds before its competitors. That can result in large profits, but they largely come at the expense of others in the market. The social value of having the trade happen a few milliseconds earlier is negligible, but the private returns can be enormous. Similarly, some types of advertising may be aimed primarily at shifting market shares in a zero-sum way rather than increasing total market size or improving the match of products with customers. Relatedly, technology could allow for improved price discrimination and targeting, enabling sellers to capture consumer surplus from

---

[47] P. Milgrom and J. Roberts, 1996, "The LeChatelier Principle," *American Economic Review* 86(1):173–179.

buyers. Again, this can be very profitable without increasing total welfare. These kinds of negative business spillovers tend to be less of an issue in highly competitive markets, but AI could increase concentration, which would increase the potential for rent and thus rent-seeking behavior. More ominously, AI could create negative externalities by increasing cybersecurity risks and costs, by violating customer privacy, or by increasing the number and strength of homemade weapons or toxins.

Measurement issues are a sixth factor that should be considered when assessing the effects of a new technology on productivity, at least as it is conventionally reported. In particular, there are many benefits that are not captured in gross domestic product (GDP) and therefore are also missing from productivity. For instance, an AI-enabled innovation that leads to a new therapeutic drug may have some small direct effects on GDP when that drug is sold, but there may be even more important indirect effects if the drug leads to longer, healthier lives. Those health benefits generally will not show up in GDP or productivity. Health care is the top area for AI investment according to the 2023 edition of the AI Index report.[48] In addition, many new products create far more consumer surplus than revenue. For instance, a free or low-cost version of a digital AI assistant might generate little or no business revenue but significant benefits for its users. In most cases, the small increase in revenue would be reflected in GDP, but the larger increase in consumer surplus generally would not be. William Nordhaus has estimated that more than 95 percent of the benefits of technological innovations ultimately end up in the hands of consumers not sellers.[49]

There are several alternative measures of well-being, including some that specifically focus on measuring consumer surplus.[50,51] However, for now GDP and productivity are the primary metrics of economic growth used in the national accounts and by business, government, and the media.

The seventh factor to consider is substantial *heterogeneity* in the productivity effect of a new technology across sectors, firms, workers, and tasks. As noted earlier, there is evidence of a growing gap in the revenue productivity of the top 5 percent of firms in an industry in a given year ("the best") compared to the remainder of firms ("the

---

[48] N. Maslej, L. Fattorini, E. Brynjolfsson, et al., 2023, "The AI Index 2023 Annual Report," AI Index Steering Committee, Institute for Human-Centered AI, Stanford University, April, https://aiindex.stanford.edu/ai-index-report-2023.

[49] W. Nordhaus, 2004, "Schumpeterian Profits in the American Economy: Theory and Measurement," NBER Working Paper No. 10433, National Bureau of Economic Research.

[50] M. Fleurbaey, 2009, "Beyond GDP: The Quest for a Measure of Social Welfare," *Journal of Economic Literature* 47(4):1029–1075.

[51] E. Brynjolfsson, A. Collis, W.E. Diewert, F. Eggers, and K.J. Fox, 2019, "GDP-B: Accounting for the Value of New and Free Goods in the Digital Economy," National Bureau of Economic Research Working Paper No. w25695.

rest").[52] While this could be owing to a variety of causes,[53] it may reflect a growing gap between leaders and laggards in technology adoption and use. If AI exacerbates this trend, then looking only at average productivity may miss the growing heterogeneity in performance.

Last, it should be noted that the economy is not static, so the *dynamic effects* of technology are the eighth and final factor that should be considered.[54] In the long run, the rate of change in productivity is more important than its level. AI can boost innovation itself, leading to a faster rate of change, not just a one-time boost. Over time, even small changes in the rate of growth compound to become significant. One promising aspect of recent AI advances is that tools like LLMs make it easier for larger and more diverse groups of people to contribute to innovation. For instance, the prompts used to direct LLMs can be written in English and do not require learning programming languages like Python or C. Furthermore, even in applications where such languages are needed, coding can increasingly be done using natural language interfaces, leveraging tools such as GitHub Copilot.

In sum, these eight factors provide a framework for understanding how AI, like other technologies, can affect productivity and well-being. Hulten's theorem can provide the initial first-order estimate, based on the first two factors, highlighting that the aggregate effect is a function of all eight factors.

It is possible to develop estimates of some of these effects that can help put upper and lower bounds on the likely productivity impact of AI. That said, there will be uncertainties in all of the variables, so this framework is important less for the sake of getting precise predictions and more for getting a sense of where the main sources of uncertainty are and where the biggest policy levers are likely to be.

The following subsections go into more detail on each of these factors.

Factor 1: Share of the Economy Potentially Affected by AI

A major reason AI may significantly boost labor productivity growth is that it has potential applications in so many parts of the economy. Generative AI along with other types of AI and robotics have the potential to affect activities that today encompass a majority

---

[52] See, for example, D. Andrews, C. Criscuolo, and P. Gal, 2015, "Frontier Firms, Technology Diffusion and Public Policy: Micro Evidence from OECD Countries," OECD Productivity Working Paper No. 2, OECD Publishing, https://doi.org/10.1787/5jrql2q2jj7b-en; and E. Brynjolfsson, A. McAfee, M. Sorell, and F. Zhu, 2008, "Scale Without Mass: Business Process Replication and Industry Dynamics," Harvard Business School Technology and Operations Management Unit Research Paper No. 07-016, September 30, http://dx.doi.org/10.2139/ssrn.980568.

[53] Revenue productivity dispersion is revenue per unit input, and it potentially reflects many factors, including (1) rising dispersion of distortions and/or frictions impeding the equalization of marginal revenue products (e.g., rising uncertainty, adjustment costs); (2) rising dispersion of markups; (3) rising dispersion in fundamentals in the presence of a given set of frictions/distortions impeding the equalization of marginal revenue products; (4) rising correlation between fundamentals and distortions/frictions (e.g., markups rising especially for the largest firms); and (5) rising dispersion in within-industry differences in production processes.

[54] M.N. Baily, E. Brynjolfsson, and A. Korinek, 2023, "Machines of Mind: The Case for an AI-Powered Productivity Boom," Brookings Institution, May 10, https://www.brookings.edu/articles/machines-of-mind-the-case-for-an-ai-powered-productivity-boom.

of worker time. There is no perfect way to assess the tasks that will be affected. Eloundou and colleagues assess the alignment of occupations with LLM capabilities and find that LLMs alone could affect 80 percent of the U.S. workforce to some degree and affect, either as a complement or substitute, over half of the tasks done by 19 percent of the workforce.[55] Furthermore, there are other types of AI, including machine learning used for classification and prediction tasks, that are suitable for thousands of other tasks.[56] The net effect of AI on tasks will thus be quite widespread.

The set of tasks that can be affected by AI has expanded significantly over the past decade. The costly process of creating computer programs via labor-intensive manual coding is increasingly being replaced by automating machine learning algorithms.[57]

Supervised machine learning progress has been rapid owing to the availability of vast amounts of training data, which capture valuable and previously unnoticed regularities, often beyond human notice or even comprehension. In this way, tacit knowledge can be codified by creating usable software. These techniques work best when there are large amounts of input data (X) that can be mapped to labeled output data (Y). The machine learning algorithm can then find the relationships (X→Y) and, depending on the application, classify the outputs into categories or make predictions about outcomes. Table 3-1 gives some examples.

Foundation models,[58] which include LLMs and other forms of generative AI, are the latest AI breakthrough. Investment in generative AI is a small fraction of total investments in AI but is growing rapidly, and generative AI is already expanding the possibilities of what AI overall can achieve. It is important to note that to date much of the investment in generative AI is concentrated in a handful of highly digitized tech giants and platform companies along with venture capital–financed firms in the United States.

Unlike other technological advances in recent decades that automated many routine physical and cognitive tasks done by humans, generative AI systems will mostly affect cognitive work—both routine tasks and nonroutine tasks. Routine tasks are ones that follow explicit rules and procedures. In contrast, the rules and steps in nonroutine

---

[55] T. Eloundou, S. Manning, P. Mishkin, and D. Rock, 2023, "GPTs Are GPTs: An Early Look at the Labor Market Impact Potential of Large Language Models," arXiv preprint, arXiv:2303.10130.

[56] E. Brynjolfsson and T. Mitchell, 2017, "What Can Machine Learning Do? Workforce Implications," *Science* 358:1530–1534, https://doi.org/10.1126/science.aap8062; E.W. Felten, M. Raj, and R. Seamans, 2023, "Occupational Heterogeneity in Exposure to Generative AI," April 10, http://dx.doi.org/10.2139/ssrn.4414065; E. Felten, M. Raj, and R. Seamans, 2021, "Occupational, Industry, and Geographic Exposure to Artificial Intelligence: A Novel Dataset and Its Potential Uses," *Strategic Management Journal* 42(12):2195–2217, https://doi.org/10.1002/smj.3286; and C.B. Frey and M.A. Osborne, 2017, "The Future of Employment: How Susceptible Are Jobs to Computerisation?" *Technological Forecasting and Social Change* 114:254–280.

[57] E. Brynjolfsson and T. Mitchell, 2017, "What Can Machine Learning Do? Workforce Implications," *Science* 358:1530–1534, https://doi.org/10.1126/science.aap8062.

[58] As discussed in Chapter 1, foundation models are an approach for building AI systems in which a machine learning model is initially trained on a large amount of unlabeled data and can then be adapted to many applications. LLMs like GPT and Bard are examples of foundation models, and tools built around LLMs include ChatGPT. LLMs generate new content, making them a form of "generative AI," along with tools like Midjourney and DALL·E, which create images, and Copilot, which helps coders write software.

TABLE 3-1 Examples of Machine Learning Applications

Input X	Output Y	Application
Voice recording	Transcript	Speech recognition
Historical market data	Future market data	Trading bots
Photograph	Caption	Image tagging
Store transaction	Are the transaction details fraudulent?	Fraud detection
Purchase	Future purchase	Customer history-based behavior retention
Car locations and speed	Traffic flow	Traffic lights
Faces	Names	Face recognition
Chemical properties	Clinical effectiveness	Drug discovery

SOURCE: Created based on data from E. Brynjolfsson and A. Mcafee, 2017, "The Business of Artificial Intelligence: What It Can—and Cannot—Do for Your Organization," *Harvard Business Review*, July 18, https://hbr.org/2017/07/the-business-of-artificial-intelligence.

tasks cannot be codified. Systems based on foundation models can accomplish a growing number of nonroutine cognitive tasks that used to be done by cognitive workers. These tasks include composing fluent prose based on bullet points, summarizing documents, brainstorming, planning, and translating information from one language to another. These tasks include many tasks in administrative support, engineering services, financial and business operations, management, and sales. Many of these tasks are currently performed by workers with strong educational credentials, including bachelor's and graduate degrees. People who were relatively immune to previous waves of automation like creative writers, graphic artists, lawyers, doctors, accountants, and even chief executive officers are now being affected. Furthermore, AI's capabilities continue to evolve rapidly, suggesting that new effects are likely to emerge rapidly.

A useful approach to understanding the effects of these technologies is the task-based approach. Occupations consist of distinct tasks—according to O*NET, typically from 15 to 30 separate tasks. Rather than automating an entire occupation, AI will typically affect only some tasks in each occupation. For instance, applying the task-based approach, Brynjolfsson and colleagues found that of the 950 occupations they studied, there were none in which machine learning "ran the table" and affected all of the tasks, but AI could affect at least some tasks in most occupations.[59]

As noted above, using this task-based approach, Eloundou and colleagues estimated that "around 80% of the U.S. workforce could have at least 10% of their work

---

[59] E. Brynjolfsson, T. Mitchell, and D. Rock, 2018, "What Can Machines Learn and What Does It Mean for Occupations and the Economy?" pp. 43–47 in *AEA Papers and Proceedings*, Vol. 108, American Economic Association.

tasks affected by the introduction of LLMs, while approximately 19% of workers may see at least 50% of their tasks impacted," using a threshold of a 50 percent reduction in the time required to complete a task while maintaining quality.[60] Even when a task is exposed, labor may remain indispensable for that task, even as overall productivity grows. There may be a transition period, with LLMs initially complementing tasks within occupations before automating them over time.[61]

Overall, Eloundou and colleagues found significant task exposure in occupations and employment in all industries, with wide sectoral heterogeneity and the highest relative exposures in the information processing industries and in hospitals. Manufacturing, agriculture, and mining show lower exposure. In contrast to the results from Acemoglu cited earlier, exposure appears to be uncorrelated with both recent factor productivity growth and labor productivity growth by sector. LLMs and related technologies could improve productivity in health care and education, two huge and perennially lagging productivity sectors. There is also growing evidence that AI can reduce the cost and duration of new drug discovery, another area in need of a productivity boost.

A recent study by Goldman Sachs estimated that generative AI can substitute for humans in about 25 percent of current tasks.[62] The estimated effects vary significantly by job type and industry sector. Higher effects are expected in administrative and office support, legal services, business and financial operations, and management and sales. Lower effects are expected in physically intensive professions such as maintenance and construction and in services such as personal care and food and hospitality services. Only some of the tasks of most jobs are exposed to generative AI automation, ranging from jobs with 50 percent or more of the tasks exposed to generative AI automation—like legal services, sales, and business and financial services—to jobs with less than 49 percent of the tasks exposed to AI automation—like production, construction, personal services, and health care. The Goldman Sachs study conjectures that AI is likely to substitute for humans in jobs with high degrees of task exposure and to complement humans in jobs with lower degrees of task exposure.

Recent research by the McKinsey Global Institute (MGI) concludes that generative AI is likely to have the largest impact on four business functions—customer operations, marketing and sales, software engineering, and R&D. Using a detailed analysis of how generative AI could transform these four use cases, MGI estimates that applying generative AI could increase productivity in customer care by between 30 and 45 percent of

---

[60] T. Eloundou, S. Manning, P. Mishkin, and D. Rock, 2023, "GPTs Are GPTs: An Early Look at the Labor Market Impact Potential of Large Language Models," arXiv preprint, arXiv:2303.10130.

[61] M.-H. Huang and R.T. Rust, 2018, "Artificial Intelligence in Service," *Journal of Service Research* 21(2):155–172, https://doi.org/10.1177/1094670517752459.

[62] Goldman Sachs, 2023, "Top of Mind: Generative AI: Hype or Truly Transformative?" *Goldman Sachs Global Macro Research*, Issue 120, July 5, https://www.goldmansachs.com/intelligence/pages/top-of-mind/generative-ai-hype-or-truly-transformative/report.pdf.

current function costs; could increase sales productivity by about 3 to 5 percent of current global sales expenditures; could increase the productivity for marketing between 5 and 15 percent of total marketing spending; could increase the productivity of software engineering from 20 to 45 percent of current annual spending; and could increase productivity in product R&D between 10 percent and 15 percent of overall R&D costs.[63]

A May 2024 paper by Acemoglu is more pessimistic about the magnitude of impacts of new advances in AI. Using existing estimates of AI exposure and task-level productivity improvements, it projects more modest macroeconomic impacts, with a maximum increase of 0.66 percent in TFP over a decade. The paper further suggests that these estimates might be overstated, as early evidence focuses on easy-to-learn tasks. By contrast, many future impacts will stem from hard-to-learn tasks, which are influenced by numerous context-dependent factors.[64]

The automotive, finance, and health care sectors are among those most likely to be affected by generative AI. In the automotive sector, generative AI will improve safety and reduce accidents, a central goal of automobile producers; will enable and accelerate the introduction of autonomous vehicles; will personalize vehicles to customer requirements; and will increase the efficiency of costly marketing and advertising functions. In finance, generative AI is building on traditional AI capabilities already adopted for task automation, algorithmic trading and asset management, fraud detection, and personalized services. In health care, prior to the generative AI breakthrough, AI was already affecting administrative services and insurance, diagnosis and treatment, and patient engagement and adherence.[65] Generative AI has the potential to affect all parts of health care—providers, payers, pharmaceutical and medical equipment producers, and services and operations.[66]

Education, parts of health care, and other forms of personal care are productivity laggards compared to the rest of the economy. Many of the tasks in these sectors have lower exposure to AI than tasks in legal and accounting services and financial services. Moreover, many of these tasks require both physical and social interactions with humans. AI could increase productivity in these perennially low productivity sectors and mitigate the Baumol effect. Chapter 5 provides examples of AI productivity enhancements in education.

---

[63] M. Chui, E. Hazan, R. Roberts, et al., 2023, "The Economic Potential of Generative AI: The Next Productivity Frontier," McKinsey & Company, June 14, https://www.mckinsey.com/capabilities/mckinsey-digital/our-insights/the-economic-potential-of-generative-ai-the-next-productivity-frontier.

[64] D. Acemoglu, 2024, "The Simple Macroeconomics of AI," NBER Working Paper No. 32487, May, National Bureau of Economic Research, http://www.nber.org/papers/w32487.

[65] T. Davenport and R. Kalakota, 2019, "The Potential for Artificial Intelligence in Healthcare," *Future Healthcare Journal* 6(2):94–98.

[66] M. Huddle, J. Kellar, K. Srikumar, K. Deepak, and D. Martines, 2023, "Generative AI Will Transform Health Care Sooner Than You Think," Boston Consulting Group, June 22, https://www.bcg.com/publications/2023/how-generative-ai-is-transforming-health-care-sooner-than-expected.

Last, there is evidence that adoption of earlier AI systems by firms had a significant effect on within-firm worker average productivity growth, adding 2–3 percentage points annually.[67] More recent AI systems could have a similar significant effect on average worker productivity over time. But it is dangerous to predict aggregate productivity effects based on case studies. For instance, it took decades for the productivity effects of computers to show up in aggregate growth and productivity.

Factor 2: Productivity Effects in Specific Applications

Even if AI affects many sectors of the economy, the total productivity impact may be limited if it is only a "so-so" technology that barely improves on existing systems—that adds to corporate profits and substitutes for humans without adding much to productivity.[68] In a number of case studies, however, the productivity impact has already been quite large. If these cases generalize, that portends well for aggregate productivity growth.

Some of the key effects of generative AI can be observed in a paper about the phased roll-out of an LLM-based system designed to assist thousands of contact center workers.[69] The research compared agents who had access to this system with those who did not. The researchers discovered average productivity gains of 14 percent within just a few months (Figure 3-10). Customer satisfaction increased, and an analysis of millions of transcripts revealed a positive shift in sentiment: consumers used more happy words and fewer angry words. Simultaneously, employee turnover decreased among those who used the system. Moreover, managerial roles evolved, with broader spans of control and fewer interventions needed.

Interestingly, the results showed very disparate effects on different types of workers. Productivity increased by more than 35 percent for the newest workers as well as the least skilled workers but showed almost no change for the most experienced and skilled employees.

How did the system achieve these results and change the organization? The key lies in the fact that while earlier types of software required painstaking coding by humans who needed to fully understand the processes they were detailing, machine learning systems like this one can capture tacit knowledge by examining the relationships among inputs and outputs. This opens up many new processes that were previously learned only through on-the-job experience. Specifically, this system analyzed millions of transcripts of customer interactions and identified the common patterns in

---

[67] Goldman Sachs, 2023, "Top of Mind: Generative AI: Hype or Truly Transformative?" *Goldman Sachs Global Macro Research*, Issue 120, July 5, https://www.goldmansachs.com/intelligence/pages/top-of-mind/generative-ai-hype-or-truly-transformative/report.pdf.

[68] D. Acemoglu and P. Restrepo, 2019, "Automation and New Tasks: How Technology Displaces and Reinstates Labor," *Journal of Economic Perspectives* 33(2):3–30, https://doi.org/10.1257/jep.33.2.3.

[69] E. Brynjolfsson, D. Li, and L.R. Raymond, 2023, "Generative AI at Work," National Bureau of Economic Research Working Paper No. w31161.

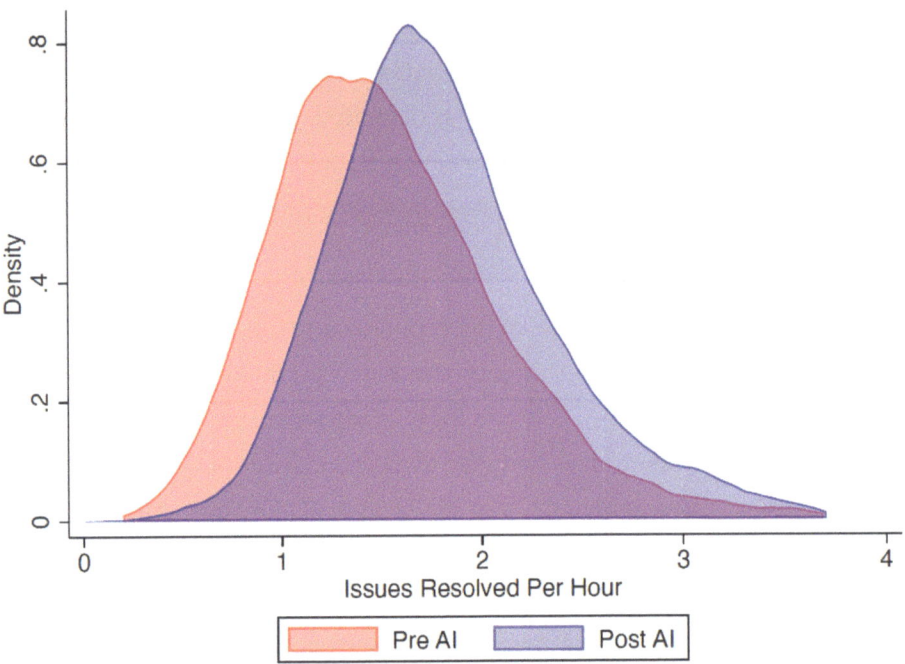

FIGURE 3-10 Generative artificial intelligence (AI) leads to productivity improvements for contact center workers.
SOURCE: E. Brynjolfsson, D. Li, and L.R. Raymond, 2023, "Generative AI at Work," National Bureau of Economic Research Working Paper No. w31161, https://arxiv.org/abs/2304.11771v1. CC-BY-NC-ND 4.0 DEED.

successful exchanges. These tended to match the skills of the most skilled and experienced workers, so they benefited less than the newer workers. The system's success can be attributed partly to the company founders' strategic decision to develop a technology designed to augment workers rather than attempting to create a fully automated replacement.

Other interesting examples of the productivity effects of machine learning systems are medical image recognition and machine translation. A convolutional neural network trained on 129,450 medical images and 2,032 different diseases was able to diagnose different types of cancer at a level that matched or exceeded 21 board-certified dermatologists.[70] The authors argue that AI could provide low-cost access to diagnostic care to billions of smartphone users, a dramatic increase in dermatology productivity. AI is also being used in radiology to improve diagnostic performance, help radiologists to prioritize images, and reduce the time it takes to read images. Recent studies have shown improved diagnostic performance with reduced reading times for images with AI in mammography and bone fracture analysis and treatment. Overall reading

---

[70] A. Esteva, B. Kuprel, R.A. Novoa, et al., 2017, "Dermatologist-Level Classification of Skin Cancer with Deep Neural Networks," *Nature* 542(7639):115–118, https://doi.org/10.1038/nature21056.

times—a measure of productivity—shortened when radiologists used AI, but abnormalities detected by AI could lengthen these times.[71] That said, productivity benefits are not guaranteed, even when machines are very good at the relevant tasks. Agarwal and colleagues conducted an experiment with radiologists that varied the availability of AI assistance.[72] They found that radiologists "do not fully capitalize on the potential gains from AI assistance."

The trading platform eBay mediates about $14 billion of cross-board trade among 200 countries. It trained a machine learning–based translation system to translate listings for various language pairs, improving on their prior systems. Because the system was rolled out in a staggered fashion across different countries, it was possible to estimate the causal effects of the system on international trade carried out on the platform. The new machine learning translation system increased trade by 10.9 percent.[73] Because prior research found that trade decreases in proportion to distance between countries, this was the economic equivalent of reducing the distance between the treated country pairs by 26 percent, a massive productivity gain for participants on the platform from a piece of software.[74]

There is a growing body of literature that estimates generative AI's productivity effects on many other occupations or tasks. Noy and Zhang find that many writing tasks can be completed twice as fast.[75] Korinek provides 25 use cases where economists can be significantly more productive using LLMs.[76] Peng and colleagues find that software engineers can write code up to twice as fast using Codex, a tool based on the LLM GPT-3's earlier version.[77] Dell'Acqua and colleagues draw on data from a preregistered experiment involving 758 consultants doing 18 distinct tasks either with or without access to GPT-4 to find that consultants using AI completed 12 percent more tasks on average and completed tasks 25 percent more quickly, and that their output was 40 percent higher in quality compared to a control group.[78]

---

[71] H.J. Shin, K. Han, L. Ryu, and E.-K. Kim, 2023, "The Impact of Artificial Intelligence on the Reading Times of Radiologists for Chest Radiographs," *NPJ Digital Medicine* 6(1):82.

[72] N. Agarwal, A. Moehring, P. Rajpurkar, and T. Salz, 2023, "Combining Human Expertise with Artificial Intelligence: Experimental Evidence from Radiology," NBER Working Paper No. w31422, http://dx.doi.org/10.2139/ssrn.4505053.

[73] E. Brynjolfsson, X. Hui, and M. Liu, 2018, "Does Machine Translation Affect International Trade? Evidence from a Large Digital Platform," NBER Working Paper 24917, National Bureau of Economic Research.

[74] A. Lendle, M. Olarreaga, S. Schropp, and P.-L. Vézina, 2016, "There Goes Gravity: eBay and the Death of Distance," *Economic Journal* 126:406–441, https://doi.org/10.1111/ecoj.12286.

[75] S. Noy and W. Zhang, 2023, "Experimental Evidence on the Productivity Effects of Generative Artificial Intelligence," *Science* 381:187–192, https://doi.org/10.1126/science.adh2586.

[76] A. Korinek, 2023, "Language Models and Cognitive Automation for Economic Research," NBER Working Paper No. 30957, National Bureau of Economic Research.

[77] S. Peng, E. Kalliamvakou, P. Cihon, and M. Demirer, 2023, "The Impact of AI on Developer Productivity: Evidence from GitHub Copilot," arXiv preprint, arXiv:2302.06590.

[78] F. Dell'Acqua, E. McFowland III, E. Mollick, et al., 2023, "Navigating the Jagged Technological Frontier: Field Experimental Evidence of the Effects of AI on Knowledge Worker Productivity and Quality," Harvard Business School Working Paper, No. 24-013, September.

Although much of the research on AI's effects on productivity is conducted in laboratory settings or as case studies, the contact center example shows that such gains in specific tasks can lead to substantial benefits in real-world situations. If there are comparable productivity effects in other knowledge and information work activities as AI is introduced, this would lead to significant gains in aggregate productivity. Generative AI, for example, could increase the productivity of workers who work with text—including reports, marketing, and coding—and those who use images, like graphic artists, designers, and engineers, among others.

Factor 3: Complements, Bottlenecks, and Redeployment

AI can increase labor productivity through three main channels. First, through automation and the resulting substitution of human labor, AI can increase labor productivity directly by reducing the worker hours required for a given amount of output. Second, AI can complement workers, making them more productive in their tasks. Third, the redeployment of the capacity of workers freed up by AI automation into other equally or more productive tasks can increase productivity. This redeployment can occur through the creation of new tasks within an organization or through the reallocation and reemployment of workers displaced by AI automation to both existing and new tasks and occupations. Some of the reemployment of displaced workers will emerge in response to higher aggregate demand and labor demand resulting from the productivity and income gains of nondisplaced workers. Some of the reemployment will result directly from the effects of AI automation on the creation of new jobs and occupations.

Thus, harnessing the productivity benefits of AI in the tasks and occupations where it can be applied is not simply a matter of substituting for labor. Instead, it is likely to require investment in worker skills and training, as well as other complements, and the creation of new occupations and redeployment of labor.

First, consider complementary investments and innovations that will be necessary to provide workers with the skills and training necessary to work with AI systems and to qualify for the new tasks and occupations they create over time. AI, like other general-purpose technologies, will also require complementary investments and innovations in both tangible and intangible capital and in new forms of organizations. For example, systems for diagnosing disease from medical images, such as the dermatology and mammography examples described above, have made impressive progress. In late 2016, AI pioneer Geoffrey Hinton famously said, "People should stop training radiologists now. It's just completely obvious within 5 years deep learning is going to do better than radiologists…. It might be 10 years, but we've got plenty of radiologists already."[79]

---

[79] G. Hinton, 2016, "On Radiology," 2016 Machine Learning and Market for Intelligence Conference, Toronto, ON, https://www.youtube.com/watch?v=2HMPRXstSvQ&t=29s.

The American College of Radiology's AI Central site lists more than 200 Food and Drug Administration–approved radiology AI algorithms.[80] However, actual adoption of these algorithms has been slow. In fact, 2021 was a record year for postings on the American College of Radiology's job board; job postings continued to be high into early 2022, at more than double the rate of 2019.[81]

One reason for the increased job postings is that according to the Occupational Information Network (O*NET), radiologists perform 30 distinct tasks, and only one of them is reading medical images. The evidence suggests that some of the tasks performed by radiologists are subject to automation by AI while others are unaffected by AI. To the extent these other tasks are essential, human radiologists, or at least someone else doing those tasks, will be necessary. Furthermore, the other tasks can become bottlenecks, limiting the productivity gains from speeding up one part of the job. In addition, the automation of some tasks will save time, but imaging use will also increase; overall, the demand for radiology and for humans doing radiology tasks could increase if demand is sufficiently elastic.

Second, the creation of entirely new tasks and occupations as a result of AI is also likely. In fact, more than 60 percent of employment in 2018 was in occupations that did not exist in 1940.[82] This implies that more than 85 percent of the employment growth over the past 80 years arises from the technology-driven creation of new tasks and occupations.[83] The ICT revolution of the past 30 years introduced new occupations like web page design and software engineering that complemented the technology.

One consequence of the need for complementary innovation and investment and the bottlenecks and redeployments is that decades of technological advancement have not made it more difficult for workers to find jobs, as measured by the unemployment rate. However, fluctuations in labor demand are reflected in wage levels more than in employment opportunities. For many workers, the wage effects have been negative. For example, Acemoglu and Restrepo find that 50 percent to 70 percent of the changes in the wage structure in the United States over the past 40 years is accounted for by relative wage declines for workers specializing in routine tasks in industries undergoing rapid automation.[84]

---

[80] M. Windsor, 2022, "This Radiologist Is Helping Doctors See Through the Hype to an AI Future," *UAB Reporter*, December 5, https://www.uab.edu/reporter/people/achievements/item/9925-this-radiologist-is-helping-doctors-see-through-the-hype-to-an-ai-future.

[81] S. Baginski, 2022, "2022 Radiologist Job Market Update: High Volume, High Pay, and a Search for High Quality of Life," vRad, Eden Prairie, MN, May 2, https://blog.vrad.com/2022-radiologist-job-market-update-rrc.

[82] D. Autor, C.M. Chin, A. Salomons, and B. Seegmiller, 2024, "New Frontiers: The Origins and Content of New Work, 1940–2018," *Quarterly Journal of Economics* 139(3):1399–1465, https://doi.org/10.1093/qje/qjae008.

[83] J. Hatzius, J. Briggs, D. Kodnani, and G. Pierdomenico, 2023, "Global Economics Analyst: The Potentially Large Effects of Artificial Intelligence on Economic Growth," Goldman Sachs, March 26, https://www.gspublishing.com/content/research/en/reports/2023/03/27/d64e052b-0f6e-45d7-967b-d7be35fabd16.html.

[84] D. Acemoglu and P. Restrepo, 2022, "Tasks, Automation, and the Rise in U.S. Wage Inequality," *Econometrica* 90:1973–2016, https://doi.org/10.3982/ECTA19815.

Factor 4: Time Lags

Although AI's effects on productivity growth may be substantial, it may take years for them to spread throughout the economy. Time lags vary for AI adoption.

In particular, the need for the complementary investments discussed in the previous section may temporarily delay or even reverse some productivity gains, as conventionally measured.[85] For instance, it took 30–40 years for factories to experience significant productivity gains from electricity.[86] Those gains were achieved only when factories reorganized around the flow of materials, with each machine powered by a separate electric motor instead of a central steam engine. This process of reorganization involved experimentation and an eventual shakeout process, with successful implementers expanding and unsuccessful implementers contracting and exiting.[87]

That said, for many AI systems the productivity effects could be realized more quickly than those for earlier general-purpose technologies because much of the necessary core infrastructure is already in place. The Internet, cloud computing, office software, and mobile devices are already widely used and can be updated efficiently with AI tools. Rapid adoption via this infrastructure is a major reason ChatGPT famously reached 100 million users in just 60 days. As Microsoft and Google introduce LLMs and other generative AI technologies into their office suites in the coming months, hundreds of millions of users will instantly gain access to the power of these innovations. Similarly, both the example of machine translation at eBay and the example of the LLM in the call center discussed above demonstrate that in some cases, generative AI technologies can be rapidly fielded and translate into significant productivity grains.

In fact, according to one recent study, generative AI is on pace to achieve the speed of diffusion in 1 year that took the Internet 7 years to achieve and that took electricity more than 20 years to achieve. Reaching 30 percent diffusion spillover into adjacent segments took electricity 30 years and the Internet half that time, and generative AI is on pace to halve that time yet again.[88]

---

[85] E. Brynjolfsson, D. Rock, and C. Syverson, 2021, "The Productivity J-Curve: How Intangibles Complement General Purpose Technologies," *American Economic Journal: Macroeconomics* 13(1):333–372, https://doi.org/10.1257/mac.20180386.

[86] E. Brynjolfsson, D. Rock, and C. Syverson, 2018, "Artificial Intelligence and the Modern Productivity Paradox: A Clash of Expectations and Statistics," pp. 23–57 in *The Economics of Artificial Intelligence: An Agenda*, National Bureau of Economic Research.

[87] The transformative effect of AI is multifaceted, as noted in several recent articles—for example, E. Selenko, S. Bankins, M. Shoss, J. Warburton, and S.L.D. Restubog, 2022, "Artificial Intelligence and the Future of Work: A Functional-Identity Perspective," *Current Directions in Psychological Science* 31(3):272–279, https://doi.org/10.1177/09637214221091823; and D.J. Putka, F.L. Oswald, R.N. Landers, A.S. Beatty, R.A. McCloy, and M.C. Yu, 2022, "Evaluating a Natural Language Processing Approach to Estimating KSA and Interest Job Analysis Ratings," *Journal of Business and Psychology*, advance online publication, https://doi.org/10.1007/s10869-022-09824-0.

[88] E. Stanley, 2023, "Tech Diffusion: 10 Lessons from 100 Years," Morgan Stanley Research, June 2.

Factor 5: Externalities and Rent Seeking

Many of the innovative applications of AI are beneficial not only to those implementing them but also to others, creating positive externalities. For instance, improvements in education and health are often considered public goods, with widespread benefits for the economy. A faster rate of scientific discovery can boost economic growth and improve well-being. More generally, Nordhaus has argued that while innovators may get large profits initially, in the long run, they capture "only a miniscule fraction of the social returns" from their technological advances—perhaps as little as 2.2 percent—with the rest eventually going to consumers and others.[89] If this is true for AI as well, then even the high private returns observed in some of these early case studies may not fully reflect the eventual benefits to consumers and others.

Innovations can also create negative externalities, like pollution and congestion. For instance, some have argued that deep fakes will make it harder to distinguish truth from fiction, creating an "epistemic threat."[90] When AI is used to increase engagement in social media, it might also lead to "digital addiction."[91] These and other negative externalities would make private returns an overestimate of the net productivity (or at least welfare) contribution of AI.

AI technologies can also be used for business stealing or rent seeking, which can be privately profitable but not drive productivity in the aggregate. For instance, better tools for high-frequency trading or deep fakes for fooling people could be privately lucrative innovations that do not necessarily translate into faster productivity growth. More effort repackaging existing art and literature and less secure property rights for artists, writers, and inventors may also lead to less innovative output. The regulatory environment, property rights, and types of innovation incentives will play a key role here.

Some of the most important rent-seeking effects of the technology may be between employers and employees. As with other automation technologies, AI affects human tasks through three effects: displacement (decrease in demand for labor in tasks that are automated), productivity (increase in the demand for labor in nonautomated tasks), and reinstatement (creation of new tasks for labor). Over time, but at a highly uncertain pace, displacement effects are offset by both productivity and reinstatement effects.[92]

---

[89] W. Nordhaus, 2004, "Schumpeterian Profits in the American Economy: Theory and Measurement," NBER Working Paper No. 10433, April.

[90] D. Fallis, 2021, "The Epistemic Threat of Deepfakes," *Philosophy and Technology* 34:623–643, https://doi.org/10.1007/s13347-020-00419-2.

[91] H. Allcott, M. Gentzkow, and L. Song, 2022, "Digital Addiction," *American Economic Review* 112(7):2424–2463, https://doi.org/10.1257/aer.20210867.

[92] D. Acemoglu and P. Restrepo, 2019, "Automation and New Tasks: How Technology Displaces and Reinstates Labor," *Journal of Economic Perspectives* 33(2):3–30, as summarized in L.D. Tyson and J. Zysman, 2022, "Automation, AI and Work," *Daedalus* 151(2):256–271, https://doi.org/10.1162/daed_a_01914.

However, displacement effects can be immediate and palpable, with negative effects on employment. By contrast, the benefits to labor from productivity and reinstatement effects can take years or even decades to appear, with significant adverse impacts on labor—unemployment, wage losses, and growing inequality—during that time.[93]

In the long run, automation, productivity growth, and employment move together. But there is no guarantee that productivity growth results in average or median wage growth. Indeed, throughout the information technology and Internet revolutions, the gap between productivity growth and average and median wage growth grew. Some scholars have argued that the advent of AI may mark an inflection point in this trend; AI may directly substitute for the expertise of elite professionals while complementing the practical knowledge of many middle-skill workers, such as nurses, skilled tradespeople, and paralegals.[94]

The disruption that accompanies major technological progress always leaves winners and losers, with trade-offs around the time horizons that matter to businesses, workers, citizens, and political leaders. Moreover, the costs of displacement may be felt in certain locations while the benefits of productivity and reinstatement fall elsewhere.[95] There is evidence that over the past 30 years, "while automation's displacement effects have accelerated and intensified, its productivity and reinstatement effects have been slower to materialize and smaller than expected."[96]

A key question is whether as AI drives technological change in the future, the displacement of labor will continue to outpace the creation of new employment opportunities. The answer is uncertain. Another question with an uncertain answer is whether businesses will deploy generative AI in "so-so" applications that reduce costs by replacing labor without generating much productivity growth or improvements in the quality of service—think self-checkout kiosks at stores as an example.[97] What is certain, as this example indicates, is that the productivity effects of generative AI will depend on how it is used—to create revenues, to reduce costs, or to enhance productivity.

---

[93] L.D. Tyson and J. Zysman, 2022, "Automation, AI and Work," *Daedalus* 151(2):256–271, https://doi.org/10.1162/daed_a_01914.

[94] A. Agrawal, J.S. Gans, and A. Goldfarb, 2023, "Do We Want Less Automation?" *Science* 381(6654):155–158, July 14; and D. Autor, 2024, "Applying AI to Rebuild Middle Class Jobs," NBER Working Paper No. w32140, February, National Bureau of Economic Research.

[95] S. Lund, J. Manyika, L. Hilton Segel, et al., 2019, "The Future of Work in America: People and Places, Today and Tomorrow," McKinsey Global Institute; and M. Muro, 2019, "Countering the Geographical Impacts of Automation: Computers, AI, and Place Disparities," Brookings Institution.

[96] L.D. Tyson and J. Zysman, 2022, "Automation, AI and Work," *Daedalus* 151(2):256–271, https://doi.org/10.1162/daed_a_01914.

[97] D. Acemoglu and P. Restrepo, 2019, "Automation and New Tasks: How Technology Displaces and Reinstates Labor," *Journal of Economic Perspectives* 33(2):3–30.

Factor 6: The Heterogeneous Effects of AI

Looking only at average productivity may mask important differences—some groups may be left behind even as others benefit. AI could exacerbate this trend or mitigate it, depending in part on the policies implemented.

In recent years, dispersion has generally increased. For instance, within-industry dispersion in TFP across establishments in the U.S. manufacturing sector has been rising, especially in the post-2000 period (see Figure 3-5). Although TFP is more difficult to measure at the firm level for other sectors, dispersion in labor productivity is rising across firms within industries in all sectors of the economy.[98] Andrews and colleagues provide evidence of rising productivity dispersion within industries in many OECD countries.[99] This increase in dispersion has not been well explained but may in part reflect growing digitization and information technology use among firms.[100,101]

Technological automation in recent decades has been skill or routine replacing, with the biggest impact on workers in routine middle-skill, middle-wage jobs. The result has been a "hollowing out" of such jobs that have declined as a share of total employment, along with a significant increase in the share of high-skill, high-wage jobs in total employment and a smaller increase in the share of low-skill, low-wage jobs in total employment.

AI technologies, prior to generative AI, could be characterized as "routine-biased technological change on steroids," automating both noncognitive and increasingly cognitive routine tasks.[102] But generative AI is a step change in the development of AI and its capabilities, extending beyond routine tasks to several nonroutine tasks that require human skills like finding patterns and summarizing content, generating novel solutions, and using basic creativity. Indeed, generative AI is likely to have the biggest impact on nonroutine "knowledge" work that previously had the lowest risk of automation. Generative AI could have the largest impact on high-wage, high-skill jobs that require significant educational credentials. The natural language ability of generative AI implies that occupations heavy on communicating and documenting may be disproportionately exposed.

---

[98] R.A. Decker, J. Haltiwanger, R.S. Jarmin, and J. Miranda, 2020, "Changing Business Dynamism and Productivity: Shocks Versus Responsiveness," *American Economic Review* 110(12):3952–3990, https://doi.org/10.1257/aer.20190680.

[99] D. Andrews, C. Criscuolo, and P. Gal, 2016, "The Best Versus the Rest: The Global Productivity Slowdown, Divergence Across Firms and the Role of Public Policy," OECD Productivity Working Paper No. 5, OECD Publishing, https://doi.org/10.1787/63629cc9-en.

[100] C. Atkins, O. White, A. Padhi, K. Ellingrud, A. Madgavkar, and M. Neary, 2023, "Rekindling US Productivity for a New Era," McKinsey Global Institute, February 16, https://www.mckinsey.com/mgi/our-research/rekindling-us-productivity-for-a-new-era#introduction.

[101] E. Brynjolfsson, W. Jin, and X. Wang, 2023, "Information Technology, Firm Size, and Industrial Concentration," NBER Working Paper No. w31065, National Bureau of Economic Research.

[102] L.D. Tyson and J. Zysman, 2022, "Automation, AI and Work," *Daedalus* 151(2):256–271, https://doi.org/10.1162/daed_a_01914.

It is important to note that occupations in many of the services that have been lagging in productivity growth—such as hospitality services, personal care, and some segments of health care—have less exposure to generative AI. Many of the tasks in these jobs require human interaction, social and emotional reasoning and sensing, and physical capabilities—areas in which humans continue to outperform generative AI. Many of these jobs are low-wage, low-skill jobs filled by workers without college degrees. Such services account for most of the growth in jobs predicted by the U.S. Bureau of Labor Statistics over the next decade. If demographics and consumer demand increase employment in jobs in low-productivity sectors with low exposure to AI as a share of total employment, this will limit the economy-wide aggregate productivity effects of AI.

Factor 7: Imperfect Measurement

Using GDP as the sole or principal measure of living standards can lead to an incomplete and distorted understanding of the true well-being of individuals and societies. Because productivity is simply defined as GDP divided by labor (for labor productivity) or GDP divided by the weighted sum of labor and capital (for TFP), these measures are imperfect measures of technical progress and only partial drivers of living standards.

GDP is an incomplete measure of living standards for several reasons. First, GDP fails to capture nonmonetary aspects that affect living standards, such as quality of life, environmental sustainability, and social indicators like crime rates, political stability, and social cohesion. With few exceptions, goods and services with zero price, like many digital goods, have zero weight in the GDP numbers. Likewise, GDP largely disregards the value of unpaid work, such as caregiving and household chores, which predominantly affects women and can significantly affect living standards.

Second, even for the goods and services that are measured, GDP considers only the aggregate level of economic output of a country and does not take into account distributional factors that affect well-being such as income inequality, the distribution of wealth, and access to goods like health care and education. Even if overall GDP increases, that does not guarantee equitable distribution of wealth, income, and opportunities, which can result in significant disparities in living standards among different socioeconomic groups.

Additionally, GDP growth can be driven by unsustainable practices, such as overexploitation of natural resources or increased production of goods with negative impacts on health and the environment. These practices may undermine long-term well-being and sustainability, even if they contribute to higher GDP figures in the short term.

Another metric, GDP-B, seeks to assess the benefits (specifically the changes in consumer surplus) created by goods and services, not their costs or prices. In this way, GDP-B captures the value of free digital services, such as search engines and online content, as well as household production and other unpriced services that traditional GDP calculations fail to take into account.[103] One recent study found that 10 digital goods generate more than $2.5 trillion in annual consumer welfare gains across 13 countries, with relatively larger benefits for the poorer countries and poorer individuals within countries.[104]

There are several alternative metrics of well-being that AI could affect, including the following:

- *Human Development Index*—This composite index measures achievements in health, education, and income to assess the overall well-being and development of a country.[105]
- *Gross National Happiness*—Originating from Bhutan, this measures the happiness and well-being of individuals and societies by considering factors beyond economic indicators, such as mental and emotional well-being, social connections, and environmental sustainability.[106]
- *Social Progress Index*—This index measures the extent to which a country provides for the social and environmental needs of its citizens, focusing on areas like basic human needs, health and wellness, educational access, personal freedom, and environmental sustainability.[107]
- *Better Life Index*—Developed by OECD, this index covers a wide range of factors that contribute to well-being, including income, education, health, work–life balance, social connections, and civic engagement.[108]

These metrics help provide a more comprehensive understanding of well-being by considering a broader range of factors beyond economic measures like GDP.

AI could improve many of these metrics without affecting GDP and productivity. For instance, if AI-based diagnoses were made widely available via smartphones as suggested by Esteva and colleagues,[109] perhaps at low or zero cost, then health and well-being might dramatically increase while medical spending and thus GDP would decline. Likewise, great energy efficiency and reduced resource use from better use of AI and

---

[103] E. Brynjolfsson and A. Collis, 2019, "How Should We Measure the Digital Economy," *Harvard Business Review* 97(6):140–148.

[104] E. Brynjolfsson, A. Collis, A. Liaqat, et al., 2023, "The Digital Welfare of Nations: New Measures of Welfare Gains and Inequality," NBER Working Paper No. w31670, National Bureau of Economic Research.

[105] S. Anand and A. Sen, 2003, "Human Development Index: Methodology and Measurement," pp. 138–151 in *Human Development and Capabilities: Re-imagining the University of the Twenty-First Century*, S. Parr and A. Kumar, eds., Oxford University Press.

[106] W. Bates, 2009, "Gross National Happiness," *Asian-Pacific Economic Literature* 23(2):1–16.

[107] M.E. Porter, S. Stern, and M. Green, 2014, *Social Progress Index 2014*, Social Progress Imperative.

[108] Á. Kerényi, 2011, "The Better Life Index of the Organisation for Economic Co-operation and Development," *Public Finance Quarterly* 56(4):518–538.

[109] A. Esteva, B. Kuprel, R. Novoa, et al., 2017, "Dermatologist-Level Classification of Skin Cancer with Deep Neural Networks," *Nature* 542:115–118, https://doi.org/10.1038/nature21056.

other technologies could allow us to increase living standards while reducing carbon emissions and living more lightly on the planet, often in ways that would not show up in conventional measures of productivity.[110] For instance, DeepMind used an AI-based cluster of algorithms to reduce cooling costs at data centers by 40 percent.[111]

Factor 8: Dynamic Effects

One of the most intriguing aspects of AI is that, to an increasing extent, it can be creative.[112] AI systems have come up with new strategies in simple games like chess or Go as well as new kinds of images, stories, poems, and music.[113]

In fact, there is growing evidence that these systems can contribute to business and scientific innovation as well. Thus, another major channel through which AI can affect productivity is the acceleration of invention and discovery of new goods, services, methods, and scientific knowledge itself. This process of innovation involves not only scientists and R&D but also chief executive officers and managers who deploy innovations into productive activities. It also involves cognitive workers more broadly, who not only produce current output but also invent and discover technological advances.

For example, AI can now predict protein structures, one of biology's greatest challenges. This capability is now being used to accelerate drug discovery and to shorten lengthy and costly clinical trials. AI can design tailor-made functional proteins, including a new protein structure with specific features like toughness and flexibility.[114,115] Mullainathan and Rambachan recently described how machine learning systems can be used to detect anomalies where data are inconsistent with existing theory and thus facilitate the creation of new scientific theories.[116] There are numerous other examples of how AI can accelerate scientific discovery.

Increasing the rate of innovation will have little effect on the level of productivity or output in the short run but is likely to dominate the long-run economic contributions of AI. As an example, if innovations that enhance the growth rate of productivity are 80 percent owing to cognitive work and cognitive labor becomes 25 percent more productive, then

---

[110] A. McAfee, 2019, "More from Less: The Surprising Story of How We Learned to Prosper Using Fewer Resources—And What Happens Next," Scribner.

[111] W. Knight, 2018, "Google Just Gave Control Over Data Center Cooling to an AI," *MIT Technology Review*, August 24, https://www.technologyreview.com/s/611902/google-just-gave-control-over-data-center-cooling-to-an-ai.

[112] University of Montana, 2023, "AI Tests into Top 1% for Original Creative Thinking," *ScienceDaily*, July 5, https://www.sciencedaily.com/releases/2023/07/230705154051.htm.

[113] Z. Epstein, A. Hertzmann, and the Investigators of Human Creativity, 2023, "Art and the Science of Generative AI," *Science* 380(6650):1110–1111, https://doi.org/10.1126/science.adh4451.

[114] A. Zhavoronkov, Q. Vanhaelen, and T.I. Oprea, 2020, "Will Artificial Intelligence for Drug Discovery Impact Clinical Pharmacology?" *Clinical Pharmacology and Therapeutics* 107(4):780–785, https://doi.org/10.1002/cpt.1795.

[115] B. Ni, D.L. Kaplan, and M.J. Buehler, 2023, "Generative Design of De Novo Proteins Based on Secondary-Structure Constraints Using an Attention-Based Diffusion Model," *Chem* 9(7):1828–1849.

[116] S. Mullainathan and A. Rambachan, 2024, "From Predictive Algorithms to Automatic Generation of Anomalies," NBER Working Paper No. w32422, https://ssrn.com/abstract=4826029.

this could raise the *rate of change* of the productivity growth rate by 20 percent as more innovations are created each year. These higher rates of productivity growth compound over time. More fundamentally, if one of the applications of AI is to improve AI itself,[117] future growth could increase even more, as the *change* in the rate of growth also increases.

The Net Effect on Aggregate Productivity Growth

There is considerable uncertainty surrounding each of these factors, and there is no way to be sure about AI's ultimate effects on productivity growth over the coming decade. That said, this framework suggests that they could be quite large. As an illustration, if generative AI were to make cognitive workers 50 percent more productive on average over a decade and if one assumes that cognitive work accounts for about half of all value added in the economy, this would imply a 25 percent increase in aggregate productivity from these two factors. This increase in output would be attenuated or amplified by the other factors noted and spread out over the decade.

This broad impact leads Baily and colleagues to estimate that generative AI could boost productivity by 18 percent cumulatively over the coming decade, or an average of about 1.7 percent per year beyond existing growth rates.[118] Similarly, MGI estimates that these technologies could increase annual productivity growth in the United States by 0.6 percent to 3.6 percent from 2022 to 2040, with a midpoint of 2.1 percent.[119] These estimates more than double the current estimate by the Congressional Budget Office of just 1.4 percent productivity growth for the coming decade.[120]

For comparison, productivity growth averaged 2.9 percent in the decade from 1995 to 2005, powered by advances in digital technologies like the Internet and large enterprise systems. Thus, an AI-powered increase in productivity growth to 3 percent or more is not implausible. While considerable uncertainty remains, substantial gains like this reflect the breadth of tasks affected and the potential magnitude of productivity gains in each task, as well as the other six factors enumerated above.

---

[117] As I.J. Good put it, "Let an ultra-intelligent machine be defined as a machine that can far surpass all the intellectual activities of any man however clever. Since the design of machines is one of these intellectual activities, an ultra-intelligent machine could design even better machines; there would then unquestionably be an 'intelligence explosion,' and the intelligence of man would be left far behind." See I.J. Good, 1966, "Speculations Concerning the First Ultraintelligent Machine," pp. 31–88 in *Advances in Computers*, Vol. 6, Elsevier.

[118] M.N. Baily, E. Brynjolfsson, and A. Korinek, 2023, "Machines of the Mind: The Case for an AI-Powered Productivity Boom," Brookings Institution, May 10, https://www.brookings.edu/articles/machines-of-mind-the-case-for-an-ai-powered-productivity-boom.

[119] M. Chui, E. Hazan, R. Roberts, et al., 2023, "The Economic Potential of Generative AI: The Next Productivity Frontier," McKinsey & Company, June 14, also estimates that generative AI alone could add 0.3–0.7 percentage points to U.S. productivity growth.

[120] A. Betz, 2022, "CBO's Economic Forecast: Understanding Productivity Growth," NABE Foundation 19th Annual Economic Measurement Seminar, July 19, https://www.cbo.gov/publication/58265. Globally, McKinsey Global Institute also estimates large contributions to productivity growth from these technologies. Worldwide, it predicts that they would add 0.2–3.3 percentage points to 2022–2040 and 0.1–0.6 percentage points from generative AI alone.

That said, these estimates of potential gains rest on the assumption that workers who are required to shift to other work activities and occupations as a result of AI adoption and displacement will find new ones with productivity levels at least as high as those in their previous work. Productivity gains will also require complementary investments both in worker training and skill development and in programs to support the worker transitions necessitated by shifts in activities, occupations, and sectors. Experimentation in the organizational changes best suited to implement AI will also be necessary. Such experimentation takes time, with heterogeneity in success across firms. Furthermore, these estimates of potential productivity gains do not take into account new high-productivity economic activities that may be created by AI.

Last, it is important to note that even if the potential for AI to automate or augment a particular work activity is large, the pace of AI adoption and deployment in market economies like the United States will depend on business decisions and on a comparison of the costs of AI compared to the costs of labor. As a result, AI adoption and the associated productivity gains are likely to be considerably faster in sectors and regions where wages are high and where the labor supply is growing slowly as a result of demographic changes. The slowdown in the growth of the labor supply in the United States and the other advanced industrial economies, resulting from demographic trends, will be a powerful tailwind encouraging AI adoption to offset human labor scarcity.[121]

PRODUCTIVITY, LABOR MARKETS, AND INEQUALITY

Even if AI delivers large productivity gains, an unanswered question is how the benefits of greater productivity will be shared. Will the benefits be inclusive, or will they result in more income and wealth inequality? The evidence from the information technology and Internet technological revolutions indicates reasons for concern.

During the past 20 to 30 years, real wages grew more slowly than labor productivity in the United States and the other advanced economies. This was true both during the period of strong productivity growth between the mid-1990s and 2005 and the period of slow productivity growth through 2019–2020. The gap between wage growth and productivity growth was larger for the median wage than for the average wage, reflecting growing wage inequality. And decoupling contributed to a drop in labor's share of national income to differing degrees in the advanced economies (Figure 3-11).

---

[121] H. Varian, 2020, "Automation Versus Procreation (aka Bots versus Tots)," VoxEU, https://voxeu.org/article/automation-versus-procreation-aka-bots-versus-tots.

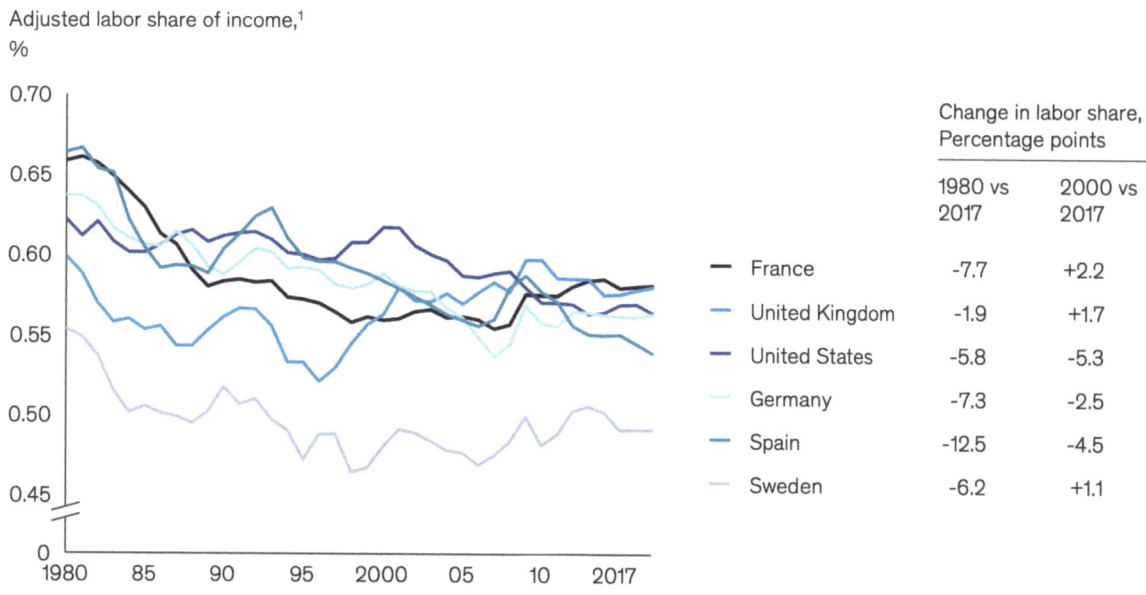

FIGURE 3-11 Declines in labor share across advanced economies since 1980.
NOTES: Footnote 1 in the figure: "Adjusted labor share for total economy over GDP at market prices from AMECO, based on ratio of total compensation of employees to GDP multiplied by the ratio of total employment to the number of employees (salaried people). This helps account for income of self-employed households assuming that their wage is similar to salaried households." AMECO is the annual macro-economic database of the European Commission's Directorate General for Economic and Financial Affairs.
SOURCE: Exhibit 1 from J. Manyika, J. Mischke, J. Bughin, L. Woetzel, M. Krishnan, and S. Cudre, 2019, "A New Look at the Declining Labor Share of Income in the United States," May, McKinsey Global Institute, https://www.mckinsey.com/featured-insights/employment-and-growth/a-new-look-at-the-declining-labor-share-of-income-in-the-united-states. Copyright © 2024 McKinsey & Company. All rights reserved. Reprinted by permission.

Economists have identified many factors behind the decline in the labor share of income and the decoupling of productivity growth and wage growth.[122,123] These include both macroeconomic factors—such as skill or routine-biased technological change, globalization, and the decline in workers covered by collective bargaining—and microeconomic factors—such as increasing concentration in product and labor markets and growing differences in firms' productivity, profits, and wages.[124,125]

---

[122] M. Pak and C. Schwellnus, 2019, "Labour Share Developments Over the Past Two Decades: The Role of Public Policies," OECD Economics Department Working Paper No. 1541, OECD Publishing, https://doi.org/10.1787/b21e518b-en.

[123] A. De Serres and C. Schwellnus, 2018, "A General Equilibrium (LM and PM Reforms) Perspective to Inequality," pp. 66–86 in *Inequality and Structural Reforms: Methodological Concerns and Lessons from Policy*, C. Astarita and G. D'Adamo, eds., European Economy Discussion Paper No. 71, European Commission.

[124] C. Schwellnus, M. Pak, P.-A. Pionnier, and E. Crivellaro, 2018, "Labour Share Developments Over the Past Two Decades: The Role of Technological Progress, Globalisation and 'Winner-Takes-Most' Dynamics," OECD Economics Department Working Paper No. 1503, OECD Publishing, Paris, https://doi.org/10.1787/3eb9f9ed-en.

[125] L. Tyson and M. Spence, 2017, "Exploring the Effects of Technology on Income and Wealth Inequality," pp. 170–173 in *After Piketty: The Agenda for Economics and Inequality*, H. Boushey, J. B. DeLong, and M. Steinbaum, eds., Harvard University Press.

The question for the future is whether the potential significant productivity gains from generative AI will be reflected in real wage gains or the decoupling of wage and productivity growth and the decline in labor's share of national income will persist.

In the United States and other market economies, profit-motivated businesses will decide how and whether to deploy AI systems based on the incentives they face. As Daron Acemoglu and Simon Johnson have emphasized in their recent book *Power and Progress: Our 1000-Year Struggle Over Technology and Prosperity*, the governance of these institutions and policies can shape these incentives.[126] As companies invest in AI, they must choose whether to emphasize AI to substitute for labor or to complement labor. For example, a call center can use AI technology to complement its human operators or restructure its processes so that AI technologies substitute for these operators.[127] However, much of the focus among technologists, business executives, and policy makers, intentionally or unintentionally, has been to develop AI systems that mimic and thus substitute for human labor rather than complement it.[128]

DRIVERS, BARRIERS, AND RISKS OF ARTIFICIAL INTELLIGENCE ADOPTION

Although there is reason for optimism about the pace at which AI technology will reshape work and significantly boost productivity, there are also reasons for caution. AI adoption may not proceed as rapidly as many expect or hope. As noted above, there are eight factors that will affect the size and the timing of AI's effect on aggregate productivity.

As discussed in the explanations of the productivity slowdown, structural changes imply headwinds to productivity growth. These include declining dynamism, rising concentration, rising market power, and rising markups of price over cost at the largest firms. Young and small firms have played an outsized role in driving the kinds of innovations that have large GDP growth effects relative to large, incumbent firms.[129] The latter face the innovator's dilemma. Major innovations can cannibalize the market for the incumbents' current set of products. Relatedly, large incumbents have incentives to acquire young and small innovative firms to deter the adverse impact on their product

---

[126] D. Acemoglu and S. Johnson, 2023, *Power and Progress: Our 1000-Year Struggle Over Technology and Prosperity*, PublicAffairs.

[127] M.N. Baily, E. Brynjofsson, and A. Korinek, 2023, "Machines of Mind: The Case for an AI-Powered Productivity Boom," Center on Regulation and Markets, Brookings Institution, May 10, https://www.brookings.edu/articles/machines-of-mind-the-case-for-an-ai-powered-productivity-boom.

[128] E. Brynjolfsson, 2022, "The Turing Trap: The Promise and Peril of Human-Like Artificial Intelligence," *Daedalus* 151(2):272–287.

[129] U. Akcigit and W.R. Kerr, 2018, "Growth Through Heterogeneous Innovations," *Journal of Political Economy* 126(4):1374–1443.

base.[130] And it is large incumbents that are the most digitized firms with the highest productivity growth rates and that have the infrastructure in place for rapid adoption and deployment of new AI systems. Indeed, five major global firms and a handful of venture capital firms are currently responsible for most of the investment in AI systems. The danger that AI will drive further productivity gaps between a few large leading firms and the rest of the firms in each sector is real, along with the danger of increasing market concentration.

International research collaborations have been central to advances in AI. A potential decline in open international collaboration, motivated by national security and economic competitiveness concerns, could impact the future pace and patterns of AI innovation.

Legal, institutional, and regulatory issues also imply significant hurdles in the implementation of AI in specific sectors and applications. Although generative AI may be new, existing laws on data protection and copyright protection have significant implications for its use. AI thrives and depends on access to information, but access to medical records, legal records, and financial records is controlled by laws and regulations. More broadly, privacy and copyright restrictions are another barrier to access the data required for AI models. AI poses risks of intellectual property infringement; in the United States, courts are already looking at a variety of issues including patent and trademark infringements by AI creators and the use of unlicensed content for training data.

A 2023 survey of 443 midsize and large law firms conducted by the Thomson Reuters Institute found a clear openness to using AI tools but also caution. Firms cited concerns about the accuracy of AI, noting that they would be liable for errors and omissions, and about the confidentiality of client material that would be needed as training data for natural language models. Firms also expressed concern about nonhumans doing certain types of legal work. One survey respondent argued that attorneys "are guided by ethical rules that take heartfelt understanding that simply cannot be programmed by algorithm."[131]

Antiquated software and often bespoke electronic medical record systems could slow the adoption of AI in the health care sector. The opacity of some AI systems is a barrier to trust by health care providers and could lengthen the time to adoption.[132] In addition, the opaque nature could raise liability issues and challenges in determining which providers get reimbursed for which services in the course of complex patient treatment. The confidentiality of the medical records needed to train AI models is potentially a major barrier to widespread adoption.

---

[130] C. Cunningham, F. Ederer, and S. Ma, 2021, "Killer Acquisitions," *Journal of Political Economy* 129(3):649–702.
[131] Thomson Reuters Institute, 2023, "ChatGPT and Generative AI Within Law Firms," https://www.thomsonreuters.com/en-us/posts/wp-content/uploads/sites/20/2023/04/2023-Chat-GPT-Generative-AI-in-Law-Firms.pdf.
[132] J. Adler-Milstein, N. Aggarwal, M. Ahmed, et al., 2022, "Meeting the Moment: Addressing Barriers and Facilitating Clinical Adoption of Artificial Intelligence in Medical Diagnosis," *NAM Perspectives*, September 29.

Bespoke AI enterprise models could be a solution to confidentiality concerns among law firms and health care providers. But there are important questions related to ownership of training data, where those data are stored, and who can access them. Enterprise solutions may not be as useful given more limited training data, and the costs to firms of using enterprise solutions will be higher than using publicly available AI tools.

Liability and associated regulatory issues are also likely to be a hurdle. In the 2017 National Academies' report on information technology, wide deployment of driverless vehicles was anticipated in the near future.[133] In addition to a variety of technical challenges, that discussion did not fully appreciate the liability and in turn insurance issues associated with driverless vehicles. Such liability issues are likely to slow the implementations of AI in a variety of autonomous equipment.

Another potential obstacle that may slow the pace of adoption is consumer trust. Misinformation and disinformation—for example, deep fakes of political leaders—could increase the level of distrust of generative AI tools in general. Given the rapid advancements in AI technology, it is conceivable that the ability of AI to perform tasks—for example, heart surgery—may advance faster than consumer preferences to be serviced by a machine and not a human.

Last, there is growing concern among the public and policy makers about serious risks created by AI.[134] These risks, not all of which are well understood, include risks to privacy, risks of discrimination and bias, risks of AI-powered digital addiction, risks to democracy and political stability, ethical risks, national security risks, cybersecurity risks, and risks of military arms races driven by new AI weapons.

Privacy protection can lead to both positive and negative effects on individuals and society, creating complex trade-offs that are particularly relevant in the context of AI. Privacy safeguards can protect individuals from harms, but restricting personal data flows can also impede the development and effectiveness of AI systems (which often rely heavily on large data sets for training) that would provide individuals and society with benefits. Privacy-enhancing technologies that anonymize or limit access to personal data may reduce privacy risks, but they often come at the cost of reduced AI performance in applications such as personalized recommendations and predictive analytics. The

---

[133] National Academies of Sciences, Engineering, and Medicine, 2017, *Information Technology and the U.S. Workforce: Where Are We and Where Do We Go from Here?* The National Academies Press, https://doi.org/10.17226/24649.

[134] A. Tong, 2023, "AI Threatens Humanity's Future, 61% of Americans Say: Reuters/Ipsos Poll," *Reuters*, May 17, https://www.reuters.com/technology/ai-threatens-humanitys-future-61-americans-say-reutersipsos-2023-05-17. The European Commission announced that "unacceptable risk AI systems are systems considered a threat to people and will be banned." See U. von der Leyen, 2023, "State of the Union Address by President von der Leyen," European Commission, https://ec.europa.eu/commission/presscorner/detail/ov/speech_23_4426.

challenge is thus one of striking the right balance in an array of contexts, which requires careful analysis to navigate the nuanced trade-offs in each.[135]

Some see more existential risks on the horizon. A recent open letter from some leading AI experts warned that "mitigating the risk of extinction from AI should be a global priority alongside other societal-scale risks such as pandemics and nuclear war."[136]

Different societies will adopt different norms on some of these risks, such as privacy and other personal rights, depending on their cultural contexts and values. However, many of these risks are common to all societies. In a recent *Foreign Affairs* essay, Ian Bremmer and Mustafa Suleyman argue that the coming wave of technological innovation will "initiate a seismic shift in the structure and balance of global power as it threatens the status of nation-states as the world's primary geopolitical actors."[137] They characterize AI as a global commons problem that will require a global AI governance structure.

In response to the risks posed by AI and after many other nations have jumped ahead on AI governance proposals, the Biden administration recently issued an executive order as a first step to assessing regulation for the responsible development and deployment of AI. This executive order covers a broad range of issues, leaning heavily on safety, privacy, civil liberties, and rights. Among other things, the order proposes that companies working on advanced AI systems, measured by compute performance that has not yet been achieved in existing models, be required to share their safety tests and develop safety and security standards through the National Institute of Standards and Technology. The proposed reporting requirements are mild, and the compute standard means that they are likely to affect only a few large corporations.

---

[135] A. Acquisti, C. Taylor, and L. Wagman, 2016, "The Economics of Privacy," *Journal of Economic Literature* 54(2):442–492.

[136] Center for AI Safety, "Statement on AI Risk," https://www.safe.ai/statement-on-ai-risk.

[137] I. Bremmer and M. Suleyman, 2023, "The AI Power Paradox: Can States Learn to Govern Artificial Intelligence—Before It's Too Late?" *Foreign Affairs* 102:26.

4

Artificial Intelligence and the Workforce

Despite widespread popular and academic concern that artificial intelligence (AI) and robotics are ushering in a jobless future, the industrialized world is currently awash in jobs.[1] Three years after the onset of the deepest recession since the Great Depression, the U.S. unemployment rate has returned to its historically low prepandemic level of 3.5 percent, and, similarly, labor force participation and employment-to-population rates have nearly fully recovered.[2] A comparable situation is unfolding across many industrialized countries. At the end of 2022, average Organisation for Economic Co-operation and Development (OECD)-wide employment and labor force participation rates were at their highest recorded levels, with half of all OECD countries exceeding previous high-water marks on both metrics.[3]

It is difficult to predict how unemployment rates may change in the years to come. The Congressional Budget Office projects that the U.S. population will grow at a glacial rate of 0.3 percent between 2023 and 2053, one-third the pace prevailing during the

---

[1] On the possibility of a jobless future, see J. Rifkin, 1995, *The End of Work: The Decline of the Global Labor Force and the Dawn of the Post-Market Era*, GP Putnam's Sons; M.R. Ford, 1995, *The Rise of the Robots: Technology and the Threat of Mass Unemployment*, Basic Books; C.B. Frey and M.A. Osborne, 2017, "The Future of Employment: How Susceptible Are Jobs to Computerisation?" *Technological Forecasting and Social Change* 114:254–280; D. Susskind, 2020, *A World Without Work: Technology, Automation and How We Should Respond*, Penguin UK; A. Korinek and M. Juelfs, 2022, "Preparing for the (Non-Existent?) Future of Work," NBER Working Paper No. w30172, June.

[2] U.S. Bureau of Labor Statistics, 2023, "BLS Employment Situation Summary, April 7, 2023," https://www.bls.gov/news.release/empsit.nr0.htm.

[3] OECD, 2023, "Labour Market Situation: OECD Employment and Labour Force Participation Rates Reach Record Highs in the Fourth Quarter of 2022, April, https://www.oecd.org/sdd/labour-stats/labour-market-situation-oecd-updated-april-2023.htm. Note that these labor force participation and employment-to-population series commenced in 2005 and 2008, respectively, so the historical comparison window is comparatively short.

prior four decades and below any sustained growth rate seen since the Census Bureau began tracking these statistics in 1900.[4] This backdrop of mounting labor scarcity would seem to diminish prospects for widespread technological unemployment.

Although broad forecasts of AI's effects on total labor demand are generated regularly by consultancies and are reported credulously by the press, such forecasts are highly speculative. An extraordinarily highly cited 2017 academic study by Frey and Osborne projected that "47% of total U.S. employment is in the high risk category" for automation, where "high probability occupations are likely to be substituted by computer capital relatively soon."[5] No such occupational apocalypse has come to pass. To take a specific example, one might have anticipated that the advent of accounting, bookkeeping, payroll, and tax preparation software over the past several decades would have eroded employment in accounting, bookkeeping, payroll, and tax preparation services. Indeed, Frey and Osborne placed the probability of computerization of each of these four categories at 97 percent or above. Instead, U.S. employment in this group of occupations grew by 19 percent in the 7 years since the publication of Frey and Osborne's paper and doubled between 1990 and 2024 from 0.6 million to 1.2 million workers (more than twice the growth rate of overall nonfarm employment).[6]

A key theme of this report, and this chapter in particular, is that the most relevant concern for present and future workers is not whether AI will eliminate jobs in net but rather how it will shape the labor market value of expertise—specifically, whether it will augment the value of the skills and expertise that workers possess (or will acquire) or instead erode that value by providing cheaper machine substitutes. The most pernicious prospect that AI and robotics hold for the labor market is that they could substantially erode the value of human expertise—certainly within specific domains and perhaps more broadly. Shifts in the market value of human expertise are where the labor market effects of technical change generally, and AI specifically, may first be seen.

---

[4] Congressional Budget Office, 2023, "The Demographic Outlook: 2023–2053," January, www.cbo.gov/publication/58612; W.S. Frey, 2021, "U.S. Population Growth Has Nearly Flatlined, New Census Data Shows," Brookings Institution, December, https://www.brookings.edu/research/u-s-population-growth-has-nearly-flatlined-new-census-data-shows. The United States is on a relatively favorable trajectory. The United Nations projects that most industrialized countries will commence population decline during the 21st century. And populations are already falling in multiple continental European countries as well as in Japan and China. The United Nations report states, "Whereas the populations of Australia and New Zealand, Northern Africa and Western Asia, and Oceania (excluding Australia and New Zealand) are expected to experience slower, but still positive, growth through the end of the century, the populations of Eastern and South-Eastern Asia, Central and Southern Asia, Latin America and the Caribbean, and Europe and Northern America are projected to reach their peak size and to begin to decline before 2100." See United Nations: Department of Economic and Social Affairs, 2022, "World Population Prospects 2022," https://www.un.org/development/desa/pd/sites/www.un.org.development.desa.pd/files/wpp2022_summary_of_results.pdf; and EuroNews with AFP, 2023, "The Countries Where Population Is Declining," EuroNews, January 20, https://www.euronews.com/2023/01/17/the-countries-where-population-is-declining.

[5] C.B. Frey and M.A. Osborne, 2017, "The Future of Employment: How Susceptible Are Jobs to Computerisation?" Technological Forecasting and Social Change 114:254–280.

[6] On employment in accounting, tax preparation, bookkeeping, and payroll services, see https://fred.stlouisfed.org/graph/?g=1oMKn. On nonfarm employment, see https://fred.stlouisfed.org/graph/?g=1oMKB.

To define terms, "expertise" denotes a specific body of knowledge or competency required to accomplish a particular objective—for example, baking a loaf of bread, taking vital signs, or coding an app (Box 4-1).[7] Human expertise commands a market premium to the degree that it is, first, necessary for accomplishing valuable objectives and, second, not possessed by most people. This scarcity may arise because the relevant skills are costly or time-intensive to acquire (e.g., training to become a surgeon, pilot, or cabinetmaker); certain talents are intrinsically rare (e.g., gifted athletes, musicians, or mathematicians); market conditions create temporary scarcity (e.g., surging demand for COBOL programmers during the run-up to Y2K); or legal and regulatory barriers limit the number of trained or certified workers (e.g., residency training in medical specialties such as endocrinology).

> **BOX 4-1 Defining Concepts Related to Expertise**
>
> The following are other related terms frequently used in discussions of technology and labor markets:
>
> - *Skill* formally means the ability to do something well. Economists often use skill in a unidimensional sense: a worker is low-skilled, mid-skilled, or high-skilled. This is too simplistic, however: one can be highly skilled in carpentry and unskilled in software development, or vice versa. But making this distinction requires specifying what someone invoking the term is "skilled in," which means specifying what expertise the worker possesses. In that case, the term "skill" adds little value, whereas the term "expertise" unambiguously refers to skill in a specific domain.
>
> - *Education and credentials* are means of acquiring and certifying expertise. But expertise is often acquired through on-the-job experience and noncredentialed training, so education and credentials pertain to only a subset of the expertise that workers possess.
>
> - *Occupations* provide a useful shorthand to denote broad categories of work, often conveying both specific skill sets and formal certification (e.g., attorney, master plumber). At the same time, occupational categories are not as crisp as they sometimes appear. One reason is that the set of specific duties ("tasks") in occupations changes over time, even without any change in occupational titles. Prior to the advent of office computing, for example, secretarial duties typically included answering phones, taking shorthand, filing papers, and typing. Aside from typing, contemporary clerical workers do few of these traditional tasks, but they increasingly do complex technical and organizational tasks like expense accounting and event planning. A second reason is that the set of occupational categories evolves and expands as technologies, tastes, and demographics change. There were, for example, essentially no

---

[7] Many dictionaries define expertise as expert skill or knowledge in a particular field—which is essentially tautological. For example, see https://www.merriam-webster.com/dictionary/expertise, where expertise is defined as "the skill of an expert."

BOX 4-1 Continued

software developers in the United States before the advent of commercial computing in the 1950s, yet at present there are more than 1.5 million.[a] Autor and colleagues estimate that the majority of current employment (more than 60 percent) is currently found in new job specialties introduced since 1940.[b] This chapter uses dozens of occupational examples for illustrative purposes, while recognizing that the expertise required by specific occupations is not static and that new occupations come into existence as new forms of expertise gain relevance.

- *Tasks*, in economic parlance, are the constituent building blocks of work: workers apply skills to accomplish tasks that produce desired outputs. A job may comprise dozens or hundreds of tasks, depending on how broadly or narrowly tasks are defined. A burgeoning economic literature uses the concept of tasks to describe the interplay between technological change, occupational structure, and skill demands.[c] The concepts of tasks and expertise are closely related; one can think of tasks as checklists of items to be accomplished (the "what"), while expertise is the know-how required to accomplish those items on the list ("the how").

- *Routine tasks*, as used in economics literature, are physically or cognitively repetitive tasks that follow tightly scripted codifiable procedures.[d] For the purposes of this report, one can equate "mass expertise" with the ability to execute routine tasks. The term "expertise" is used throughout this chapter to distinguish different domains of expertise that do not map tightly to the routine/nonroutine distinction, including artisanal expertise, elite expertise, and translational expertise.

- *Automation* refers to technological advances that facilitate the substitution of capital for labor at a widening range of tasks or productive processes. Concretely, when a task that was formerly done by workers is delegated to machines, that task is automated.

- *Augmentation* is a case where a technology enables workers to work more effectively, perform higher-quality work, or accomplish previously infeasible tasks.

---

[a] See U.S. Bureau of Labor Statistics, 2023, "Occupational Employment and Wage Statistics: 15-1252 Software Developers," https://www.bls.gov/oes/current/oes151252.htm.

[b] D. Autor, C.M. Chin, A. Salomons, and B. Seegmiller, 2024, "New Frontiers: The Origins and Content of New Work," 1940–2018, *Quarterly Journal of Economics* 139(3):1399–1465, https://doi.org/10.1093/qje/qjae008.

[c] See, among other sources, D.H. Autor, F. Levy, and R.J. Murnane, 2003, "The Skill Content of Recent Technological Change: An Empirical Exploration," *The Quarterly Journal of Economics* 118(4):1279–1333; F. Levy and R.J. Murnane, 2005, *The New Division of Labor,* Princeton University Press; D. Acemoglu and D. Autor, 2011, "Skills, Tasks and Technologies: Implications for Employment and Earnings," pp. 1043–1171 in *Handbook of Labor Economics*, Vol. 4, Elsevier; and D. Acemoglu and P. Restrepo, 2019, "Automation and New Tasks: How Technology Displaces and Reinstates Labor," *Journal of Economic Perspectives* 33(2):3–30.

[d] This terminology originates in D.H. Autor, F. Levy, and R.J. Murnane, 2003, "The Skill Content of Recent Technological Change: An Empirical Exploration," *The Quarterly Journal of Economics* 118(4):1279–1333.

Much of the value of labor in industrialized economies derives from the scarcity of expertise rather than from the scarcity of workers per se. Consider, for example, the jobs of air traffic controller and crossing guard. Both make rapid-fire, life-or-death decisions to avert collisions between vehicles, passengers, and bystanders. Despite their fundamental similarities, the median annual pay of air traffic controllers in 2021 ($131,000) was more than four times the corresponding remuneration for crossing guards ($31,500). The key difference separating these jobs is expertise. In most of the United States, working as a crossing guard requires no formal training or certification. Conversely, the job of air traffic controller requires an associate's or bachelor's degree in air traffic control complemented by several years of on-the-job apprenticeship.[8] These training requirements potentially give rise to scarcity. If an unexpectedly urgent need arose for crossing guards, most air traffic controllers could presumably fill these roles. If an urgent need for air traffic controllers arose, the reverse would not be true.[9]

Jobs for which mass expertise suffices—such as table-waiting, cleaning and janitorial services, manual labor, and (even) child care—tend to pay poorly, not just in the United States but in all industrialized countries.[10] The low pay in these jobs does not reflect a lack of intrinsic value of the services they provide but rather the abundance of workers who are able to do this work.[11]

Expertise is often acquired through formal education, but the two are not synonymous. Much expertise is acquired through training and experience rather than through schooling. Many occupations in the skilled trades—electrical work, plumbing, heating and cooling, construction, manufacturing production, and so on—do not require formal education beyond post-secondary schooling but are mastered through intensive apprenticeships. Certification for many health vocations—such as dental hygienists, magnetic resonance imaging technologists, and diagnostic medical sonographers—requires an associate's degree but not a bachelor's degree. All of these occupations (trades workers,

---

[8] On crossing guards, see https://www.bls.gov/ooh/about/data-for-occupations-not-covered-in-detail.htm. On air traffic controllers, see https://www.bls.gov/ooh/transportation-and-material-moving/air-traffic-controllers.htm.

[9] The fact that expertise is both scarce and necessary to produce a good or service does not guarantee that this expertise will be highly rewarded. The product or service enabled by this expertise must also have significant market value (e.g., expertise in slide rule mathematics is no basis for a career). But occupations that require little expertise are poorly paid as a rule.

[10] G. Mason and W. Salverda, 2010, "Low Pay, Working Conditions, and Living Standards," pp. 35–90 in *Low-Wage Work in the Wealthy World*, J. Gautié and J. Schmitt, eds., Russell Sage Foundation, http://www.jstor.org/stable/10.7758/9781610446303.6.

[11] That does not mean the wage will be zero; workers can choose not to work at all. But wage levels in jobs that require only generic skill sets will not depend primarily on the supply of suitably trained workers but rather on the set of alternative options available to workers with generic skills, a point that goes back to W.J. Baumol, 1967, "Macroeconomics of Unbalanced Growth: The Anatomy of Urban Crisis," *The American Economic Review* 57(3):415–426. Provided that workers are necessary to perform these generic work tasks, and that consumers do not find non-labor-using substitutes for them or choose to forego these services altogether, earnings in this type of work will tend to rise with societal incomes. Thus, as Baumol observed, earnings of hair stylists, while typically low, have roughly kept pace with overall economic growth.

health technicians) are relatively well paid, reflecting the expertise they require.[12] Expertise does not by itself guarantee high pay, of course; the product or service enabled by this expertise must also have significant market value. For this reason, expertise in data science is a sound basis for a wide range of careers, whereas expertise in historical baseball statistics is not.

The objective of this chapter is to assess the implications of rapid advances in AI for the nature of work and the jobs available to workers. The chapter is framed around the demand for expertise because AI is most likely to impact the labor market profoundly by reshaping this demand. The chapter addresses three central questions:

1. *Substitution*: What expertise is likely to be substituted or made obsolete?
2. *Complementarity*: What expertise is likely to be augmented or newly demanded?
3. *Transition*: How feasible will it be for workers to acquire newly valuable expertise?

As is evident, none of these questions directly concern the impact of AI on *aggregate* employment or unemployment. However, there is ample reason to believe that AI, at least initially, will affect the value of expertise in a multitude of dimensions, and this will be consequential for worker welfare.

Although this report focuses on the United States, similar lessons likely apply to many other industrialized countries—though not necessarily to low- and middle-income countries. One topic on which this chapter will *not* focus is the demand for AI developers specifically—that is, people who build AI systems. Building AI systems is expert work, of course, and it is reasonable to expect there to be much more of it. But it will not be a large part of overall employment. Consider the example of software developers: Despite decades of sustained growth in investment in computer technology, slightly less than 1 percent of the U.S. workforce is currently employed in software development.[13] If this fraction were to double to 2 percent, this would still comprise a smaller share of the workforce than is currently employed as fast food and counter workers.[14]

Before applying the expertise framework to assess the potential labor market impacts of AI, it is first used to interpret the labor market impacts of the two preceding technological revolutions: the Industrial Revolution and the computer revolution. This framing will both put AI in context with earlier technological eras and demonstrate that

---

[12] These examples are drawn from the U.S. Bureau of Labor Statistics, 2024, "Occupational Outlook Handbook," https://www.bls.gov/ooh.

[13] As noted earlier, employment in software development was 1.53 million in May 2022 (see https://www.bls.gov/oes/current/oes151252.htm), whereas overall U.S. employment was 158.3 million in June 2022 (see Summary Table A of "News Release: The Employment Situation—July 2023," USDL-23-1689, https://www.bls.gov/news.release/pdf/empsit.pdf).

[14] U.S. Bureau of Labor Statistics, 2023, "Occupational Employment and Wage Statistics: 35-3023 Fast Food and Counter Workers," https://www.bls.gov/oes/current/oes353023.htm.

the lens of expertise brings key elements into focus across multiple eras of economic history. The chapter begins explaining how technological change simultaneously erodes and augments demand for expertise.

Alongside highlighting these potential employment consequences, the final section of this chapter considers other *nonemployment* risks arising from the widespread adoption of AI including algorithmic fairness and discrimination, worker surveillance and privacy, and issues around the ownership of creative output and intellectual property.

THE ROLE OF TECHNOLOGY IN ERODING AND AUGMENTING DEMAND FOR EXPERTISE

The term "expertise" refers to capacities that reside in people. Yet, the *value* of expertise is often inseparable from the tools and technologies that are used by experts. For example, it is self-evident that the tools used by air traffic controllers enhance rather than erode the value of their expert knowledge: absent radar, the Global Positioning System (GPS), and two-way radios, air traffic controllers could do little more than stare at the sky. Similarly, the expertise of plumbers, electricians, and medical technicians would be less valuable—and in some cases irrelevant—absent the tools with which that expertise is applied. The principle is a general one: tools often augment the value of expertise by increasing workers' capabilities and conserving their time.

But not all technologies augment the value of expertise; some render it superfluous. For example, the market value of taxi drivers' exhaustive and painstakingly acquired knowledge of the streets and alleys of London was diminished when GPS-enabled ride-hailing apps made that expertise widely available through smartphones. Although there are currently as many London cabbies as ever, their earnings dropped by about 10 percent when Uber entered the market.[15] Similarly, the roll-out of an AI-based taxi-routing program in Yokohama, Japan, erased the routing advantage of expert versus novice drivers, largely eliminating the value of expertise.[16] In the foreseeable future, the job of air traffic control may be handled primarily by AI, potentially eroding the earnings potential of air traffic controllers. Where technology eliminates the need for human expertise, this generally yields efficiency gains and reduces costs for consumers and

---

[15] T. Berger, C. Chen, and C.B. Frey, 2018, "Drivers of Disruption? Estimating the Uber Effect," *European Economic Review* 110:197–210. Consistent with falling barriers to expertise, the number of self-employed drivers who did not have the traditional London taxi credential rose steeply.

[16] K. Kanazawa, D. Kawaguchi, H. Shigeoka, and Y. Watanabe, 2022, "AI, Skill, and Productivity: The Case of Taxi Drivers," NBER Working Paper No. w30612, National Bureau of Economic Research.

businesses. But this will in many cases lessen the earnings and employment prospects of workers whose expert skills are made less scarce.[17]

In reality, a stream of technological advances—from automatic transmissions to tax preparation software—continuously erodes the value of expertise by simplifying and automating formerly expert tasks. These technologies are effective: the expertise required to perform simple bookkeeping calculations, for example, was once highly coveted and handsomely remunerated but is now abundantly supplied, is heavily automated, and commands almost no skill premium.[18]

One can see this phenomenon writ large in the U.S. labor market, as shown in Figure 4-1. Despite substantial economic growth over the past four decades, real wages of noncollege workers[19] (especially noncollege men) fell steeply from approximately 1980 to 2010 as these workers were displaced from skilled manufacturing and mid-level administrative jobs into generic personal service positions requiring little formal expertise.[20]

Yet, despite ongoing technological advances that simplify and automate formerly expert work, the return to formal skills—one form of expertise—has been rising for decades. Why has the expertise-commodifying effect of innovation not overwhelmed its augmenting effect? This extinction of expertise—or, more precisely, of its market value—*would* very likely occur were it not for a central countervailing force: the domain of expertise is continually expanding. Many of the most highly paid jobs in industrialized economies—oncologists, software engineers, patent lawyers, therapists, movie stars—did not exist until specific technological or social innovations created a need for them. Prior to the era of air transport, for example, there was neither a market demand for nor supply of air traffic controller skills. Less than 1 year ago, the job of "prompt engineering"—crafting text queries for chatbots that produce optimal outputs—was essentially nonexistent. It is now in high demand.[21]

Very few occupations are entirely eliminated by automation (though the occupation of elevator operator serves as the exception that proves the rule).[22] But some

---

[17] R.E. Susskind and D. Susskind, 2015, *The Future of the Professions: How Technology Will Transform the Work of Human Experts*, Oxford University Press.

[18] C. Goldin and L.F. Katz, 1995, "The Decline of Non-Competing Groups: Changes in the Premium to Education, 1890 to 1940," NBER Working Paper No. 5202.

[19] That is, workers with less than a bachelor's degree.

[20] Only in the past decade have earnings of noncollege men regained most of the ground that they lost after 1980. Real earnings declines were, fortunately, shallower and not as enduring among noncollege women. See D. Autor and D. Dorn, 2013, "The Growth of Low-Skill Service Jobs and the Polarization of the U.S. Labor Market," *American Economic Review* 103(5):1553–1597; D. Autor, 2019, "Work of the Past, Work of the Future," *AEA Papers and Proceedings* 109:1–32; and D. Acemoglu and P. Restrepo, 2022, "Tasks, Automation, and the Rise in U.S. Wage Inequality," *Econometrica* 90(5):1973–2016.

[21] A. Mok, 2023, "'Prompt Engineering' Is One of the Hottest Jobs in Generative AI. Here's How It Works," *Business Insider*, March 1, https://www.businessinsider.com/prompt-engineering-ai-chatgpt-jobs-explained-2023-3; and Wikipedia, 2023, "Prompt Engineer," Wikimedia Foundation, March 10, https://en.wikipedia.org/wiki/Prompt_engineering.

[22] Only one occupation has been fully automated in the post-war period—elevator operators. See E. Bessen, 2016, "How Computer Automation Affects Occupations: Technology, Jobs, and Skills," Boston University School of Law, Law and Economics Research Paper No. 15-49, October 3, http://dx.doi.org/10.2139/ssrn.2690435.

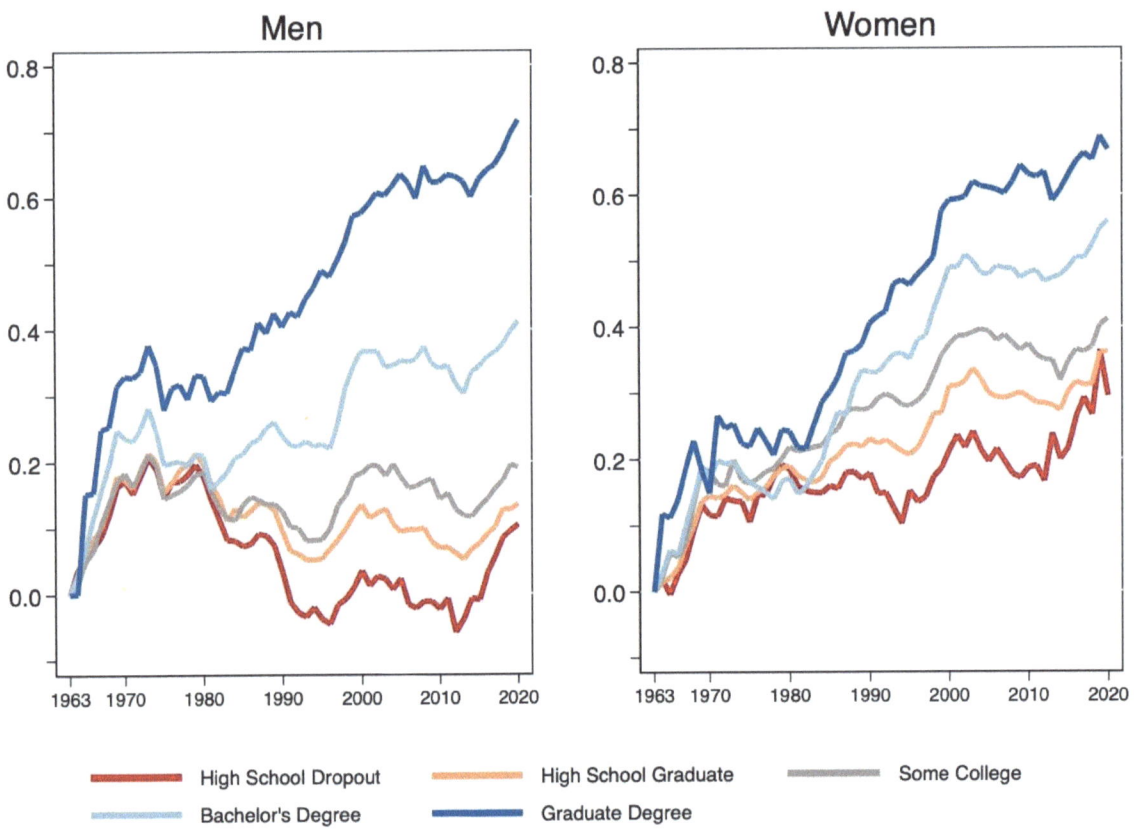

FIGURE 4-1 Percentage change in real hourly wages of working-age men and women by education level, 1963–2020.
SOURCE: D. Autor, 2019, "Work of the Past, Work of the Future," *AEA Papers and Proceedings* 109:1–32, https://doi.org/10.1257/pandp.20191110. Copyright American Economic Association; reproduced with permission of the AEA Papers and Proceedings.

occupations shrink to near insignificance in the face of technological shifts, and those that remain may be distinct from what preceded them. Between 1920 and 1940, automation of the switchboard operator occupation, one of the most common occupations for American women, resulted in significant displacement, with a small remaining core of operators who performed high-level services.[23] In the metropolitan areas where these job contractions were concentrated, however, these losses were offset by employment growth in middle-skill clerical jobs and lower-skill service jobs, including new categories of work—jobs that employed workers of similar demographic characteristics to those who worked as switchboard operators in the prior generation.

These examples may be familiar, but the point is general. The creation of demand for new expertise is a critical force that counterbalances the tendency of

---

[23] J. Feigenbaum and D.P. Gross, 2024, "Answering the Call of Automation: How the Labor Market Adjusted to Mechanizing Telephone Operation," *The Quarterly Journal of Economics* 139(3):1879–1939.

automation to erode the value of old expertise.[24] Figure 4-2 documents that more than half (60 percent) of the job activities that U.S. workers performed in 2018 were not present—had not yet been *invented*—as of 1940. What makes work "new" is that it requires expertise that was not previously in demand or perhaps did not exist (e.g., pediatric oncology, AI prompt engineering, or pneumatic hammering). Human expertise has remained valuable not because it is timeless but because it is continually changing. The force of innovation has been central to this replenishment. But this is not the only force: rising wealth, changing demographics, and changing tastes also play central roles.[25]

Both automation of traditional work and new task creation occur simultaneously, but there is no reason to assume that these forces exactly offset one another. For much of the 20th century, these forces were in rough balance—new technologies not only displaced existing tasks but also complemented humans, generating new tasks and enabling humans to perform higher-quality work. This balance underpinned the period's wage and employment growth and shared prosperity.

Sometime after approximately 1970, for reasons that are not well understood, this balance was lost. Automation maintained its pace or even accelerated over the following decades, but new task creation slowed, especially for those workers without 4-year degrees.[26] Computerization displaced noncollege workers from factories and offices, and blue-collar workers were displaced by import competition.[27] Although employment is rising in health and skilled personal service occupations that may ultimately constitute a "new middle," this growth has not yet fully offset the loss of equivalently well-paid traditional middle-skill jobs, particularly among noncollege males.[28] Non-college-educated workers increasingly have taken shelter in low-paid service sector jobs such as food service, security, cleaning, and entertainment. Their work is socially valuable, as above,

---

[24] D. Acemoglu and P. Restrepo, 2018, "The Race Between Man and Machine: Implications of Technology for Growth, Factor Shares, and Employment," *American Economic Review* 108(6):1488–1542; and D. Autor, C. Chin, A.M. Salomons, and B. Seegmiller, 2022, "New Frontiers: The Origins and Content of New Work, 1940–2018," NBER Working Paper No. 30389, August.

[25] D. Autor, C. Chin, A.M. Salomons, and B. Seegmiller, 2022, "New Frontiers: The Origins and Content of New Work, 1940–2018," NBER Working Paper No. 30389, August.

[26] D. Acemoglu and P. Restrepo, 2019, "Automation and New Tasks: How Technology Displaces and Reinstates Labor," *Journal of Economic Perspectives* 33(2):3–30; D. Autor, C.M. Chin, A. Salomons, and B. Seegmiller, 2022, "New Frontiers: The Origins and Content of New Work, 1940–2018," NBER Working Paper No. w30389, August; and D. Acemoglu and S. Johnson, 2023, *Power and Progress: Our 1000-Year Struggle Over Technology and Prosperity*, PublicAffairs.

[27] D.H. Autor, D. Dorn, and G.H. Hanson, 2013, "The China Syndrome: Local Labor Market Effects of Import Competition in the United States," *American Economic Review* 103(6):2121–2168.

[28] Examples of this new middle include "sales representatives, truck drivers, managers of personal service workers, heating and air conditioning mechanics and installers, computer support specialists, self-enrichment education teachers, event planners, health technologists and technicians, massage therapists, social workers, marriage and family counselors, audiovisual technicians, paralegals, healthcare social workers, chefs and head cooks, and food service managers." See M.R. Strain, 2020, "The Middle Class Is Changing, Not Dying." Discourse, April 20, https://www.discoursemagazine.com/p/the-middle-class-is-changing-not-dying.

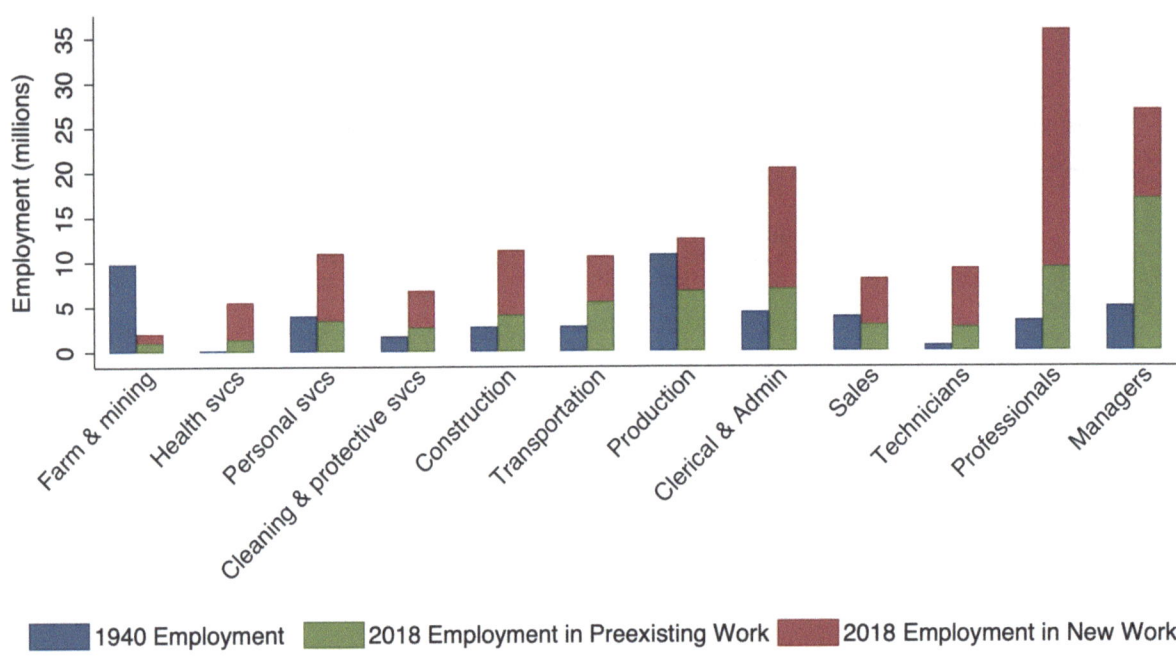

FIGURE 4-2 Employment counts by broad occupation in 1940 and 2018, distinguishing between titles present in 1940 and those subsequently added.
SOURCE: D. Autor, C.M. Chin, A. Salomons, and B. Seegmiller, 2024, "New Frontiers: The Origins and Content of New Work, 1940–2018," *Quarterly Journal of Economics* 139(3):1399–1465, https://doi.org/10.1093/qje/qjae008.

but because the positions require little in the way of specialized education, training, or expertise, they pay poorly.[29]

This expertise framework helps shed light on the following key questions:

- Is AI likely to raise wages or lower them, and for whom?
- Will AI further expand wage inequality or potentially reduce it?
- Will AI make worker expertise more valuable, or will it make it less necessary?
- What types of expertise are likely to be displaced by AI automation, and what types of expertise are likely to be made more valuable?

Before turning to AI, it is instructive to consider two prior technological revolutions: the Industrial Revolution and the computer revolution.

Table 4-1 provides an overview of the impact of each of these eras on the demand for expertise, and Table 4-2 provides a rubric for different types of expertise.

---

[29] D. Acemoglu, D. Autor, and S Johnson, 2023, "Can We Have Pro-Worker AI? Choosing a Path of Machines in Service of Minds," MIT Shaping the Future of Work Initiative Policy Memo, September 19, https://shapingwork.mit.edu/wp-content/uploads/2023/09/Pro-Worker-AI-Policy-Memo.pdf.

TABLE 4-1 Impacts of Three Technological Eras on the Demand for Expertise

	Expertise Substituted/ Made Obsolete	**Expertise Augmented/ Newly Demanded**	**Ease of Acquiring Needed Expertise**
Industrial era	Artisanal expertise (e.g., weaving, shoemaking, clock-making).	*Mass expertise.* Learning rules and mastering tools for manufacturing/production and office/ information tasks ("accomplishing routine tasks").	Literacy and numeracy needed. Owing to high school movement, workers well prepared to acquire industrial era mass expertise.
Information era	Mass expertise. Expertise in learning rules and mastering tools (i.e., carrying out routine tasks).	*Elite expertise.* Combining expert knowledge with acquired judgment to make high-stakes decisions in nonstandard cases. Needed for abstract decision making, communications, and management. Elite expertise becomes the bottleneck when routine tasks are automated.	Often requires a college degree or significant post-secondary education plus years of hands-on supervised practice or apprenticeship (e.g., medical doctor, pilot). Less than one-third of workers qualified.
Artificial intelligence era	May substitute for some "elite expertise"—making it less scarce.	*Translational expertise.* Combining expert judgment with inputs and guidance from artificial intelligence to carry out "elite expert" tasks.	May require foundational training in subject expertise (e.g., law, medicine) plus acquired judgment without necessarily requiring professional levels of post-secondary education.

TABLE 4-2 Types of Expertise: A Rubric

	Definition	**Educational Requirements**	**Representative Occupations**
Artisanal expertise	Mastery of full sequence of steps for producing a product.	Apprenticeship	Blacksmith, wheelwright, clockmaker
Mass expertise	Executing precise rules-based tasks (routine tasks) in production or office environments. Learning rules, mastering tools.	Typically, high school education and on-the-job training/experience	Production worker, machinist, typist, bookkeeper
Elite expertise	Combining formal training with acquired judgment to make high-stakes decisions (nonroutine cognitive tasks).	Often 4-year college degree plus graduate or professional degree	Medical doctor, lawyer, scientist, engineer, nurse, architect
Translational expertise	Combining foundational technical knowledge with supporting tools to accomplish high-stakes tasks.	Likely post-secondary vocational training that may not require a 4-year degree	Nurse practitioner, tradesperson, construction contractor

DEMAND FOR EXPERTISE IN THE INDUSTRIAL REVOLUTION

Although the Industrial Revolution is a monumentally broad topic, the discussion here will summarize its implications for work in the simplest possible terms. Prior to the Industrial Revolution, there was no concept of mass production. Most goods were handmade one at a time by skilled craftspeople (artisans). No two instances of the same item—be it a horseshoe, a wagon wheel, or a work boot—were identical. Artisanal work was generally expertise-intensive. The artisan was responsible for producing the complete product, not simply for accomplishing a few steps along the way.

This changed in the 18th and 19th centuries as industries mastered a new form of work organization that became known as mass production.[30] Mass production involved breaking the complex work of artisans into discreet, self-contained, and often quite simple steps that could be carried out mechanistically by a team of production workers, often abetted by machinery and overseen by managers.[31] As a case in point, the Ford Motor Company's River Rouge production plant, an archetype of mass production, employed more than 100,000 workers at its peak.[32]

The transition from artisanal to mass production profoundly changed the demand for worker expertise—what expertise was needed, who supplied it, and what wages it commanded. Most directly, mass production *reduced* demand for artisanal labor by providing a faster, cheaper production system that combined high-tech machinery, managerial expertise, and vast numbers of comparatively unskilled workers.[33] Although the skilled British weavers and textile workers who rose up in protest against mechanization in the 19th century—the eponymous Luddites—are frequently derided for their naive fear of technology, these fears were not misplaced. As the economic historian Joel Mokyr and colleagues wrote in 2015, "The handloom weavers and frame knitters with their little workshops were quite rapidly wiped out by factories after 1815."[34]

But mass production did not merely displace existing expertise. It created enormous demand for new forms of expertise. Initially, this demand was most concentrated on uneducated, untrained workers who could perform repetitive production steps. Whereas skilled artisans were almost necessarily adults—reflecting the years of

---

[30] D. Hounshell, 1984, *From the American System to Mass Production, 1800–1932: The Development of Manufacturing Technology in the United States*, No. 4, Johns Hopkins University Press.

[31] For detailed examples, see J. Atack, R.A. Margo, and P.W. Rhode, 2019, "Automation of Manufacturing in the Late Nineteenth Century: The Hand and Machine Labor Study," *Journal of Economic Perspectives* 33(2):51–70.

[32] Ford Motor Company, n.d., "Company Timeline: 1917," https://corporate.ford.com/about/history/company-timeline.html.

[33] C. Goldin and L.F. Katz, 1998, "The Origins of Technology-Skill Complementarity," *The Quarterly Journal of Economics* 113(3):693–732.

[34] J. Mokyr, C. Vickers, and N.L. Ziebarth, 2015, "The History of Technological Anxiety and the Future of Economic Growth: Is This Time Different?" *Journal of Economic Perspectives* 29(3):31–50. Mokyr and colleagues were in turn drawing on D. Bythell, 1969, *The Handloom Weavers: A Study in the English Cotton Industry During the Industrial Revolution*, Cambridge University Press.

apprenticeship required to master their trades—early factories made abundant use of children and unmarried women. Conditions in early factories were often grueling, dangerous, and exhausting. And the only essential capacities needed were physical dexterity and willingness to work (or inability to *not* work) under punishing conditions, often for extremely low pay.[35]

But these initial abysmal conditions improved in the early 20th century as a consequence of three powerful undercurrents. First, the enormous productivity gains stemming from the Industrial Revolution generated vast wealth while reducing the cost of everyday products, leading to a surge in demand. Households could for the first time afford luxuries such as full wardrobes, factory-made household goods, and new industrial products, including electric toasters and irons. The rapid expansion of industrial activity created new demand for labor and bid up wages. Rising incomes in turn enabled a change of norms, spurring laws restricting child labor and mitigating dangerous working conditions. This further promoted rising living standards.

Second, and as important, while early factory work required little skill or training, as new products and new production techniques emerged, workers operating and maintaining complex equipment needed expertise and training to carry out their work, such as skills in machining, fitting, welding, chemical processes, textiles, dyeing, calibrating precision instruments, and so on.[36] The growing need for expertise was not limited to production workers. The demand for educated and highly trained workers rose across the board in maintenance, engineering, production infrastructure, product design, logistics, accounting, communications, sales, and management to coordinate these many sophisticated parts. Whereas mass production was initially expertise-displacing, relying primarily on cadres of untrained workers accomplishing rote tasks under brutal conditions, it ultimately generated demand for mass expertise. Workers increasingly required experience, training, and formal knowledge to master and manage sophisticated tools and valuable materials in a complex environment.[37] In a phrase, workers needed to master tools and follow rules. (In contemporary economic parlance, many of these rule-and-tool activities would be classified as "routine tasks." Similarly, mass expertise could be defined as the skill to carry out routine tasks in production and office environments.)

Ultimately, although the rise of mass production eclipsed a substantial stock of artisanal expertise, the demand for new expertise that it generated proved vastly larger than these displacement effects. Much of the expertise required was *novel*. There had

---

[35] In Britain, textile workers were often orphans who were placed in indentured servitude to the mill, which provided food and boarding and, perhaps, education until the children were released at age 18.

[36] Of course, the design and integration of early industrial era tools and factories required mechanical expertise that was exceedingly rare in the late 18th and early 19th centuries. See M. Kelly, J. Mokyr, and C.Ó. Gráda, 2023, "The Mechanics of the Industrial Revolution," *Journal of Political Economy* 131(1):59–94.

[37] C. Goldin and L.F. Katz, 1998, "The Origins of Technology-Skill Complementarity," *The Quarterly Journal of Economics* 113(3):693–732.

been no demand for electricians until electricity found industrial and consumer uses. There were no skilled machinists prior to the invention of the machines that they operated. And there were no production engineers prior to the rise of mass production. In short, much of the expertise made valuable by the era of mass production was not required and did not *exist* before changes in technology and work organization made that expertise essential for delivering goods and services. The new ideas, institutions, and technologies of the Industrial Revolution thus spurred a vast expansion of the breadth and depth of expertise required of workers.

Third, the Industrial Revolution did not simply change industry. It fundamentally reshaped the basket of goods and services produced and consumed by citizens of industrializing countries. Even at the height of U.S. industrial activity in the early 1950s, less than 40 percent of employment was in industry (i.e., manufacturing, mining, and utilities) and only about 10 percent was in agriculture.[38] The remainder was in services, a residual sector that encompasses everything from education to finance, insurance, real estate, business services, health care, food and hospitality, transportation, power generation, and travel (among other examples). Services comprised only one-third of employment in 1900 but encompassed more than half by 1950 and nearly four-fifths by 2020. The growth of services also generated vast new demands for labor and accompanying demands for new expertise. Many of these services were not themselves a direct product of the Industrial Revolution. But the transformative economic growth stemming from the Industrial Revolution allowed countries to focus their resources on these service activities, many of which would be considered nonessential in a poorer society. For example, while it would be a stretch to claim that the advent of mass production *created* the movie industry, neither the technology for producing and projecting movies nor the mass market consumer audience that was willing and able to pay for them would have been conceivable absent the rise in living standards that mass production afforded.[39]

This section thus far has addressed two of the three questions posed at the beginning of this chapter: What expertise was replaced (artisanal expertise), and what expertise was newly demanded by the Industrial Revolution (mass expertise)? The answer to the third question—relating to the feasibility of acquiring newly required expertise—is crucial to understanding why the Industrial Revolution created so much mass prosperity. Much of the expert work created in the industrial era demanded specific training and experience. Yet, workers typically needed no more than a high school education to enter these specialties. This fact was critically important because during the early 20th century,

---

[38] L. Johnston, 2012, "The Growth of the Service Sector in Historical Perspective: Explaining Trends in US Sectoral Output and Employment, 1840–1990," unpublished manuscript, College of Saint Benedict, Saint John's University.

[39] Clark makes the case that demand for services rises relative to demand for goods as societies get wealthier. See C. Clark, 1957, *The Conditions of Economic Progress*, London, Macmillan.

most of the United States moved to institute universal, publicly funded secondary school education.[40] A large and growing fraction of U.S. adults was therefore equipped with the foundational formal skills needed to enter the expert occupations that were on the rise. To be clear, a high school education did not guarantee entry into the middle class, nor did high school–educated workers earn as much as those with college or post-college degrees. Moreover, discrimination against minorities and women denied a large fraction of the population access to these opportunities.[41] But the excellence of U.S. public education in this era enabled a significant portion of the U.S. workforce—those who were not the targets of systemic discrimination—to make a successful transition into 20th century industry and services. Absent that educational foundation, it is unlikely that the United States would have reaped the same rapid, broadly shared income growth in the ensuing decades.[42]

DEMAND FOR EXPERTISE IN THE COMPUTER ERA BEFORE ARTIFICIAL INTELLIGENCE

Stemming from the innovations pioneered during World War II, the computer era reshaped this mass expertise trajectory. Like other general-purpose technologies that preceded it (e.g., electricity, the steam engine), the digital computer was highly applicable to a vast number of products, processes, and workplace settings. Relative to all technologies that had preceded it, however, the computer's unique power was its ability to execute cognitive and manual tasks cheaply, reliably, and rapidly that were encoded in explicit, deterministic rules—that is, programs. This might seem prosaic: Do all machines not simply follow deterministic rules? At one level, yes. Machines do what they are built to do unless they are malfunctioning. But at another level, no. Distinct from prior machines, computers are symbolic processors that access, analyze, and act upon abstract information.[43] Prior to the computer era, there was essentially only one tool for processing abstract information: the human mind. And not just any mind would do. Often, literacy and numeracy were required.

---

[40] C. Goldin and L.F. Katz, 2009, *The Race Between Education and Technology*, Harvard University Press.

[41] D. Autor, C. Goldin, and L.F. Katz, 2020, "Extending the Race Between Education and Technology," *AEA Papers and Proceedings* 110:347–351.

[42] Between 1947 and 1973, the rate of real mean family income growth was roughly identical across all five quintiles of the U.S. household income distribution, as well as among the top 5 percent of households. After 1973, this pattern skewed radically, with almost all income growth occurring among the top 40 percent, and especially the top 20 percent and 10 percent, of the income distribution. See C. Goldin and L.F. Katz, 2007, "Long-Run Changes in the Wage Structure: Narrowing, Widening, Polarizing," *Brookings Papers on Economic Activity* 38:135–168. However, income levels, wealth, and access to opportunity differed radically between Black and White Americans owing to both historical and contemporary discrimination.

[43] E. Brynjolfsson and L.M. Hitt, 2000, "Beyond Computation: Information Technology, Organizational Transformation and Business Performance," *Journal of Economic Perspectives* 14(4):23–48.

The widespread adoption of powerful, inexpensive machines that could perform symbolic processing led to a seismic shift in the expertise demanded of workers. To understand how this worked, it is useful to conceptualize a job as performing a series of tasks required to accomplish a specific goal. Consider the tasks involved in writing a research report—such as assembling and managing a research team; collecting data; developing and testing hypotheses; performing calculations; drafting, editing, and proofreading; and distributing the report to readers. Before computers, most research and writing tasks would have been accomplished manually, aided by books, adding machines, typewriters, and postal mail. Human expertise would have been critical in such tasks as leading research teams, interpreting data, developing and testing hypotheses, calculating quantitative implications, and report writing.[44]

Computerization enabled the reassignment of a crucial set of tasks from humans to machines—in the above example, organizing data, performing calculations, proofreading text for misspellings, and distributing results. Now computers accomplish a well-delineated subset of tasks—that is, precise replicable steps that can be specified fully in advance. These are what economists typically refer to as "routine tasks" and what coders refer to as "programs."[45] Because a computer programmer must specify the sequence of steps required to accomplish a task before a computer can execute it, routine tasks are well suited to computerization. The cost of executing these programmed instructions has fallen dramatically. A 2007 paper by William Nordhaus estimated that the cost of performing a given computational task has fallen at least 1.7 trillion-fold since the predawn of the computer age, with most of that decline occurring since 1980.[46]

The spectacular fall in the cost of computing—accompanied by stunning improvements in speed and miniaturization—created powerful economic incentives for firms to use machines rather than workers to perform routine job tasks. This was a major step forward for productivity. But it was a mixed blessing for many workers because, in many instances, computers proved more proficient and far less expensive than workers in mastering tools and following rules. In the precomputer era, workers who specialized in skilled office and production tasks were the embodiment of the "mass expertise" of the industrial era. As computing advanced, it eroded the value of that mass expertise by displacing some of the core routine tasks that these workers performed. This catalyzed a contraction in the share of employment found in middle-skill production, office,

---

[44] D. Autor, K. Basu, Z. Qureshi, and D. Rodrik, 2022, "An Inclusive Future? Technology, New Dynamics, and Policy Challenges," Brookings Institution's Global Forum on Democracy and Technology, May 31, https://www.brookings.edu/articles/an-inclusive-future-technology-new-dynamics-and-policy-challenges.

[45] D.H. Autor, F. Levy, and R.J. Murnane, 2003, "The Skill Content of Recent Technological Change: An Empirical Exploration," *The Quarterly Journal of Economics* 118(4):1279–1333; F. Levy and R.J. Murnane, 2005, *The New Division of Labor*, Princeton University Press.

[46] W.D. Nordhaus, 2007, "Two Centuries of Productivity Growth in Computing," *The Journal of Economic History* 67(1):128–159.

administrative, and sales occupations (Figure 4-3).[47] The routine tasks once supplied by these workers were still needed—in fact, such tasks were used ever more intensively as their cost fell—but they were now performed by machines.

The wage consequences of routine task displacement were stark. Workers whose industries and occupations were most exposed to the automation of routine tasks saw sharp falls in their real earnings from 1980 forward, as shown in Panel A of Figure 4-4. Those most affected were disproportionately workers with a high school education but no post-secondary schooling, a group that—not by coincidence—fared extremely poorly overall during the past four decades (see Figure 4-1). Notably, this downward-sloping relationship between routine task–exposure and wage declines was absent before 1980, prior to the advent of large-scale commercial computerization (Figure 4-4, Panel B). This adds to the case that it was computerization specifically—not some other force—that depressed the earnings of workers who were specialized in routine task–intensive jobs. Computerization was therefore a critical force (though not the only factor) in the displacement and devaluation of the "mass expertise" that the industrial era had robustly demanded.

Not all tasks are, however, suited to computer execution. Many critical tasks follow rules and procedures that are known neither to computer programmers nor to the people who regularly perform them. The scientist and philosopher Michael Polanyi observed in 1966 that "we know more than we can tell," meaning that people's tacit knowledge often exceeds their explicit formal understanding.[48] Making a persuasive argument, telling a joke, riding a bicycle, or recognizing an adult's face in a baby photograph are subtle and complex undertakings that people seemingly accomplish with little effort without ever understanding precisely how. Mastery of these so-called "nonroutine" tasks is attained not through formal education (i.e., by learning the rules) but instead by learning-by-doing. A child learning to ride a bicycle does not need to study the physics of gyroscopes. But for a computer to control a motorized bicycle, a programmer would (in the pre-AI era) need to specify all the relevant instructions in advance. This observation—that human beings instinctively understand and perform many tasks, yet they cannot articulate the specific rules or procedures involved—is often referred to as Polanyi's paradox.[49]

The capacity of computers to execute routine tasks with unprecedented speed at minimal cost proved highly complementary to managerial, professional, and technical

---

[47] Similar evidence for European Union countries is found in M. Goos, A. Manning, and A. Salomons, 2014, "Explaining Job Polarization: Routine-Biased Technological Change and Offshoring," *American Economic Review* 104(8):2509–2526.

[48] M. Polanyi, 1966, *The Tacit Dimension*, University of Chicago Press.

[49] D. Autor, 2014, "Polanyi's Paradox and the Shape of Employment Growth," *Proceedings of the Federal Reserve Bank of Kansas City*, Jackson Hole Economic Policy Symposium, August.

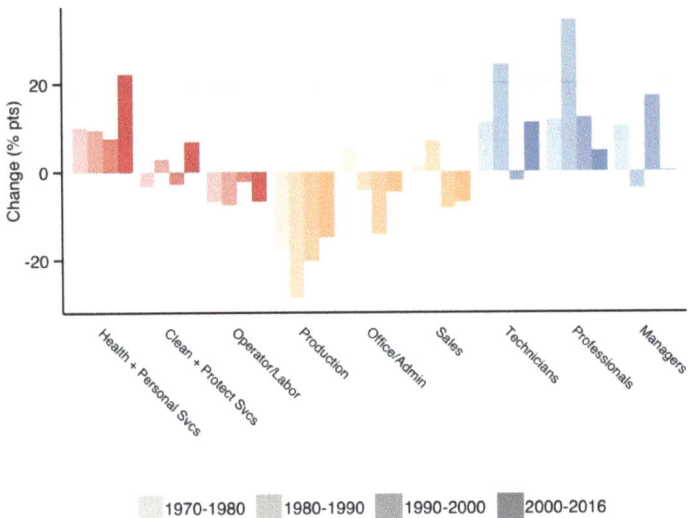

FIGURE 4-3 Percent changes in employment shares among working-age adults in the United States by occupation, 1970–2016.
SOURCE: D. Autor, 2019, "Work of the Past, Work of the Future," *AEA Papers and Proceedings* 109:1–32, https://doi.org/10.1257/pandp.20191110. Copyright American Economic Association; reproduced with permission of the AEA Papers and Proceedings.

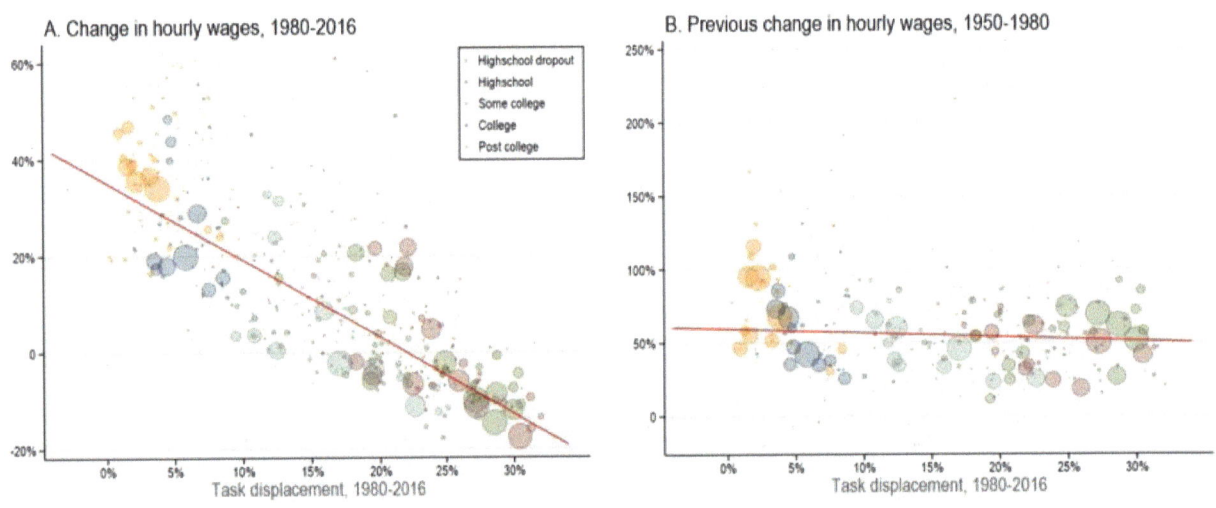

FIGURE 4-4 Changes in real hourly wages versus task displacement in the United States, 1980–2016 and 1950–1980, by educational attainment. Task displacement based on observed labor share declines (%), 1980–2016.
SOURCE: D. Acemoglu and P. Restrepo, 2022, "Tasks, Automation, and the Rise in U.S. Wage Inequality," *Econometrica* 90(5):1973–2016, https://doi.org/10.3982/ECTA19815. CC BY-NC-ND 4.0 DEED.

workers—whose work is concentrated in nonroutine abstract and interpersonal tasks.[50] This complementarity arises because professional workers regularly make high-stakes decisions that are tailored to specific circumstances—for example, diagnosing a patient, crafting a legal brief, leading a team or organization, designing a building, or engineering a software product. For such tasks, knowing the rules is necessary but not sufficient; professionals must combine domain-specific knowledge with judgment and creativity to devise appropriate responses to novel problems. The discussion here refers to this as "elite expertise": the technical knowledge and acquired judgment needed to make high-stakes, one-off decisions. Computerization complements elite expertise by enabling professionals to spend less of their time acquiring information and conducting routine analysis and more of their time interpreting and applying that information. It thus augments the accuracy, productivity, and thoroughness of professional decision making, rendering professional expertise more valuable. It is therefore no coincidence that the earnings of workers with 4-year and *especially* graduate degrees (in law, medicine, science, engineering, design, and management) rose steeply as computerization advanced.

These advances in routine task execution came at a cost to others. Computerization augmented the value of elite expertise in part by automating away the mass expertise of the workers on whom professionals used to rely. This created inequality in opportunity because entry into the professions is expensive, requiring both high levels of formal education—often in the form of graduate degrees and professional credentials—and significant time spent in training—for example, medical residencies, postdoctoral fellowships, junior status in law or academia, management of small organizations, and so on. In the era of mass production, the advancing high school movement dovetailed with the skill demands of the industrializing economy, so the supply of high school–educated workers kept pace with the rapidly rising demand. To use the terminology of Goldin and Katz, in the "race between education and technology" in the early decades of the 20th century, education decidedly won that heat.[51] But there was no corresponding college movement on the scale of the high school movement to meet the rising demands for elite expertise in the computer era. Instead, the rising demand for elite expertise in this period contributed to rising inequality, with earnings growth concentrated among the educated elite.

Not all nonroutine tasks require elite expertise, however. Some tasks—such as cleaning rooms, waiting tables, picking items in a warehouse, driving a vehicle in city traffic, or assisting elderly people with daily living—rely on dexterity, simple

---

[50] On the value of social skills, see D.J. Deming, 2017, "The Growing Importance of Social Skills in the Labor Market," *The Quarterly Journal of Economics* 132(4):1593–1640.

[51] For a deep historical account, see C. Goldin and L.F. Katz, 2009, *The Race Between Education and Technology*, Harvard University Press.

communication, and common sense.⁵² Because these nonroutine manual (or "service") tasks draw on substantial reservoirs of tacit knowledge, they have proved stubbornly difficult to automate. Yet, because the vast majority of workers can master these tasks with modest training, the workers performing service tasks typically earn low wages.

Computerization did not improve this situation. Although computerization neither automates the central tasks of nonroutine manual work nor strongly augments the workers doing these tasks, it substantially affected this work *indirectly*—in many cases not positively. As the automation of routine tasks eroded employment in clerical, administrative, and production occupations, many of the noncollege workers who would have performed this work were increasingly shunted into hands-on service occupations such as food service, cleaning and janitorial services, security, and personal care. This placed downward pressure on wages in this (already) low-wage work, providing an additional force for rising inequality.⁵³

Applying the three questions posed at the beginning of this chapter to the computer era helps to weave together these threads:

1. What expertise was substituted or made obsolete in the computer era? *Mass expertise.* Expertise in carrying out middle-skilled, routine-intensive tasks in offices and factories was devalued as computers could carry out this work faster, cheaper, and more accurately than the workers they replaced.⁵⁴

2. What expertise was augmented or newly demanded? *Elite expertise.* Abstract reasoning, strong interpersonal and leadership skills, and expertise in high-stakes, situation-specific decision making were more valuable as computers automated the routine components of these tasks. As the value of expert nonroutine tasks rose, workers with graduate degrees ("elite expertise") were the biggest beneficiaries.

3. How feasible was it for workers to acquire newly valuable expertise? *Acquiring elite expertise is costly in time and money.* If workers could have entered growing, highly educated professions rapidly, many would have benefited from the

---

⁵² Although half-a-dozen years ago, autonomous vehicles were predicted to overtake and replace human drivers rapidly, the problem has proved much harder than anticipated because the complexity of high-stakes nonroutine decision making required is immense; even experienced drivers find the process almost effortless. See S.E. Shladover, 2021, "'Self-Driving' Cars Begin to Emerge from a Cloud of Hype," *Scientific American*, September 21, https://www.scientificamerican.com/article/self-driving-cars-begin-to-emerge-from-a-cloud-of-hype.

⁵³ D. Acemoglu and P. Restrepo, 2022, "Tasks, Automation, and the Rise in US Wage Inequality," *Econometrica* 90(5):1973–2016.

⁵⁴ By contrast, dexterous physical tasks that are performed in relatively fluid, nonstandardized environments, such as construction sites, homes, or restaurants, have not been subject to automation because the lack of environmental control makes these tasks nonroutine. As Herbert Simon wrote in 1960, "Environmental control is a substitute for flexibility." Factories enable automation by reducing the need for flexibility. This is far harder to accomplish on construction sites. See H.A. Simon, 1960, "The Corporation: Will It Be Managed by Machines?" pp. 17–55 in *Management and the Corporations*, M.L. Anshen and G.L. Bach, eds., McGraw-Hill.

labor market changes wrought by computerization. But the virtuous synergy between public education and new demands for expertise seen in the early 20th century was absent during the computer revolution. Mass education did not provide the needed number of 4-year degrees that would have allowed workers to enter expanding professions, often through graduate training, and that would have been required to maintain the shape of the earnings distribution. Moreover, college enrollment among U.S. adults, especially U.S. males, responded with remarkable sluggishness to the rising demand for educated workers after 1980.[55] Rather than catalyzing a new era of "mass expertise," computerization instead bolstered a decades-long trend of rising inequality. Workers with expertise in professional, technical, and managerial tasks saw their skills become even more valuable. Workers lacking elite expertise were increasingly relegated to nonexpert service work as the broad middle set of occupations was eroded by automation. Thus, in the long-running race between education and technology, education lost decisively in these decades.

DEMAND FOR EXPERTISE IN THE ARTIFICIAL INTELLIGENCE ERA

Earlier chapters discussed the technical attributes of AI. This chapter discusses its implications for the operation of the labor markets—specifically, its potential impact on the demand for expertise. These potential impacts stem from one attribute that AI possesses and previous technologies lacked: the capacity to master and execute nonroutine tasks. While in the pre-AI era engineers struggled to program computers to accomplish tasks that humans understand only tacitly, this is no longer an intrinsic obstacle for AI. AI learns by example, mastering tasks without explicit instruction and acquiring capabilities that it was not designed to perform. In short, AI can infer tacit relationships, meaning that it has made substantial progress toward overcoming Polanyi's paradox.

To understand the power of this tacit learning capability, consider one simple application: identifying pictures of chairs. Although it seems trivial, explicitly defining what makes a chair a chair is extraordinarily challenging: Must it have legs and, if so, how many? Must it have a back? What range of heights is acceptable? Must it be comfortable, and what makes a chair comfortable? Writing the rules for this problem is maddening.[56]

---

[55] D. Autor, 2014, "Skills, Education, and the Rise of Earnings Inequality Among the 'Other 99 Percent,'" *Science* 344(6186):843–851.

[56] See D. Autor, 2022, "The Labor Market Impacts of Technological Change: From Unbridled Enthusiasm to Qualified Optimism to Vast Uncertainty," NBER Working Paper No. 30074, May.

If written too narrowly, they will exclude stools and rocking chairs. If written too broadly, they will include tables and countertops. In a well-known paper, Grabner and colleagues argue that the fundamental problem is that what makes a chair a chair is its suitability for sitting upon.[57] What makes something "suitable" for sitting upon is as elusive as the original problem. Given this morass, this chair classification task would be categorized as "nonroutine" for purposes of conventional computing—a human task rather than a machine task.

Fast forward to the present, and AI can "solve" this classification problem but not by following explicitly programmed rules. Rather, AI infers the solution inductively by training on examples. Given a suitable database of tagged images and sufficient computing power, AI can infer what image attributes are statistically associated with the label "chair" and can then use that information to classify untagged images of chairs with a high degree of accuracy.[58] It can then refine this typology as its outputs are affirmed or corrected by human users. In general, the rules that AI uses for this classification remain tacit. Nowhere in the learning process does AI formally codify or reveal the underlying features (i.e., rules) that constitute "chair-ness." The classification instead emerges from layers of learned statistical associations with no human-interpretable window into that decision-making process. This absence of transparency, which David Autor refers to as "Polanyi's revenge"—"computers now know more than they can tell us"—creates a new set of challenges touched upon briefly below.[59]

Three key properties emerge from AI's capacity to infer tacit relationships:

1. *AI tools can learn and adapt.* AI, when based on machine learning, acquires capabilities from examples, draws inferences from unstructured information, and generalizes acquired capacities across domains—for example, large language models (LLMs) can craft prose, explain jokes, and write computer code. This capacity is distinct from prior technologies that were, in a fundamental sense, scripted to execute prespecified actions that were encoded mechanically or symbolically.

2. *AI tools are generative.* AI can produce novel output that would be judged by many casual observers and professional experts to be competent; useful; and in some cases, creative. While some earlier pre-AI software packages

---

[57] H. Grabner, J. Gall, and L. Van Gool, 2011, "What Makes a Chair a Chair?" pp. 1529–1536 in *Proceedings of the 2011 IEEE Conference on Computer Vision and Pattern Recognition*, IEEE Computer Society, https://doi.org/10.1109/CVPR.2011.5995327.

[58] E. Brynjolfsson and T. Mitchell, 2017, "What Can Machine Learning Do? Workforce Implications," *Science* 358(6370):1530–1534; E. Brynjolfsson, T. Mitchell, and D. Rock, 2018, "What Can Machines Learn, and What Does It Mean for Occupations and the Economy?" *AEA Papers and Proceedings* 108:43–47.

[59] D. Autor, 2022, "The Labor Market Impacts of Technological Change: From Unbridled Enthusiasm to Qualified Optimism to Vast Uncertainty," NBER Working Paper No. 30074, May.

generated music, prose, and original graphical art, the results were highly programmatic. Works created by contemporary AI tools are in many cases on par with human creations.
3. *AI tools may alter the order of operations between human ideation, expertise creation, and subsequent expertise erosion (i.e., automation).* Historically, human expertise has preceded and was necessary for subsequent automation. New technologies were conceived by inventors, engineers, and designers; deployed using novel tools and expertise; and (if successful) broadly adopted, along with supporting expertise. Over the longer run, these technological innovations might be automated as the relevant processes and knowledge are codified and routinized.

A corollary to the third property is that AI will likely reverse this flow of innovation. In numerous conceivable cases, AI will solve problems that presently confound current understanding. Humans will then be left to decipher how AI solved the problem and how this solution actually works.[60] The same logic applies to other well-known examples, such as AI's progress on the epochal problem of protein folding[61] or its mastery of open-ended games like Go. It is highly plausible that frontier innovations will increasingly precede, and perhaps defy, human understanding. Humans will then face a substantial challenge both in understanding how AI systems accomplish tasks and in supervising AI systems to thwart erroneous or dangerous decisions.

These challenges are already visible in the complex interaction between partially autonomous vehicles and their human drivers. In the vast majority of typical driving settings, partially autonomous vehicles are arguably more attentive and less error-prone than human drivers. But they are susceptible to making catastrophic errors that an attentive driver would not make—for example, driving at highway speed into a roadside safety vehicle, as some Tesla vehicles have done.[62] In theory, the combination of human drivers and partially autonomous vehicles should be safer than either operating alone. In reality, because drivers have difficulty sustaining passive attention, they are often ill-prepared to accept an emergency "handoff" when required. This problem will likely become more acute as the proficiency of autonomous vehicles improves and the attentiveness and even the underlying driving expertise of human drivers atrophy.

---

[60] For a vivid example of this process in the case of judicial bail decisions, see J. Ludwig and S. Mullainathan, 2023, "Machine Learning as a Tool for Hypothesis Generation," NBER Working Paper No. w31017, March.
[61] R.F. Service, 2020, "'The Game Has Changed.' AI Triumphs at Protein Folding," *Science* 370(6521):1144–1145.
[62] F. Siddiqui, R. Lerman, and J.B. Merrill, 2022, "Teslas Running Autopilot Involved in 273 Crashes Reported Since Last Year," *Washington Post*, June 15.

Implications of Artificial Intelligence for the Demand for Expertise

Before applying the three-part rubric to consider how demand for human expertise may be reshaped in the AI era, two major caveats are needed. First, this report was written in the early years of what appears to be a revolution in machine capabilities. There is almost no representative or authoritative evidence so far to guide forecasts of how the widespread adoption and continued advancement of AI may affect work and workers. Second, commentators and experts of all stripes—social and natural scientists, historians, and journalists—have an almost unblemished record of *incorrectly* forecasting the long-run consequences of technological innovations. For example, Aristotle prophesied in the fourth century BC that if "the shuttle would weave and the plectrum touch the lyre without a hand to guide them, chief workmen would not want servants, nor masters slaves."[63] But slavery was not universally abolished for more than 150 years after the 1785 invention of the power loom,[64] and in some places, it even persists today.[65] The study committee does not claim greater foresight than Aristotle.

As important, in attempting to forecast the "consequences" of technological change, there is a risk of portraying the future as a fate to be divined rather than an expedition to be undertaken. This would be an error. Both the technologies developed and the manner in which they are used—for exploitation or emancipation, for broadening prosperity or concentrating wealth—are determined foremost not by the technologies themselves but by the incentives and institutions in which they are created and deployed.[66] For example, scientific mastery of controlled nuclear fission in the 1940s enabled nations to produce both massively destructive weapons and carbon-neutral electricity generation plants. Eight decades on, countries have prioritized these technologies differently. North Korea possesses an arsenal of nuclear weapons but no civilian nuclear power plants. Japan, the only country against which an offensive nuclear weapon has been used, possesses no nuclear weapons and 12 civilian nuclear power plants in current operation.[67]

AI is far more malleable and broadly applicable than nuclear technology; hence, the range of both constructive and destructive uses is far wider. Some nations already use AI to surveil their populations heavily, squelch viewpoints that depart from official

---

[63] Aristotle. *Politics,* Translated by H. Rackham, Harvard University Press, 1932, book 1, section 1253b.
[64] M. Cartwright, 2023, "The Textile Industry in the British Industrial Revolution" in *World History Encyclopedia*, https://www.worldhistory.org/article/2183/the-textile-industry-in-the-british-industrial-rev and M.A. Klein, 2002, *Historical Dictionary of Slavery and Abolition*, Scarecrow Press, p. 22.
[65] International Labour Organization, 2024, "Joining Forces to End Forced Labor," September 9, https://www.ilo.org/publications/joining-forces-end-forced-labour.
[66] For an in-depth treatment of this topic, see D. Acemoglu and S. Johnson, 2023, *Power and Progress: Our 1000-Year Struggle Over Technology and Prosperity*, PublicAffairs.
[67] Arms Control Association, 2024, "Nuclear Weapons: Who Has What at a Glance," July, https://www.armscontrol.org/factsheets/nuclear-weapons-who-has-what-glance and International Atomic Energy Agency, 2024, "Country Nuclear Power Profiles," AIEA Non-serial Publications, https://cnpp.iaea.org/public.

narratives, and identify (and subsequently punish) dissidents—and they are exporting these capabilities rapidly to like-minded autocracies.[68] In other settings, the same underlying AI technologies are used to advance medical drug discovery (including the development of COVID-19 vaccines), enable real-time translation of spoken languages, and provide free online tutoring in frontier educational subjects.

What these examples highlight is that the potential effects of AI on the work of the future depend critically on what objectives individuals, corporations, educational institutions, and governments pursue; what investments they make; and even what vision of the future guides these decisions. The discussion below considers *possible* paths for how labor markets may be shaped by the development and deployment of AI, recognizing that none of these paths are inevitable. The fact that some paths are more desirable than others provides a strong impetus for choosing policies carefully.

What Expertise Will Be Substituted or Made Obsolete?

It is reasonable to assume that AI tools will likely soon equal or exceed human capacities in numerous "elite expert" tasks (at substantially lower cost): writing business and legal documents; digesting, distilling, and synthesizing research; producing presentations, charts, illustrations, and animations; performing state-of-the-art medical diagnoses and providing treatment plans; solving engineering and design problems; managing complex systems such as power grids, server clusters, and air traffic control systems; and developing educational content.[69]

The rapid progress of AI in these domains is illustrated in Figure 4-5, which shows that OpenAI's ChatGPT v4.0 LLM is currently able to score above the 80th percentile on numerous high school Advanced Placement exams (statistics, macroeconomics, microeconomics, and psychology) as well as on the Uniform Bar Examination, the quantitative reasoning section of the Graduate Record Examination, and the mathematics section of the SAT.[70] While acing standardized tests is not equivalent to practicing successfully in a professional environment (i.e., lawyers do not take standardized tests for a living), these results strongly suggest that LLMs will be able to carry out some of the core nonroutine tasks of highly paid professionals in the years ahead.

---

[68] M. Beraja, A. Kao, D.Y. Yang, and N. Yuchtman, 2021, "AI-tocracy," NBER Working Paper No. 29466, November, National Bureau of Economic Research, http://www.nber.org/papers/w29466.

[69] Relatedly, Daniel Rock and colleagues used a decade of data from private-sector posting sources to create a geometric analysis of change in occupations. They found that digital technologies are densifying the occupational landscape—increasing occupations by as much as 4 percent per year with less "distance" as defined by specific skill needs between occupations. If this were to hold during the introduction of generative AI, it would add emphasis to the potential value of expansive access to targeted training. See D. Rock, 2022, "Work2Vec: Measuring the Latent Structure of the Labor Market," ESCoE Economic Measurement Webinars, https://escoe-website.s3.amazonaws.com/wp-content/uploads/2022/01/25103832/Daniel-Rock-Slides.pdf.

[70] This model was state of the art as of March 2023. Readers of this report will surely encounter more powerful successors to this model.

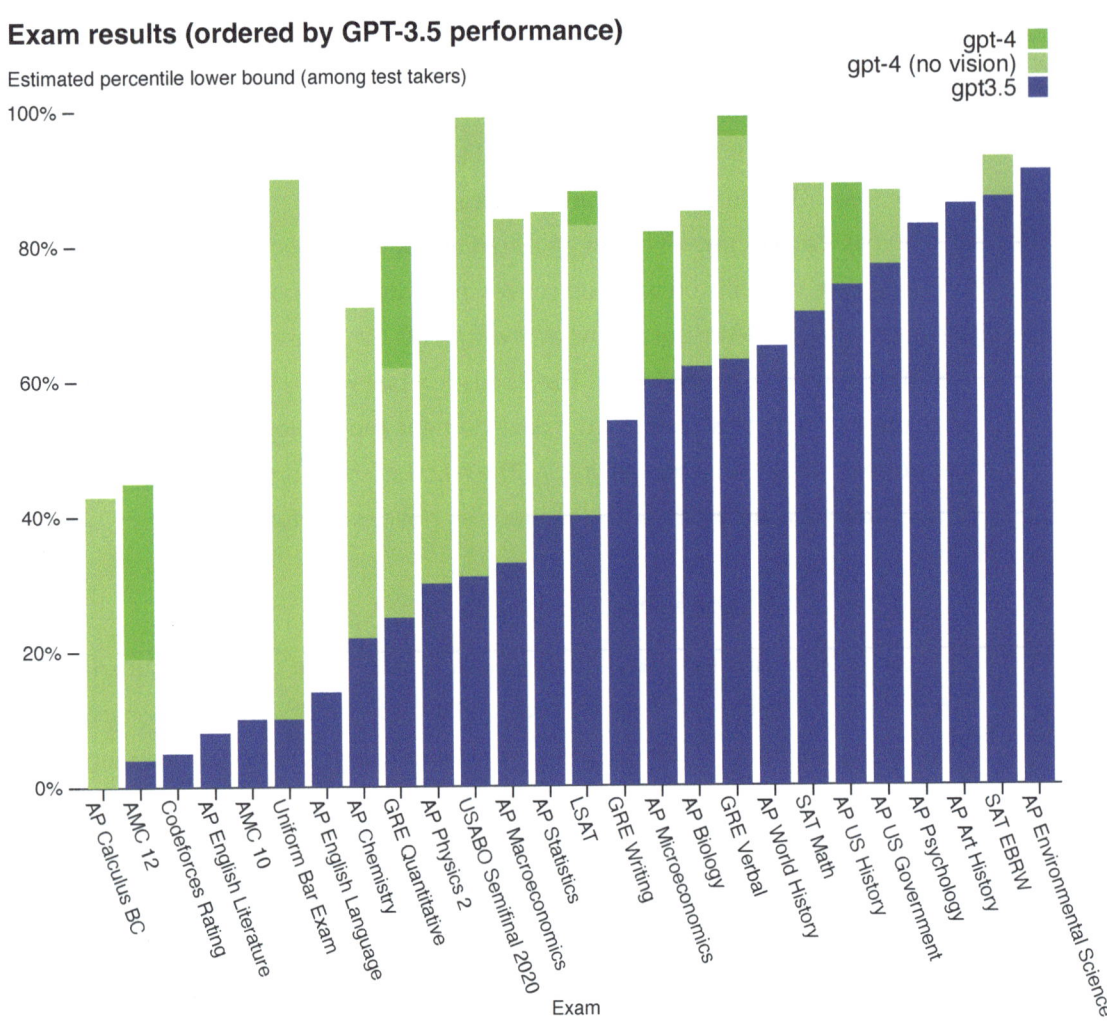

FIGURE 4-5 Scores of ChatGPT 3.5 and ChatGPT 4 on high-stakes exams: percentile scores relative to the population of test takers.
SOURCE: OpenAI, J. Achiam, S. Adler, et al., 2023, "GPT-4 Technical Report," https://doi.org/10.48550/arXiv.2303.08774.

This does not mean that human expertise will be superfluous. For instance, expertise will be needed to develop, implement, maintain, and upgrade AI. More generally, expertise will be required at the frontier of every field—medicine, law, engineering, design, and laboratory and natural sciences, among many others. It is much more likely that AI will accomplish a growing fraction of "conventional" cases, even as human expertise remains essential in frontier and nonstandard cases. There will be significant heterogeneity in tasks within the broader category of AI technologies, with some amenable to full automation and many others requiring significant human expertise and involvement.

AI will also speed progress in robotics. But the era in which it is feasible and cost-effective to deploy robots to perform physically demanding tasks in unpredictable real-world environments—rather than in tightly controlled factory settings—remains further away. If that sounds unduly pessimistic, consider the faltering rate of technological progress toward fully autonomous driving—despite tremendous investment in that goal and widespread pronouncements of imminent technological mastery. Note further that driving an automobile requires far less physical dexterity and cognitive flexibility than, for example, installing plumbing, landscaping a house, assisting an elderly person to bathe, cooking a meal from fresh ingredients, or cleaning up after that meal is over. This observation suggests that a vast set of nonroutine manual tasks, particularly those performed in variable and unpredictable environments, will require human labor and expertise for quite some time. Here too, the committee expects uneven progress with robotics continuing to advance in many predictable workplace environments, such as factories and warehouses, where the requirements for flexibility and situational adaptability are far less demanding. Note that there is also some possibility, as discussed in Chapter 2, that a new generation of multimodal foundation models—trained on text, video, voice, and sounds—could yield sudden advances in AI abilities to model the physical world and corresponding advances in robotics.

Given these assessments, AI is likely to *substitute* for human labor in two broad categories of tasks:

1. AI will speed the rate of automation of "mass expertise" (i.e., learning rules, mastering tools) by enabling machines to complete the "last mile" of tasks that were previously out of reach—for example, taking retail inventory at a convenience store; stocking a warehouse; or boxing small, irregular objects in a direct-to-consumer sales warehouse.
2. More profoundly, AI will enable partial automation of many high-value intellectual services supplied by workers with elite expertise in fields such as law, medicine, engineering, education, architecture, tax accounting, research, and so on. Many forms of elite expertise may become more accessible and less expensive in the AI era.

These observations are consonant with a growing set of studies that seeks to classify which workplace tasks, occupations, and industries are most "exposed" to AI—meaning that they are engaged in tasks that appear within the realm of AI's capabilities.[71] A consistent result from this body of work is that AI's potential to replicate the core tasks of occupations is generally greater for high-education, high-wage occupations—though perhaps not for the most highly educated occupations—and generally less for low-education, low-wage occupations, particularly those that engage in physical tasks in high-variability environments (i.e., not assembly lines and warehouses), as is also discussed in Chapter 3.

The predictions above for which tasks AI can readily substitute are in the committee's estimation credible and relatively uncontroversial. But this is the least challenging part of forecasting the labor market consequences of widespread AI deployment. At the onset of prior technological revolutions, it was comparatively easy for contemporaries to predict that the Industrial Revolution would displace artisanal expertise—the Luddites seem to have caught on to this idea quickly—or that the computer era would displace worker expertise in routine clerical and production tasks. Similarly, it is self-evident that AI will substitute for some of the nonroutine cognitive labor tasks supplied by professional workers. It is a far greater challenge to anticipate what forms of worker expertise will be *augmented* (i.e., made more valuable) by the deployment of AI and, similarly, what novel forms of expertise will be newly demanded to support the products, processes, services, and work modalities enabled by this technological revolution.

The next section develops three scenarios that cover a range of cases. They are potentially relevant over the next 5–15 years and could unfold by 2040 or sooner.

What Expertise Will Be Augmented or Newly Demanded?

Scenario 1: Further Occupational Polarization

Advances in AI could extend the reach of automation to "routine-like" tasks, thus prolonging or accelerating the decades-long trend of occupational polarization shown earlier in Figure 4-3.[72] In this scenario, the substitution of AI for human tasks would radiate outward from the current locus of computer automation. This would enable machines

---

[71] E. Brynjolfsson, T. Mitchell, and D. Rock, 2018, "What Can Machines Learn, and What Does It Mean for Occupations and the Economy?" *AEA Papers and Proceedings* 108:43–47; E. Felten, M. Raj, and R. Seamans, 2018, "A Method to Link Advances in Artificial Intelligence to Occupational Abilities," *AEA Papers and Proceedings* 108:54–57; E. Felten, M. Raj, and R. Seamans, 2019, "The Effect of Artificial Intelligence on Human Labor: An Ability-Based Approach," *Academy of Management Proceedings* 1; E. Felten, M. Raj, and R. Seamans, 2021, "Occupational, Industry, and Geographic Exposure to Artificial Intelligence: A Novel Dataset and Its Potential Uses," *Strategic Management Journal* 42(12):2195–2217; E. Felten, M. Raj, and R. Seamans, 2023, "Occupational Heterogeneity in Exposure to Generative AI," Social Science Research Network, https://dx.doi.org/10.2139/ssrn.4414065; M. Webb, 2020, "The Impact of Artificial Intelligence on the Labor Market," unpublished manuscript, Stanford University; and T. Eloundou, S. Manning, P. Mishkin, and D. Rock, 2023, "GPTs Are GPTs: An Early Look at the Labor Market Impact Potential of Large Language Models," arXiv preprint, arXiv:2303.10130, March 27.

[72] These tasks are labeled "routine-like" because they are not routine in the sense of following fully codifiable procedures that are amenable to classical computing. But these "routine-like" tasks are arguably adjacent to those routine tasks because the nonroutine component is not highly expertise-intensive.

to take on a larger set of nonroutine managerial tasks, such as evaluating worker performance, and a larger set of nonroutine manual tasks, such as operating a burger grill or fryolator in the assembly-line-like production environment of a fast-food restaurant.

By substituting for a broader set of middle-skill tasks, AI would further amplify the value of the "elite expertise" that is characteristic of professional occupations, similar to what the adoption of computers has done in recent decades. Owing to AI's additional capabilities in nonroutine tasks, substitution would reach further into the ranks of white-collar work, enabling some "college" tasks to be automated. The definition of what constitutes "elite" work would therefore ratchet upward.[73]

Machines might perform the first pass of medical diagnosis tasks, legal brief–writing tasks, engineering design tasks, syllabus development, or data analysis. But the final pass would still require human review, refinement, and improvement. "Elite experts" would therefore be called upon to complete the job. Presumably, this final step would require the *most capable* experts, given that AI has already completed the journeyman-level work. In this scenario, the demand for increasingly rarified "elite expertise" would rise; tasks performed by workers with "mass expertise" would be further imperiled by automation; and downward wage pressure on the earnings of workers in nonexpert service work would intensify as another wave of middle-tier workers is displaced from white- and blue-collar jobs.[74]

There are reasons for skepticism about this scenario, however. The foundational claim that "elite experts" will be indispensable for performing the "final draft" of many nonroutine tasks appears suspect. It is plausible, instead, that machines will exceed human performance even without elite supervision in producing many conventional professional products, such as legal briefs, marketing presentations, summaries of reports or meetings, letters of promotion or termination, news stories summarizing sporting events, or earnings reports. Rather than elite expertise becoming a gatekeeper for many professional products, it may become increasingly optional—called for only when the stakes are high or the appropriate course of action is highly uncertain.

More broadly, if the defining feature of classical computing is that it is uniquely capable of carrying out routine tasks rapidly, then the defining feature of AI is that it excels at mastering nonroutine tasks. Indeed, AI in its current incarnation is poorly suited to accomplishing canonical routine tasks: witness the unreliability of LLMs in distinguishing facts that the model has learned from fictions that its probabilistic reasoning hallucinates. Recognizing that AI and classical computing have profoundly different strengths

---

[73] Tyson and Zysman memorably refer to this scenario as "routine-biased technological change on steroids." See L.D. Tyson and J. Zysman, 2022, "Automation, AI and Work," *Daedalus* 151(2):256–271.

[74] As noted in Chapter 1, demand for such service tasks is very likely to grow with the aging of the population, which is occurring rapidly in the United States and throughout the industrialized world. Nevertheless, service tasks are expected to remain generally low in the pay scale across industrialized countries because these tasks use primarily generic, nonexpert skills.

and weaknesses, it would be surprising if these technologies had the same implications for the division of labor between workers and machines.

Scenario 2: The Elimination of Expertise

A second scenario is that advancements in AI and in AI-enabled machines (such as dexterous robotics) grow so capable and inexpensive in the years ahead that they come to outcompete humans across essentially every domain, effectively reducing the value of human labor to near zero. This scenario is ubiquitous in dystopian science fiction (e.g., the well-known 2008 animated movie *Wall-E*). Despite its origins in fiction, this scenario *is* economically coherent and has gained renewed currency in academic debate.[75] Four decades ago, the Nobel laureate economist Wassily Leontief forecast that "progressive introduction of new computerized, automated, and robotized equipment can be expected to reduce the role of labor ... similar to the process by which the introduction of tractors and other machinery first reduced and then completely eliminated horses and other draft animals."[76] Leontief's argument was not that humanity would run out of work (what economists call a "lump of labor" fallacy) but rather that workers would become unemployable in that work if machines could do the same tasks better, faster, and cheaper.

This scenario envisions what Nobel Prize–winning economist Herbert Simon labeled a "problem of intolerable abundance"—too much labor available too cheaply.[77] To understand the challenge that this could create, observe that the labor market serves two distinct but interdependent functions in market economies. First, it allocates people to jobs in which they produce the goods and services on which society depends. Second, it provides the primary means of income distribution. Absent chattel slavery, indentured servitude, and labor coercion, citizens possess an inalienable right to their own labor. This enables most (but far from all) adults to earn a living by providing (more precisely, selling) their labor to employers (including to themselves in the form of self-employment). In 2019, $6 in every $10 of U.S. gross national product was paid to workers as wages and fringe compensation—that is, labor's share of national income was about 60 percent.[78]

---

[75] See, for example, D. Susskind, 2020, *A World Without Work: Technology, Automation and How We Should Respond*, Penguin UK; and A. Korinek and M. Juelfs, 2022, "Preparing for the (Non-Existent?) Future of Work," NBER Working Paper No. w30172, June.

[76] W.W. Leontief, 1983, "The Distribution of Work and Income," *Scientific American* 247(3):188–205, September.

[77] In a letter published on March 16, 1966, in the *New York Review of Books*, Herbert Simon wrote, "Insofar as they are economic problems at all, the world's problems in this generation and the next are problems of scarcity, not of intolerable abundance. The bogeyman of automation consumes worrying capacity that should be saved for real problems—like population, poverty, the bomb, and our own neuroses."

[78] University of Groningen and University of California, Davis, n.d., "Share of Labour Compensation in GDP at Current National Prices for United States," retrieved from FRED, Federal Reserve Bank of St. Louis, https://fred.stlouisfed.org/series/LABSHPUSA156NRUG, accessed June 29, 2024.

If advances in AI were to cause labor's share to fall to zero—or even to fall by half—a formidable distributional challenge would be created.[79] Although, in theory, nations would be immensely wealthier if all work were performed by machines and citizens were free to pursue other interests, these nations would be gravely challenged to implement an alternative means of income distribution. Distinct from the inalienable right to one's own labor, ownership rights to material resources *are* highly "alienable" and hence often the subject of civil conflict. Allocating the ownership and distribution of these material resources absent claims based on labor ownership would likely create severe governance problems.[80] Although these challenges are outside the scope of this report, they are a reminder that a future without work appears far from utopian.

The committee does not, however, believe that AI will displace most human labor tasks in the near future. First, as noted above, a vast set of dexterous blue-collar and in-person service tasks appears likely to remain out of the reach of cost-effective automation for many years to come. Second, as highlighted in Chapter 1, industrialized countries face decades of sustained demographic scarcity. This scarcity creates a headwind against rising unemployment, even if labor demand were declining.[81] Last, the full automation scenario assumes that novel work requiring new expertise and aptitudes that humans but not machines possess will *not* be created. Although it is difficult to predict what such work might be, history suggests that human society will nevertheless be effective at creating it. Were that not the case, the transition to manufacturing and services from agriculture in the 19th and 20th centuries, or the substantial occupational reallocations wrought by the past four decades of computerization, might have led to sustained increases in joblessness. Instead, employment rates are currently reaching multidecade highs across the industrialized world.

But *complete automation* is an extreme case in a broader set of plausible scenarios. AI certainly will enable machines to displace a broader set of human tasks than was possible in the pre-AI era. The consequences of that displacement do not fundamentally depend on *how much* work is displaced; they depend instead on the value of labor (i.e., the value of expertise) in the tasks that remain, the extent of new expert tasks created and demanded, the rate at which people are displaced from existing work, their capacity

---

[79] Labor's share of national income has fallen by 3 to 10 percentage points in many industrialized countries during the past three decades, but it is not clear that this fall is owing to automation. See D. Autor, D. Dorn, L.F. Katz, C. Patterson, and J. Van Reenen, 2020, "The Fall of the Labor Share and the Rise of Superstar Firms," *The Quarterly Journal of Economics* 135(2):645–709.

[80] This problem is known to economists and political scientists as the "resource curse": nations with large, geographically concentrated national resources (such as fossil fuels or valuable minerals) tend to experience slower economic growth, higher levels of corruption, weaker institutions, and inferior development outcomes compared to countries with fewer natural resources. See M.L. Ross, 2015, "What Have We Learned About the Resource Curse?" *Annual Review of Political Science* 18:239–259.

[81] This scarcity also accelerates the rate of automation, however. See D. Acemoglu and P. Restrepo, 2022, "Demographics and Automation," *The Review of Economic Studies* 89(1):1–44.

to retrain to acquire newly valuable expertise, the rate at which they can acquire these skills, and the productivity gains that stem from automation itself.

Scenario 3: Reinstatement of Mass Expertise

This scenario is speculative but plausible and attainable but not inevitable. It rests on the hypothesis that the future of expertise may borrow attributes from both elite and mass expertise.

Mass Expertise Versus Elite Expertise

The key distinction between mass expertise and elite expertise is the types of problems to which they are applied. Consider a set of canonical mass expertise tasks: proofreading a document, managing an expense account, operating a computerized lathe, or installing electrical circuitry. Workers' expertise is indispensable for performing these tasks correctly and efficiently. But, owing to the tight parameters of these tasks, increased worker expertise is unlikely to produce qualitatively better results. Expense accounts are either error-free or they are not; electrical installations are either neat, safe, and up to code or they are not.

Contrast these cases with canonical elite expertise tasks such as managing a patient's cancer care, writing a legal brief, drafting an advertising campaign, architecting a building, or leading a team or organization. There is not a single correct or best way to perform these tasks, nor is there an upper bound on how well they can be done. Each is a high-stakes, one-off case where the range of potential outcomes spans from extraordinary to catastrophic. Achieving excellent results requires both subject matter expertise and professional judgment. The latter component is usually acquired through experience. Elite professionals are generally not assigned high-stakes cases until they have first demonstrated mastery in a supervised apprenticeship or in a lower-stakes professional assignment (e.g., medical resident, junior law partner, postdoctoral researcher, division manager).

How might AI change this picture? As previously mentioned, it is likely that AI will soon take on the "last mile" of many mass expertise tasks, particularly cognitive tasks (e.g., expense accounting) and manual and physical tasks performed in a controlled, predictable setting (e.g., operating a computerized lathe) but not tasks performed in highly variable real-world settings (e.g., installing electrical wiring). In these cases, AI's impacts are primarily incremental, expanding the range of tasks where classical computing already holds a comparative advantage. What remains unanswered—and potentially is more novel—is how the emerging capability of AI to perform "elite" tasks (e.g., writing, medical diagnosis, software development, legal analysis, engineering) might enable changes in the demands for human expertise in carrying out these tasks.

By making elite expertise more accessible and less expensive, AI can be used to complement the judgment, ingenuity, creativity, and interpersonal acumen of workers engaged in elite tasks while simultaneously reducing the extent of expert knowledge required to perform them. That is, applied effectively, the hypothesis is that AI could enable less-expert workers to carry out more expert tasks.

A Motivating Example

As a motivating example (not from the AI realm), consider the job of nurse practitioner (NP). NPs are registered nurses who have earned an additional master's degree and passed a certification exam. NPs diagnose and treat illness, practicing either independently or as part of a health care team. Some focus on health promotion and disease prevention while others perform, order, or interpret diagnostic tests. NPs also may prescribe medication. The NP occupation was founded in the mid-1960s but did not become prevalent until the past two decades. NP employment more than tripled between 2011 and 2022, with approximately 300,000 NPs working at present, and is projected to increase by 40 percent in the next decade—far above the growth rate of overall employment. Simultaneously, the range of tasks performed by NPs has broadened substantially, and NPs' earnings have risen. In 2021, the median salary for NPs was $123,000.[82] NPs exemplify the above definition of professionals: They confront high-stakes, one-off cases, where the set of potential outcomes ranges from extraordinary to catastrophic. They provide diagnostic, treatment, and prescribing services that were once within the exclusive dominion of medical doctors (MDs).

What enabled the reallocation (or sharing) of high-stakes tasks from MDs to NPs? In part, medical professionals perceived a care shortcoming in the health care system, recognized that the skills of registered nurses were underused, and chose to pioneer a new professional occupation. This in turn required a supporting set of training institutions and (eventually) a change in the scope of medical practice rules.[83] Information technologies, combined with improved training, also facilitated this new division of labor. For example, a 2012 study reported that information and communications technology (ICT) plays a critical role in enabling NPs to deliver advanced practice care: "ICT supported the advanced practice dimension of the NP role in two ways: availability and completeness of electronic patient information enhanced timeliness and quality

---

[82] It is challenging to find consistent time-series data on NP employment in the United States. The U.S. Bureau of Labor Statistics reports an increase from 81,000 NPs in 2011 to 224,000 in 2022. See U.S. Bureau of Labor Statistics, n.d., "Employed Full Time: Wage and Salary Workers: Nurse Practitioners Occupations: 16 Years and Over," retrieved from FRED, Federal Reserve Bank of St. Louis, https://fred.stlouisfed.org/series/LEU0257870000A, accessed June 29, 2024.

[83] P. Asubonteng, K.J. McCleary, and G. Munchus, 1995, "Nurse Practitioners in the USA—Their Past, Present and Future: Some Implications for the Health Care Management Delivery System," *Health Manpower Management* 21(3):3–10.

of diagnostic and therapeutic decision-making, expediting patient access to appropriate care."[84]

Looking forward, it is a near-certainty that AI will further *augment* this occupation, enabling NPs to perform a broader variety of expert tasks. Indeed, one can imagine a future in which a student would attend a 4-year program to obtain a bachelor's of science degree in health care followed by an apprenticeship in medical practice. When training is complete, a certified health care worker, assisted by AI, could perform a far larger set of diagnostic and care tasks than is currently feasible.[85]

The NP occupation provides a focal example of how a technology such as AI could be used to *complement* the expertise of nonelite workers. Specifically, by providing relevant frontier expertise, guidance, and a set of digital guardrails, AI could enable less-expert workers to perform more expert tasks.

Note that the claim is *not* that AI can enable untrained, nonexpert workers to carry out expert tasks. It is not plausible that "any worker" overseen by AI could perform the tasks of NPs or MDs (or legal counsels, architects, engineers, managers of large organizations, etc.). The claim instead is that AI can reduce the demand for frontier expertise in some high-stakes tasks, thereby enabling trained workers to play a greater practical role in translating between elite knowledge and everyday practice. Concretely, AI could provide guidance and guardrails for workers who grasp the totality of the specific case or challenge they are confronting; exercise judgment; and communicate dexterously with coworkers, clients, and third parties. This model, if successful, would reinstate a form of "mass expert" work—the type of work that was arguably more prevalent prior to the computer revolution.

To develop this idea further, consider again the example of NPs. Efficacy as an NP requires three complementary skill sets:

1. *Technical knowledge*—Foundational technical and scientific knowledge of human biology, anatomy, physiology, epidemiology, psychology, and so on. This enables analytical thinking about diagnostic information, symptoms, treatments, and so on.
2. *Procedural knowledge*—Protocols for executing specific medical procedures—for example, taking vital signs, drawing blood, inserting a catheter, performing cardiopulmonary resuscitation, staunching bleeding, and so on. Such

---

[84] J. Li, J. Westbrook, J. Callen, and A. Georgiou, 2012, "The Role of ICT in Supporting Disruptive Innovation: A Multi-Site Qualitative Study of Nurse Practitioners in Emergency Departments," *BMC Medical Informatics and Decision Making* 12:1–8.

[85] The growth of the NP occupation offers a relatively uncommon large-scale case where high-stakes professional tasks—diagnosing, treating, and prescribing—were reallocated (or co-assigned) from the most elite professional workers (MDs) to another set of professionals (NPs) with somewhat less elite (though still substantial) formal expertise and training.

protocols are the standard rules and tools used for delivering medical care. Protocols reduce the probability of error and establish rules and lines of authority for contingencies that might arise.

3. *Expert judgment*—Expert judgment intermediates between formal knowledge and hands-on practice. Because the stakes in patient care are high and the "correct" steps are not fully specified, expert judgment is required to draw a link from the domain of technical and procedural knowledge to any specific practical instance—for example, evaluating whether a patient needs routine versus emergency care, determining which diagnostic tests should be administered, knowing when to probe for specific symptoms that the patient might not report, deciding whether or not to execute a risky life-saving procedure, and so on. Expert judgment is almost invariably gained through supervised learning, where established experts advise, coach, and (critically) prevent consequential errors by novices. Expert judgment is arguably closely related to tacit knowledge: expertise that is acquired through experience rather than explicit instruction.

The hypothesis here is that by serving as a *substitute* for some technical and procedural knowledge, AI can serve as a *complement* to NPs' expert judgment:

- *AI can supplement (or substitute for) technical knowledge.* The reservoir of medical knowledge is vast and constantly expanding. Because it is impossible for a single expert to master the entire medical frontier, the field of medicine contains a large and continually expanding set of specialties. It is, however, entirely feasible for AI tools to absorb the reservoir of frontier medical knowledge. As AI tools develop, they will be increasingly useful for surfacing the relevant knowledge at the appropriate time. Indeed, while professionals already have access to vast repositories of professional journals and databases, significant expertise is often required simply to use these tools. By responding to natural language and contextual queries to surface frontier expertise, AI can make expert knowledge far more accessible. These tools may reduce the quantity of technical knowledge that health care workers are required to master. Human experts will still be needed at the frontier of every medical field, but the modal health care worker may require *less* frontier expertise if many specific technical details can be supplemented by AI.
- *AI can likely substitute for procedural knowledge.* Many medical procedures (and technical procedures generally) require a health care worker to follow a specified series of steps. AI can provide guidance for carrying out unfamiliar

procedures. But executing such steps almost always requires practice and judgment. An untrained adult cannot safely insert a catheter by following instructions on a computer screen. An experienced medical worker could, however, likely use a new medical device—or a new type of catheter—by following instructions and guidance provided by AI. AI can likely supplement or substitute for procedural knowledge, but this capability is useful primarily to workers who have the expertise (i.e., the expert judgment) to carry out such procedures.

- *AI can likely complement expert judgment.* By supplementing technical and procedural knowledge, AI can enable workers who possess expert judgment to perform a broader range of expert tasks. Concretely, it is extremely unlikely that an untrained adult could safely perform the caregiving duties of an NP, regardless of what AI tools were available to provide guidance, coaching, and supervision. The potential for catastrophic error would be extremely high, and the untrained worker would not have the capacity to respond should such an error arise. Conversely, it is highly plausible that an NP could safely perform a broader range of procedures if supported by AI. What distinguishes these scenarios is expert judgment. Expert judgment enables experienced workers to make high-stakes decisions in their domain of expertise, even in unfamiliar cases. Stated succinctly, the hypothesis is that AI could *complement* expert judgment, enabling those possessing it to accomplish a broader set of tasks.

These claims are difficult to evaluate in the abstract, but consider a few occupations for which expert judgment is prevalent: electrician, software developer, chef, attorney, architect, aircraft mechanic, and store manager. Is it plausible that AI could fully substitute for the expertise of workers in performing the primary tasks of these occupations? If the answer were "yes," it seems likely that these occupations might eventually become economically equivalent to jobs in food service, cleaning, security, crossing guard services, and so on—work that is socially valuable but relatively poorly paid because it requires primarily mass expertise.

"No" is a more realistic answer. Each of these occupations calls on workers to apply expert judgment to translate from technical and procedural knowledge to professional practice. AI will broaden the reach of those with expert judgment rather than making their expertise superfluous:

- AI will assist electricians in tackling unfamiliar installations. Electricians will need judgment, dexterity, and mastery of appropriate tools to perform safe electrical installations.

- AI will assist software developers to write code rapidly. Developers will need to develop and review the architecture of the software they are developing.
- AI will enable chefs to master a larger range of cuisines—recommending recipes, proposing new recipes, and suggesting cooking techniques. Chefs will require judgment, dexterity, and acute taste to cook.
- AI will augment attorneys and paralegals by generating legal documents and proposing lines of argument. Attorneys will assess what lines of argument are most persuasive and will make those arguments to judges, juries, and other attorneys.
- AI will assist architects to develop and visualize designs and to perform engineering calculations. Architectural expertise will be needed to judge the suitability, practicality, and desirability of those designs.
- AI will enable aircraft mechanics to tackle a broader range of installation and repair tasks by interpreting data, proposing diagnostic tests, and searching for relevant service bulletins. Executing that mechanical work will require experience, judgment, and finesse.
- AI will assist store managers to track inventory and staffing, anticipate demand peaks and troughs, follow consumer fashions, and minimize wastage. Managers will provide leadership and coaching to workers, engage with customers, solve myriad problems, and maintain esprit de corps.

AI will serve to supplement technical and procedural knowledge for workers performing each of these occupations. It will provide information to improve performance and guardrails to reduce the likelihood of error. But it likely will not eliminate the expert judgment required, which is gained through training, coaching, and practice. This expertise will be required to intermediate between formal knowledge and hands-on practice.

Figure 4-6 presents a stylized version of this hypothesis. The horizontal axis on this figure represents the expertise that a worker brings to an expert occupation (such as those listed above), ranging from no knowledge (far left) to frontier expertise (far right). The vertical axis represents the potential for AI to augment worker performance in the high-stakes tasks in that occupation. As the figure suggests, there is potentially little opportunity for AI to augment performance of untrained workers placed in situations with high-stakes tasks. Plausibly, it may be unproductive or dangerous for untrained workers to take on such tasks even when supported by AI (e.g., an untrained worker attempting to insert a catheter or perform a high-voltage electrical installation).

At the midpoint are workers who possess some expert judgment obtained through training and experience but who are not at the frontier of their field. Here, AI

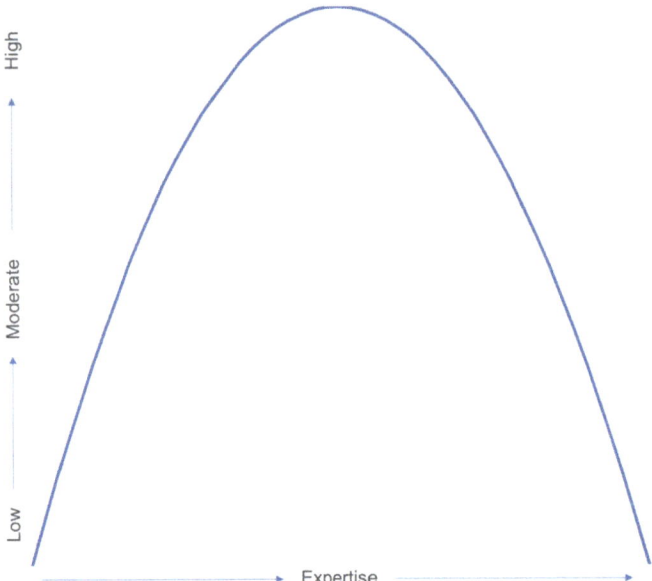

FIGURE 4-6 Hypothetical relationship between domain-specific expertise and the potential for artificial intelligence (AI) augmentation in high-stakes tasks.
NOTE: On the left-hand side of this figure, AI is unhelpful or potentially dangerous when used by novice workers for high-stakes tasks. AI is increasingly complementary to workers with relevant judgment and training. AI potentially adds less value for workers with the full complement of technical and procedural expertise as well as expert judgment (though even there, it may save time).

can potentially supplement technical and procedural knowledge, while providing guidance and guardrails for performing expert tasks. Workers will apply expert judgment in carrying out those tasks and respond appropriately in the case of unexpected outcomes (e.g., unexpected bleeding, short circuit).

AI may be less complementary to frontier experts (far right side of the figure) who are performing high-stakes tasks, simply because these experts already bring the full complement of technical and procedural knowledge plus expert judgment. However, AI may save frontier experts considerable time, enable their exploration of additional approaches and techniques, and supply novel frontier information that has only just emerged from other experts. Hence, a more ambitious version of this figure could posit *negative* augmentation (adverse impact) on the left-hand side of the figure, substantial positive augmentation at the center, and nonzero positive augmentation on the right-hand side.

EVIDENCE ON ARTIFICIAL INTELLIGENCE AND EXPERTISE

At the time of this writing, there is little rigorous, representative evidence on the potential complementarity or substitutability between AI and human expertise in workplace settings. The following are among the relevant studies.

Noy and Zhang

This study experimentally evaluated the use of generative AI (ChatGPT v3.5) by college graduates (sampled from Prolific) for professional writing tasks.[86]

- Using ChatGPT cuts work time by approximately 40 percent on professional writing tasks that take an average of 20 minutes when done using standard tools.
- The average quality of output, evaluated by a panel of double-blinded college graduates who are experts in professional writing tasks, improved slightly.
- Writing quality improved substantially more among less-skilled writers, where writing skill is measured using performance on round 1 of the task (for which ChatGPT was not used).
- This study does not fully test the hypothesis shown in Figure 4-6 because all subjects in the experiment were skilled writers. The study confirms the right-hand side of Figure 4-6 (from the midpoint of the x-axis). It does not test the left-hand side.
- Hypothesis: Had Noy and Zhang included high school graduates who were not skilled writers in their study, the graduates' performance even using ChatGPT would have remained poor.
- Interpretation: If AI completely supplants the need for expertise, then there is no complementarity. If AI supplements expertise but does not obviate the need for it, there is complementarity.

Brynjolfsson and Colleagues

This team conducted a study on the use of an AI chatbot for customer support tasks. Trained on a database of previous customer support calls, the AI chatbot provides real-time suggested responses to customer support agents. It does not directly respond to customers.[87]

---

[86] S. Noy and W. Zhang, 2023, "Experimental Evidence on the Productivity Effects of Generative Artificial Intelligence," *Science* 381(6654):187–192.

[87] E. Brynjolfsson, D. Li, and L.R. Raymond, 2023, "Generative AI at Work," NBER Working Paper No. w31161, April.

- Use of the tool increased throughput (chat resolutions per hour) by 14 percent on average, reflecting (1) a decline in the time it takes an agent to handle a chat; (2) an increase in the number of chats that an agent can handle per hour; and (3) a small increase in the fraction of chats resolved successfully.
- Customer satisfaction was not greatly affected. However, escalation requests (requests for manager assistance) fell. Use of the chatbot substantially improved how customers treat agents, as measured by sentiment analysis applied to their chats. Worker attrition declined, particularly among novices.
- Critically, and similar to the findings of Noy and Zhang, use of the tool substantially reduced productivity inequality. Less experienced workers became almost as effective as expert workers when supported by the AI tool. Agents not using the tool reached maximum productivity in approximately 10 months on average. Agents using the tool attained this productivity level after only 3 months and exceeded it thereafter.
- Like the study by Noy and Zhang, this study confirms the right-hand side of Figure 4-6 but does not test the left-hand side.
- Hypothesis: Had Brynjolfsson and colleagues included customer support workers with no training or expertise in the products they were supporting, unsatisfactory customer service results would have emerged.
- Interpretation: If AI completely supplants the need for expertise in this customer service role—so that "any worker" can do this job equally effectively with no training—this implies no expertise complementarity. If AI supplements expertise but does not obviate the need for it, this indicates complementarity (at least up to some level of expertise, as is shown in Figure 4-6).

Agarwal and Colleagues

This team conducted an experiment using diagnostic AI with professional radiologists, varying the availability of AI support and contextual information.[88]

- Providing AI did not uniformly increase diagnostic quality. Even though the AI predictions were more accurate than almost two-thirds of the participants' assessments in the experiment, AI assistance did not improve radiologists' diagnostic quality on average. Radiologists were unsuccessful, and in many cases counterproductive, in integrating their assessments with information provided by the AI.

---

[88] N. Agarwal, A. Moehring, P. Rajpurkar, and T. Salz, 2023, "Combining Human Expertise with Artificial Intelligence: Experimental Evidence from Radiology," NBER Working Paper No. w31422, July.

- Providing contextual information—information accessible to radiologists but not currently used by AI tools—*does* increase radiologists' diagnostic quality.
- Implication: AI and radiologists are substitutes not complements (in fact, radiologists often perform worse when supplemented by AI—implying negative complementarity).
- This experiment does not directly test the consequences of giving AI to "any worker" to perform radiological services.
- As the authors hypothesize, with appropriate training, radiologists would be able to use AI more effectively—yielding better results than AI or doctors alone.
- If this conjecture were proved correct, it would support the conceptual framing shown in Figure 4-6.

In summary, none of these three studies provides a conclusive confirmation or rejection of the conceptual framework above. The committee is, however, cautiously optimistic that this framework will prove relevant in a large number of instances—although certainly not in all.

HOW FEASIBLE WILL IT BE FOR WORKERS TO ACQUIRE NEWLY VALUABLE EXPERTISE?

The answer to the question of whether workers can acquire new expertise will depend on three factors. The first is the type of expertise that is newly required: primarily elite expertise, as polarization extends substantially upward into many college-educated white-collar occupations (Scenario 1); none, as all expertise is eliminated (Scenario 2); or substantial expert judgment, as AI supports the reinstatement of a new era of mass expertise (Scenario 3). The learning challenges posed by these scenarios differ dramatically.

A second factor is how effective AI proves to be as an educational tool. As will be discussed in Chapter 5, AI has the potential to make education more accessible, personalized, immersive, and cost-effective. Tools such as LLMs that can customize interactive instructional content as well as augmented and virtual reality devices that can transform education into simulation could make learning more interactive and engaging. For many tasks requiring the acquisition of expert judgment, it is highly plausible that AI could be used to create simulated environments, where workers perform high-stakes tasks in low-stakes settings. At present, simulation training is used widely in aviation, where the cost of error is potentially catastrophic and the need for ongoing practice is substantial. Commercial pilots in the United States are required to undergo 2 days of flight simulator training every 6 months to retain their certification.[89] Simulation-based training may prove particularly valuable for adults, who are generally less amenable to classroom-based instruction than younger learners.

A final factor that will prove crucial is the quality and cost of the training institutions that are made publicly and privately available to support skill acquisition. A growing body of evidence finds that training programs that are effective in enabling adults to enter skilled occupations typically "combine upfront screening, occupational and soft skills training, and wraparound services."[90] These wraparound services are often expensive because they must financially support learners during intensive training, which often precludes paid employment. Denmark, which is renowned for its capacity to support displaced workers to return to gainful employment, spends 3.1 percent of its gross domestic product (GDP) on active and passive labor market programs. By comparison, the United States spends 0.3 percent of its GDP on these programs.[91] A key lesson to draw is that new educational technology, no matter how spectacular, will not itself be sufficient to support the training needs of present and future workers, particularly displaced adult workers. Substantial public investments will be required.

WORKFORCE RISKS

Although the study committee does not foresee an imminent prospect of AI causing a vast increase in technological unemployment, advances in AI could very well put downward pressure on the wages of many workers. Alongside this risk, worker surveillance and privacy, issues around the ownership of creative output, and algorithmic fairness and discrimination are all of concern.

Many workers—for example, call center employees, truckers, and warehouse workers—have long been subject to strict output metrics. AI will expand the share of the workforce subject to strict monitoring and allow for more intrusive monitoring. For example, AI tools may be able to monitor how often white-collar workers are shopping online or checking their personal email during the workday, or to keep tabs on how many hours per day they are physically in front of their computers. AI-powered cameras with biometric feedback indicators can monitor delivery drivers' tendencies to brake

---

[89] C. Page, 2022, "How Pilots Use Flight Simulators to Prepare for Any and All Eventualities," *The Points Guy*, July 11, https://thepointsguy.com/news/how-pilots-use-flight-simulators.
[90] L.F. Katz, J. Roth, R. Hendra, and K. Schaberg, 2022, "Why Do Sectoral Employment Programs Work? Lessons from WorkAdvance," *Journal of Labor Economics* 40(S1):S249–S291.
[91] C.T. Kreiner and M. Svarer, 2022, "Danish Flexicurity: Rights and Duties," *Journal of Economic Perspectives* 36(4):81–102.

hard, speed, or look away from the road while driving.[92] An AI-powered program called Cogito reminds call-center workers to sound cheerful and upbeat when it identifies concerns with workers' tones of voice.

AI image generators like Stable Diffusion and DALL·E 2 use training data from enormous image archives. Many artists are concerned that generative AI platforms are mimicking their artistic style, creating images that are insufficiently different from the artists' original work.[93] If this were the case, AI platforms would be violating existing copyright laws. As AI capabilities advance, one can easily imagine this problem extending to authors of fiction and nonfiction, movies, and music. In addition, there are substantial unresolved legal issues around the ownership of AI-generated images and documents—for example, are they owned by the AI platform, by the user, or by any customers of the user? If one asks an AI platform to write a song in the style of Bob Dylan, does Bob Dylan have an ownership claim over the platform's output?

The output from AI solutions may perpetuate socioeconomic, racial, or gender bias due, for example, to bias in underlying training data. For example, in 2014 Amazon attempted to build a program to vet job applicants. The company's training data came from a job applicant pool that was mostly male. Amazon's model disrated résumés including the word "women's" and downgraded applicants who were graduates of two women's colleges. Amazon recognized the problem and retired the tool, but this remains a cautionary tale.[94] Buolamwini and Gebru studied commercial gender classification systems and found that error rates for darker-skinned females were substantially higher than for lighter-skinned males, potentially owing to the use of training data that were not representative of the population as a whole.[95]

Something similar could happen with health services. If training data come from people with health insurance and if optimal treatment differs between people with and without health insurance, then AI-driven treatment could show preference for the insured over the uninsured or allocate resources to patients who have historically received more intensive treatment.[96] Beyond training data, the choice or design of algorithms could inadvertently perpetuate bias.

---

[92] The Daily Telegraph, 2022, "Amazon Installs AI Cameras to Monitor Its Delivery Drivers," *The Daily Telegraph*, https://www.telegraph.co.uk/business/2022/05/22/amazon-installs-ai-cameras-monitor-delivery-drivers.

[93] See, for example, *Anderson v. Stability AI, et al.*, described in G. Karger, 2023, "AI-Generated Images: The First Lawsuit," *Science and Technology Law Review*, January 25, https://journals.library.columbia.edu/index.php/stlr/blog/view/479.

[94] J. Dastin, 2018, "Insight—Amazon Scraps Secret AI Recruiting Tool That Showed Bias Against Women," *Reuters*, October 10, https://www.reuters.com/article/world/insight-amazon-scraps-secret-ai-recruiting-tool-that-showed-bias-against-women-idUSKCN1MK0AG.

[95] J. Buolamwini and T. Gebru, 2018, "Gender Shades: Intersectional Accuracy Disparities in Commercial Gender Classification," *Proceedings of Machine Learning Research* 81:1–15.

[96] Z. Obermeyer, B. Powers, C. Vogeli, and S. Mullainathan, 2019, "Dissecting Racial Bias in an Algorithm Used to Manage the Health of Populations," *Science* 366(6464):447–453.

Socioeconomic, gender, and racial bias are serious concerns. Real-world experiences—some discussed above—demonstrate the risk that the continued adoption of AI could perpetuate these biases. But there is reason for optimism, as well. As Kleinberg and colleagues argue,

> Algorithms by their nature require a far greater level of specificity than is usually involved with human decision making, which in some sense is the ultimate "black box." With the right legal and regulatory systems in place, algorithms can serve as something akin to a Geiger counter that makes it easier to detect—and hence prevent—discrimination.[97]

The committee recognizes potential benefits but is concerned by these workforce risks. Increased worker surveillance could in some settings increase worker safety, advance workplace equity, or strengthen the link between individual worker performance and compensation. Simultaneously, stepped-up surveillance may strip workers of autonomy and discretion, shifting the balance of bargaining power from workers to firms.[98] These potential benefits and risks will need to be weighed alongside workers' rights to reasonable privacy and expectations of just treatment. The same is true of the competing interests of human content creators and generative AI outputs. Adjudication of these benefits and risks will be shaped by regulation, judicial interpretation of existing law, new laws designed to address these specific issues, and negotiations among firms and worker representatives.

Although the risks posed by surveillance, privacy invasion, and coercive monitoring are particularly salient in the case of AI, the consequences of previous technological transitions for the welfare of workers and the strength of the middle class have depended not only on the nature and application of technologies but also on the negotiation frameworks and legal institutions that have shaped the design, adoption, and uses of technology as well as the distribution of rents (economic surplus) between owners, managers, and line workers. The positive strides in middle-class prosperity that accompanied the second industrial revolution were in part due to the success of labor unions, and supporting federal and state legislation, in negotiating for higher standards of pay, reasonable hours, safe working conditions, and employment security. In more recent decades, worker bargaining power in the United States has eroded in the face of contracting labor union representations; aggressive employer mobilization against worker

---

[97] J. Kleinberg, J. Ludwig, S. Mullainathan, and C.R. Sunstein, 2020, "Algorithms as Discrimination Detectors," *Proceedings of the National Academy of Sciences* 117(48):30096–30100.

[98] A. Levy, 2022, *Data Driven*, Princeton University Press; and A. Picchi, 2021, "Amazon Apologizes for Denying That Its Drivers Pee in Bottles," *CBS News*, April 5, https://www.cbsnews.com/news/amazon-drivers-peeing-in-bottles-union-vote-worker-complaints.

organizing efforts; and the "fissuring" of the labor market, denoting the process of companies outsourcing tasks and responsibilities that were previously handled in-house to third-party contractors, subcontractors, or other external entities.[99]

Some central property rights and norms that citizens view as intrinsic (e.g., the expectation that a worker's location, movement, and activity will not be monitored in continuous time by a digital tracking device) have become increasingly contestable in the era of AI, including the definition and ownership of intellectual property, the right to privacy, and expectations about surveillance and coercive monitoring. When such rights and expectations become contestable, interested parties likely will encroach on these rights and expectations unless either regulatory or bargaining institutions intercede. The law is unlikely to prevent these interested parties from doing otherwise because laws are not generally crafted to constrain activities that are perceived as infeasible. One must anticipate that firms will violate such expectations and norms when new technological capabilities permit, not owing to malevolence but because such encroachments appear profitable.[100] Workers may also exploit newfound technological capabilities to violate employer expectations—for example, by covertly recording workplace activities or by using AI to perform unauthorized job tasks. What is clear is that well-functioning bargaining and regulatory institutions are indispensable for ensuring a socially desirable resolution of newly contestable (as well as existing) rights and expectations.[101] These issues are morally charged and socially consequential, affecting not only economic efficiency but also income distribution, political power, and civil rights. Both the pernicious uses of AI technology and its socially valuable applications are already visible and will become more potent and salient in the years ahead. The stakes are extremely high. How AI is deployed and who gains and loses from this process will depend upon the collective (and conflicting) choices of industry, governments, foreign nations, nongovernmental organizations, universities, worker organizations, and individuals.

DIRECTIONS FOR FURTHER RESEARCH

This is a highly uncertain time for forecasting the future of work. If AI lives up to the potential that many believe it holds, it is likely to reshape substantially the demand for

---

[99] D. Weil, 2014, *The Fissured Workplace: Why Work Became So Bad for So Many and What Can Be Done to Improve It*, Harvard University Press.

[100] Many salient historical examples are provided by D. Acemoglu and S. Johnson, 2023, *Power and Progress: Our 1000-Year Struggle Over Technology and Prosperity*, PublicAffairs.

[101] As noted above, this is a simple Coasean observation, not an indictment of markets per se: when the ownership of a property right (including the right to take or not take an action) is ill-defined, the market equilibrium set of actions involving this property right is likely to be inefficient because externalities in the exercise of this right will not be internalized. See R.H. Coase, 1960, "The Problem of Social Cost," *The Journal of Law and Economics* 3(October):1–44.

expertise and the demand for labor more generally. While this will be disruptive, these costs can be accompanied by substantial benefits if AI is used well. At a macroeconomic level, successful implementation of AI could improve productivity; advance science and engineering; and help humanity to tackle some of its greatest challenges, including poverty reduction, food production, mass education, climate change mitigation, and preservation of biodiversity. At a labor market level, the greatest potential—though by no means an inevitable or intrinsic consequence—of AI deployment is to improve the quality of work and the value of workers. This would mean using AI as a tool that enables a larger fraction of the workforce to perform valuable, expert work that at present is primarily only accessible to workers with elite levels of education. This would require the following:

- Developing AI tools that enable less-specialized workers to perform more-specialized work;
- Harnessing AI to make education and reskilling more immersive, more accessible, less expensive, and more effective—particularly for adults and mid-career workers; and
- Steering the development of AI toward applications that augment the value of human expertise by complementing intrinsic human strengths in holistic thinking, seasoned judgment, and rich communication with others.

5

Artificial Intelligence and Education

Improvements in access to education and rising educational attainment across successive birth cohorts have played a key role in U.S. economic growth over the past 150 years.[1] Rapid expansions in education from the high school movement in the early 20th century and from increased college access in the mid-20th century helped foster shared prosperity in the face of rapid technological change and automation from electrification and then computerization that increased the demand for more educated workers. A slowdown in educational advances and large socioeconomic status gaps in access to high-quality educational opportunities in the late 20th and early 21st centuries have contributed to rising wage and income inequality, increased college and post-college wage premiums, and stagnating earnings for noncollege workers.[2] Growing income inequality has been associated with rising achievement and educational attainment gaps between high- and low-income children in the United States in recent decades.[3] The COVID-19 pandemic generated new educational challenges with school closures and large differences across schools, neighborhoods, and families in resources and preparedness for remote learning. The result has been a substantial slowdown in learning, decline in reading and math test scores, and expanded achievement gaps in K–12 schooling by socioeconomic status and race.[4]

---

[1] C. Goldin and L.F. Katz, 2008, *The Race Between Education and Technology*, Harvard University Press.

[2] D. Autor, C. Goldin, and L.F. Katz, 2020, "Extending the Race Between Education and Technology," *AEA Papers and Proceedings* 110:347–351.

[3] G.J. Duncan, A. Kalil, and K.M. Ziol-Guest, 2017, "Increasing Inequality in Parent Incomes and Children's Schooling," *Demography* 54(5):1603–1626.

[4] The Nation's Report Card, 2022 "Reading and Mathematics Scores Decline During COVID-19 Pandemic," https://www.nationsreportcard.gov/highlights/ltt/2022; R. Jack, C. Halloran, J. Okun, and E. Oster, 2023, "Pandemic Schooling Mode and Student Test Scores: Evidence from US School Districts," *American Economic Review: Insights* 5(2):173–190; and D. Goldhaber, T.J. Kane, A. McEachin, E. Morton, T. Patterson, and D.O. Staiger, 2023, "The Consequences of Hybrid and Remote Instruction During the Pandemic," *American Economic Review: Insights* 5(3):377–392.

Technological change impacts the labor market demand for different types of expertise and tasks, thereby changing the demand for education and training. But new technologies can also impact how education and training are provided. The recent, rapid rise of artificial intelligence (AI) and large language models (LLMs), especially chatbots such as ChatGPT, has led to widespread fears among educators and parents that AI may negatively disrupt education by creating increased cheating opportunities, providing students directly with the answers so that they do not learn key concepts, and spreading misinformation.[5]

At the same time, AI has the potential to transform the education system and improve learning outcomes for K–12, post-secondary schooling, and workforce training by making education more personalized, engaging, and cost-effective. To reach this promise, public and private investments likely will be needed to increase access to high-speed Internet connections and online learning opportunities, incorporate safeguards into AI-enhanced education technology, test the effectiveness of specific uses of AI in education, and train teachers to be more comfortable with and take advantage of generative AI tools and other computer-assisted learning (CAL) technologies. Under a scenario of appropriate investments and research, AI tutors and AI-enhanced technologies could operate as collaborators with students and teachers to facilitate enhanced learning rather than AI just providing a shortcut to the answers without deeper student engagement in learning.[6] Broad access to high-quality AI tutors for students and AI teaching assistants for teachers also could help reduce the educational inequalities from differences in family and school resources that have become even starker in the wake of the COVID-19 pandemic. In the most optimistic case, all students would have a world-class and engaging virtual AI tutor with them both at school and at home; in-class assignments and homework would be adaptive and self-grading; active learning would be enhanced, and student assessments could focus more on what students can do rather what they retain in the short run; teachers would be empowered to be more creative and effective instructors and mentors; and AI could be leveraged to enhance post-secondary and lifelong learning opportunities.

This chapter will first explore what is currently known about how AI potentially can be deployed to improve learning outcomes for K–12, post-secondary schooling, and adult workforce training. It will then report on how the education system may need to adapt to current and expected changes in the training and continuing education needs of the workforce from the possible impacts of AI on skill demand and career opportunities.

---

[5] See, for example, K. Huang, 2023, "Alarmed by A.I. Chatbots, Universities Start Revamping How They Teach," *New York Times*, January 16, https://www.nytimes.com/2023/01/16/technology/chatgpt-artificial-intelligence-universities.html.

[6] For a vivid and optimistic assessment of AI's promise to positively transform education, see S. Khan, 2023, "How AI Could Save (Not Destroy) Education," TED2023, April, https://www.ted.com/talks/sal_khan_how_ai_could_save_not_destroy_education.

ARTIFICIAL INTELLIGENCE AS AN INPUT FOR EDUCATION

AI has the potential to ameliorate key problems in the education production process. Student outcomes are likely to be enhanced when students are highly motivated and actively engaged in learning, feedback is timely, students can relate to and see value in the material, lessons are immersive, and teaching is sufficiently individualized to be at the right level to push students toward their learning frontiers.[7] But heterogeneity in student backgrounds, preparation, and learning styles makes maintaining such conditions difficult in traditional classroom settings.

Education technologies incorporating AI promise to help surmount barriers in traditional education delivery in at least three ways: personalization, enhanced motivation and engagement, and more timely and broad access to frontier learning opportunities. First, CALs trained using machine learning methods on large data sets of student experiences and performances should be able to identify groups of students facing similar difficulties as well as those students able to handle more advanced material, which would permit more cost-effective personalized instruction potentially enlivened using virtual tutors (or tutoring bots) enhanced by LLMs. Such technologies can also provide teachers with dashboards to monitor individual student learning progress and virtual teaching assistants to help teachers leverage data-driven tools to target group instruction at a more appropriate level.[8]

Second, AI and virtual reality technologies can provide effective, immersive, and engaging learning experiences (including more realistic simulation environments for practical occupational training) to increase student motivation and engagement with material and in learning. Education technologies can further provide salient and timely nudges to parents, teachers, and students to try to offset behavioral biases that often lead to procrastination and disengagement from learning and create barriers to applying to and matriculating in college or training programs.[9]

Third, broader access to AI-enhanced educational technologies might particularly benefit less advantaged students and those in lower-resourced school districts and post-secondary institutions by providing them with similar learning opportunities and

---

[7] For a discussion of the promise of AI to improve education along such dimensions see Khan Academy, n.d., "A New Chapter in Education," https://www.khanacademy.org/college-careers-more/ai-for-education/x68ea37461197a514:unit-teaching-with-ai/x68ea37461197a514:getting-started-with-ai-in-the-classroom/a/ai-a-new-chapter-in-education-begins, accessed June 29, 2024.

[8] Evidence on learning gains from data-driven instruction and appropriate targeting of teaching range from high-performing U.S. charter schools to the Teaching at the Right Level approach developed by the Indian nongovernmental organization Pratham. See, for example, W. Dobbie and R.G. Fryer, Jr., 2013, "Getting Beneath the Veil of Effective Schools: Evidence from New York City," *American Economic Journal: Applied Economics* 5(4):28–60; and J-PAL, 2022, "Teaching at the Right Level to Improve Learning," https://www.povertyactionlab.org/case-study/teaching-right-level-improve-learning.

[9] On the promise and limitation of behavioral science and current nudging interventions for education see P. Oreopoulos, 2021, "Nudging and Shoving Students Toward Success," *Education Next* 21(2).

assistance to those already available to more advantaged students. Sufficient investments in AI-based CALs, broadband access, and teacher training and professional development to take advantage of the new technologies in less advantaged areas could serve to narrow large and persistent educational inequalities by family socioeconomic status and community resources. But without appropriate investments in improved access for those who are less advantaged, richer households and schools as well as more advanced learners are likely to take greater advantage of new AI-based learning tools, potentially serving to expand educational inequalities as has seemed to be the case for other recent educational technologies such as massive open online courses (MOOCs) and as experienced with remote learning for K–12 and community colleges during the COVID-19 pandemic. AI also has the potential to provide virtual tutors and better online course and program information to support online post-secondary degree programs, online credential programs (such as those offered by Coursera), and MOOCs. Still, similar complementary investments in human teaching assistants, human advisors, and more universal access to reliable broadband and appropriate digital devices will be needed to make such opportunities feasible for many adult learners and less advantaged post-secondary students.

Much research documents substantial learning gains from more personalized teaching and from access to adaptive CALs.[10] In particular, Benjamin Bloom in the 1980s highlighted large (2 standard deviations) gains of personalized one-on-one instruction by a human tutor over conventional classroom instruction in small-scale randomized controlled trials (RCTs).[11] Bloom characterized this huge learning gap between personalized and traditional classroom instruction as the "2 sigma problem" because individual instruction is sufficiently more expensive than traditional group classroom instruction, making it infeasible within the budgetary constraints of public education systems. Bloom's clarion call motivated experimentation and research to assess the effectiveness of one-on-one or small group tutoring as a supplement to classroom instruction for part of the school day or after school. A recent meta-analysis by Andrew Nickow, Phillip Oreopoulos, and Vincent Quan of well-crafted evaluations (using RCTs or regression discontinuity designs) of interventions providing human tutors to individual students or small groups of students found "consistent and substantial positive impacts on learning outcomes" typically of around 0.37 standard deviation. But these impacts are certainly not close to as dramatic as the 2 standard deviations gain of Bloom's full move to adaptive one-on-one instruction. Tutoring programs tend to have larger learning impacts

---

[10] See, for example, A.V. Banerjee, S. Cole, E. Duflo, and L. Linden, 2007, "Remedying Education: Evidence from Two Randomized Experiments in India," *Quarterly Journal of Economics* 122(3):1235–1264; and K. Muralidharan, A. Singh, and A.J. Ganimian, 2019, "Disrupting Education? Experimental Evidence on Technology-Aided Instruction in India," *American Economic Review* 109(4):1426–1460.

[11] B.S. Bloom, 1984, "The 2 Sigma Problem: The Search for Methods of Group Instruction as Effective as One-to-One Tutoring," *Educational Researcher* 13(6):4–16.

in earlier grades, when the tutors are teachers or paid paraprofessionals as opposed to volunteers and parents, and when done during the school day.[12]

Thus, more personalized instruction can greatly improve learning outcomes, but small group instruction and one-on-one instruction with human teachers and tutors are quite resource-intensive. Attempts to scale tutoring and make it more cost-effective by going online became urgent in response to school closures and learning losses from the COVID-19 pandemic in 2020–2022. Such efforts have included one-on-one virtual tutoring for disadvantaged middle school students using volunteer college students, group virtual peer tutoring (such as Schoolhouse World), and even low-touch text messages to support parents in educating their children (especially in developing countries).[13] But such online tutoring programs and low-touch attempts at helping parents personalize learning have faced challenges ranging from low uptake by children and parents to difficulties in recruiting and retaining effective human tutors.

CALs have played an increasing role in recent decades in trying to supplement and personalize learning opportunities. CALs have ranged from personal computers and tablets in the classroom to an expanding array of online educational resources. Recent RCTs evaluating educational interventions using CALs have found substantial learning gains of 0.2 to 0.4 standard deviations for well-implemented interventions but also some with little or no impacts.[14] Educational software designed to help students learn specific skills working at their own pace has shown great promise for improving learning outcomes, particularly in math. But CALs have often been clunky and unengaging for students; teachers have not been adequately trained in the use or sufficiently motivated to help students take full advantage of CALs; and the digital divide by socioeconomic status in access to computers and high-speed Internet across schools, neighborhoods, and households has meant CALs can expand educational inequality when many less advantaged students have difficulty accessing CALs and other online learning opportunities.

AI-enhanced CALs, especially those based on LLMs such as the Khan Academy's Khanmigo AI virtual tutor, show promise for replicating some of the advantages of high-quality personalized instruction and potentially being able to do so at much lower cost and at scale.[15] Students can work with LLMs and their virtual tutoring bots as collaborators and thought partners. For example, LLMs can lead students through steps

---

[12] A. Nickow, P. Oreopoulos, and V. Quan, 2020, "The Impressive Effects of Tutoring on PreK–12 Learning: A Systematic Review and Meta-Analysis of the Experimental Evidence," NBER Working Paper No. 27476.

[13] On one-on-one volunteer virtual tutoring, see M. Carlana and E. La Ferrara, 2021, "Apart But Connected: Online Tutoring and Student Outcomes During the Pandemic," Working Paper, Harvard University. On free online peer-to-peer tutoring, see https://schoolhouse.world. On SMS text message tutoring assistance for parents, see N. Angrist, P. Bergman, and M. Matsheng, 2022, "Experimental Evidence on Learning Using Low-Tech When School Is Out," *Nature Human Behavior* 6(July):941–950.

[14] M. Escueta, A.J. Nickow, P. Oreopoulos, and V. Quan, 2020, "Upgrading Education with Technology: Insights from Experimental Research," *Journal of Economic Literature* 58(4):897–996.

[15] N. Singer, 2023, "Not Just Math Quizzes: Khan Academy's Tutoring Bot Offers Playful Features," *New York Times*, June 8, https://www.nytimes.com/2023/06/08/business/khanmigo-tutor-chat.html.

of writing essays or solving math problems at a comfortable pace; help students check their own understanding and provide immediate feedback; try to engage students in deeper material; and connect the curricular material to students' own lives, interests, and goals. Students can debate their virtual tutoring bot to improve their arguments in a nonjudgmental setting. Teachers, parents, and tutors can observe student progress and provide further help if a student gets stuck. An AI tutor can also provide access to information on colleges and career options, helping to supplement the work of often highly stressed guidance counselors facing huge student loads in many U.S. public high schools.[16]

New education technologies, such as those based on generative AI, also show promise in combating the perennial problems of student boredom and apathy by making learning more immersive, interactive, and even fun. An AI assistant like Khanmigo can work alongside a student as a digital coach not only to personalize learning but also to make the activity more engaging—for example, through questions and feedback via the Socratic method or by allowing students to have discussions and debates with historical figures, pop culture icons, or characters from a literary or cinematic work. Math word problems, for example, can be rewritten by LLMs for each student, using their favorite hobby or sports team as the motivating topic.

However, inaccurate information and tutoring advice remain a concern with LLMs and AI virtual tutors. Furthermore, feedback from a virtual tutor may not be as rewarding and motivating as that from human teachers and peers. An open practical and research question is the extent to which interactions with an AI virtual tutor can be arranged to complement those with human instructors and classmates.

Augmented and virtual reality devices also may soon become more widely available to make learning more like an immersive simulation exercise or video game, increasing both realism (connection to practical real-world applications) and student engagement. Such approaches are currently used for some professional training such as flight simulation training in aviation, commercial truck driving simulated training, some community college programs, and simulation-based training to deal with high-pressure or dangerous situations for the military and the police.[17] Simulation-based training might be more attractive and effective for nontraditional students who fail to thrive in traditional classrooms and for adult learners. An important hypothesis meriting study is the extent to which the twin promises of AI-based CALs to personalize instruction (teach at the right level) and to make education more immersive reinforce each other in spurring learning gains.

---

[16] On the longer-term educational benefits of access to more effective guidance counselors, see C. Mulhern, 2023, "Beyond Teachers: Estimating Individual Guidance Counselors' Effects on Educational Attainment," Working Paper, August 23, http://papers.cmulhern.com/Counselors_Mulhern.pdf.

[17] On simulation training for the police and military, see, for example, RAND, n.d., "Simulation-Based Training: Use of Virtual Environments in Diverse Contexts," https://www.rand.org/well-being/justice-policy/projects/simulation-based-training.html, accessed June 29, 2024.

Potential downsides for educational progress from access to LLMs include students using LLMs for cheating or plagiarism, or students directly getting the answers from ChatGPT without going through the intermediate steps and failing to engage with crucial material more deeply. It is unclear at present the extent to which AI-based shortcuts for artistic and design assignments could serve to dull student creativity or free students to be more creative. Hallucinations and misinformation remain an issue for ChatGPT and other transformer-based LLMs. CALs using AI virtual tutors, such as Khanmigo, can be designed with safeguards to try to avoid such pitfalls—for example, pushing students to work out answers on their own by checking their comprehension and providing nudges and subtle hints at each stage of the problem-solving process instead of giving them the answers directly. Furthermore, students working in groups could try to critique answers provided by an LLM such as ChatGPT to help build critical decision-making and judgment skills and ferret out misinformation. In fact, Finland has integrated a program of media literacy to help students recognize misinformation online as part of its core curriculum.[18] Prompt engineering training overall and in specific domains to get more accurate information from LLMs likely will need to be integrated into educational curricula at all levels.

A further worry is that increased reliance on LLMs and virtual tutors in education could crowd out time spent interacting with human teachers and with a diverse group of other students (human peers). Less time spent in high-quality classroom social interactions with peers could have adverse impacts on the development of valuable soft skills (e.g., social interaction, communication, and teamwork skills). A key issue going forward is to find ways to integrate AI-based CALs into interactive group learning and problem-solving activities among students.

Universities, professional schools, and individual faculty are also grappling in real time with whether and how to incorporate ChatGPT and other generative AI tools into classes given the now widespread use by many students of these readily available online resources. Current policies of individual instructors range from banning any use of ChatGPT in a course to active engagement with ChatGPT in classroom discussions including critiques of the answers provided by ChatGPT. In fact, Tyler Cowen and Alex Tabarrok have already put together an initial guide for how best to use LLMs to supplement college-level instruction in economics.[19] AI-enhanced online tools have the potential to provide students with immediate feedback and guidance on projects (such as coding exercises in a computer science class), provide hints on how to improve work, automate more standardized aspects of grading and assessments, and alert faculty and

---

[18] J. Gross, 2023, "How Finland Teaches Even Youngest Pupils to Spot Misinformation," *New York Times*, January 11, p. A10.

[19] T. Cowen and A. Tabarrok, 2023, "How to Learn and Teach Economics with Large Language Models, including ChatGPT," GMU Working Paper in Economics, No. 23-18, May 12.

teaching fellows to which students need further help. Thus, generative AI tools might take over some of the more routine aspects of instruction and grading, allowing for a more efficient allocation of faculty and teaching fellow instructional time and better targeting of one-on-one or small group human tutoring. AI also threatens the viability of take-home exams and assessments and might motivate a rethinking of assessments to evaluate student learning-by-doing and the application of knowledge in novel situations rather than just demonstrating retention and mastery of course concepts.[20]

Important levers for realizing the potential of AI-enhanced CALs are getting buy-in from teachers, providing teachers with training and coaching on the new CALs and how to use them to better personalize instruction and teach at the right level, and making sure teachers have time to integrate such learning aids into their lesson plans. Inadequate teacher engagement and support could be a major bottleneck limiting the impact of AI on educational outcomes. Studies of education technology interventions often show little (or even negative) impact on student learning when technology is just plopped into a classroom with little guidance provided to teachers.[21] A recent evaluation of the Khoaching with Khan Academy program, which provides coaches ("Khoaches") to teachers in grades 3 to 8 to better use Khan instructional videos as a CAL to help offset COVID-19 pandemic learning losses, finds a central role for teacher buy-in and that training, supporting, and guiding teachers to adapt a CAL can be an effective way of generating meaningful test score gains.[22]

One potentially successful route toward teacher buy-in involves employing CALs for homework assignments rather than as alternatives to existing in-class teaching methods. For example, the CK-12 Foundation's website[23] provides a range of K–12 lessons and associated questions to test student understanding. Many teachers assign specific CK-12 lessons, and the associated questions, as homework to review and enhance the material covered in class. Teachers appreciate the fact that this CAL reduces their workload by automatically grading the homework assignments and producing a summary for the teacher regarding which topics create the most difficulty for the students. This adoption of CALs for homework thus reduces overall teacher workload without requiring changes to their current in-class teaching methods. Furthermore, once the homework is being performed online, it is easy to introduce AI technology to create more intelligent and personally customized homework. Each homework

---

[20] See D. Deming, 2023, "Generative AI Is a Black Mirror for Educators," *Forked Lightning*, September 5, https://forklightning.substack.com/p/generative-ai-is-a-black-mirror-for.

[21] See, for example, S. Beg, W. Halim, A.M. Lucas, and U. Saif, 2022, "Engaging Teachers with Technology Increased Achievement, Bypassing Teachers Did Not," *American Economic Journal: Economic Policy* 14(2):61–90.

[22] P. Oreopoulos, C. Gibbs, M. Jensen, and J. Price, 2024, "Teaching Teachers to Use Computer Assisted Learning Effectively: Experimental and Quasi-Experimental Evidence," NBER Working Paper No. w32388, National Bureau of Economic Research.

[23] The website for the CK-12 Foundation is ck12.org, accessed June 29, 2024.

question presented to the student by CK-12 depends on the earlier questions the student answered correctly or incorrectly, providing a customized sequence of questions that adapts to each student's level of understanding. Furthermore, if a student answers a question incorrectly, a hint and an opportunity to reanswer the question are provided. As of January 2023, the CK-12 system chooses which of several hints to provide to the student, based on which hints have led to the best learning outcomes for previous students who made the same mistake.[24] In this way, the more students use CK-12, the better it learns to teach future students. The CK-12 experience illustrates an important potential for CALs, namely their ability to learn to teach better based on observed outcomes of previously taught students. Such increasing returns are especially attractive given the potential scale of CALs; for example, CK-12 has already taught more than 200 million students over the past 15 years, far more than a human teacher could ever reach (or learn from) in a lifetime.

The recent COVID-19 pandemic experience with remote instruction raises worries of large disparities among students (and among educational providers) in access to high-speed Internet connections and digital devices, state-of-the-art learning technologies, and appropriate spaces for learning. A concern is that more advantaged educational institutions and students are likely to be better positioned to take advantage of new AI-based CALs. To try to prevent new educational technologies from further widening educational inequalities by socioeconomic status, a major policy issue going forward will be to make sure all schools, teachers, and students are provided broadband access, appropriate digital hardware, and proper training and support to benefit from AI-enhanced CALs and online learning opportunities.

More rigorous research also is needed to assess the actual educational efficacy and cost-effectiveness of AI-enhanced CALs. For example, there is not yet much clear evidence on the impacts on student learning of AI virtual tutors (such as Khanmigo) alone versus either no tutor or a human tutor. Educational practice would further benefit from research on whether hybrid models combining lower-intensity human tutors plus AI virtual tutors can generate learning gains equivalent to more intensive human one-on-one instruction at lower cost in K–12 schools, post-secondary education settings, and worker and professional training programs. Other important practical and research questions include (1) understanding the impacts of greater reliance on AI-based tools on student critical thinking and creativity, and (2) developing approaches to help teachers incorporate LLMs and AI-based CALs into interactive student group activities to better develop teamwork skills, improve respect for others, and foster innovation.

---

[24] R. Schmucker, N. Pachapurkar, S. Bala, M. Shah, and T. Mitchell, 2023, "Learning to Give Useful Hints: Assistance Action Evaluation and Policy Improvements," pp. 383–398 in *European Conference on Technology Enhanced Learning*, O. Viberg, I. Jivet, P.J. Muñoz-Merino, M. Perifanou, and T. Papathoma, eds., Springer Nature Switzerland.

IMPLICATIONS OF LIKELY ARTIFICIAL INTELLIGENCE IMPACTS ON THE LABOR MARKET FOR EDUCATION

Past technological revolutions have substantially altered production processes and the demand for different tasks, types of expertise, and skills, thus altering the educational and training needs of the workforce as discussed in the previous chapter. The industrial era from the late 19th to mid-20th centuries was associated with an increase in the demand for mass expertise (numeracy and literacy) to perform precise rules-based tasks in production and office jobs. Workforce education needs in the industrial era were primarily met through mass access to secondary schooling fostered by the high school movement, and supplemented by work experience and employer-provided on-the-job training.[25] The subsequent information era of advances in classical computing in the late 20th century and early 21st century was associated with the automation of many routine manual and cognitive tasks, reducing demand for the types of middle-skill production and office jobs that provided pathways to middle-class incomes in the industrial era. The automation and reduced cost of routine tasks complemented highly educated workers with college and graduate training by increasing the demand for elite expertise combining expert knowledge with acquired judgment to make high-stakes decisions in nonstandard cases. Classical computing was less able to substitute for the nonroutine manual tasks and social and interactive skills required in many in-person service jobs (e.g., home health aides, janitors, and baristas). The information era was associated with a polarization of the labor market, increased returns to college and (especially) professional and graduate degrees as well as to social and communication skills, and challenges related to resources for college preparation and access to quality colleges for students from less advantaged households.

The open question for the education system raised in Chapter 4 is that of the likely impacts of advances in AI (and the emerging "artificial intelligence era") on the labor market demand for human tasks, skills, and expertise. One scenario is that AI and robotics are largely implemented in the same manner of past classical computing gains to automate a broader range of routine cognitive and manual tasks, taking over the "last mile" of many mass expertise tasks from expense accounting to producing standardized legal documents to physical tasks in controlled and predictable settings. Under this scenario, AI would further reduce the demand for mass expertise (and some middle-skill jobs) and possibly increase the demand for elite expertise and for nonroutine in-person services emphasizing social and communication skills. Some initial evidence indicates that the surge in AI activity since 2015 has been associated with increased vacancies

---

[25] C. Goldin and L.F. Katz, 2008, *The Race Between Education and Technology*, Harvard University Press.

for AI skills themselves and reduced vacancies for previously sought skills in more AI-exposed establishments, suggesting some AI-based automation of previous tasks and increased skill requirements in new job openings.[26] An implication of this scenario for education practice is to increase preparation and access to higher education for professional positions requiring elite expertise and specialized knowledge and to further emphasize problem solving, abstract thinking, and social and communication skills.

AI-based software and products increasingly can take over certain (often routine) tasks in professional positions relying on elite expertise, from note taking and medical record inputting for physicians to standard writing tasks for lawyers and other professionals.[27] Reduced time on "paperwork" and standardized tasks can free up professionals to use their judgment and decision-making expertise on more complicated cases and to communicate and be more engaged with patients and clients. AI and large databases also can provide professionals with improved decision aides and effective copilots for handling complicated cases and decisions. Machine learning algorithms trained on large samples have the capacity to notice patterns that people might not and thereby offer promise to improve diagnoses by medical professionals and to help scientific researchers and other practicing professionals to develop and explore new hypotheses.[28] The shift to a data-rich environment with more information available to both professionals and their clients and patients may further change elite expertise jobs toward a focus on synthesizing information and making tough judgment calls based on tacit knowledge and experience as opposed to being a font of information not available to others. Such shifts in professional jobs based on elite expertise should motivate changes in curriculum in professional schools and encourage more frequent ongoing professional training to help professionals take advantage of AI-based tools to streamline more routine activities and to improve their communication and information-synthesizing skills (e.g., improving "bedside" manner for health care professionals).

A second possible scenario sketched in the previous chapter is that if AI increasingly substitutes for elite expertise, insights from elite expert knowledge will become accessible to a broader range of workers, making the expertise less scarce. AI advances and diffusion in this scenario may increase the demand for translational expertise combining foundational technical knowledge with supporting tools (likely to increasingly

---

[26] D. Acemoglu, D. Autor, J. Hazell, and P. Restrepo, 2022, "Artificial Intelligence and Jobs: Evidence from Online Vacancies," *Journal of Labor Economics* 40(S1):S293–S340.

[27] S. Lohr, 2023, "A.I. Outshines in Health Care. At Paperwork," *New York Times*, June 26, p. A1.

[28] J. Ludwig and S. Mullainathan, 2024, "Machine Learning as a Tool for Hypothesis Generation," *The Quarterly Journal of Economics* 139(2):751–827, https://doi.org/10.1093/qje/qjad055; and G. Charness, B. Jabarian, and J. List, 2023, "Generation Next: Experimentation with AI," Artefactual Field Experiments 00777, The Field Experiments Website, https://ideas.repec.org/p/feb/artefa/00777.html. On the implications of AI for medical practice see D.J. Lamas, 2023, "There's One Hard Question My Fellow Doctors and I Will Need to Answer Soon: Guest Essay," *New York Times*, July 6, https://www.nytimes.com/2023/07/06/opinion/artificial-intelligence-medicine-healthcare.html.

use AI) to accomplish high-value and complex tasks that may previously have required professional workers with elite expertise in positions such as nurse practitioners and physician assistants. AI could then, for example, assist electricians and auto mechanics in dealing with difficult and unfamiliar situations, speed up coding by software developers and allow more attention to overall software architecture, and broaden the cuisine range of chefs and caterers.

A rise in the demand for translational expertise could be met through shifts in education and training emphasis toward strong basic skills (numeracy and literacy) and social/communication skills, foundational training in specific subject expertise (e.g., law, accounting, medicine, plumbing, carpentry), and experiential learning that might end up looking more like a combination of post-secondary vocational training and a liberal arts education. The cooperative education model for higher education long used at Northeastern University that alternates semesters of academic study with full-time work to gain hands-on learning and foster translation expertise is a promising approach that could be adept at expanding post-secondary education opportunities to a broad group of students in the AI era.[29] The New York City P-TECH Grades 9–14 high school model, which combines accelerated high school course work, early college, and work-based learning experiences, could play a similar role in providing valuable labor market skills and associate's degrees.[30] Sectoral employment training programs and registered apprenticeship programs that provide occupational and soft-skills training and wrap-around services with strong connections to employers in a growing sector and input from unions and/or community groups represent another promising and flexible training model for jobs requiring translational expertise. Recent evaluations find that sectoral employment programs providing training, internships, and support service lasting from several months to 2 years have generated substantial and persistent earnings increases of 12 percent to 34 percent following training.[31]

Community college partnerships with consortia of local employers to provide training for emerging jobs with upward mobility potential also remain a crucial part of the post-secondary education system both for new high school graduates and for returning students attempting to augment or change careers.[32] And much evidence indicates that programs of wraparound support for community college students, such as the Accelerated Study in Associate Programs (ASAP) of the City University of New York,

---

[29] The website for Northeastern's cooperative education model is https://careers.northeastern.edu/cooperative-education, accessed June 29, 2024.

[30] M. Dixon and R. Rosen, 2022, *On Ramp to College: Dual Enrollment Impacts from the Evaluation of New York City's P-TECH 9-14 Schools*, MDRC.

[31] L.F. Katz, J. Roth, R. Hendra, and K. Schaberg, 2022, "Why Do Sectoral Employment Programs Work? Lessons from WorkAdvance," *Journal of Labor Economics* 40(S1):S249–S291.

[32] R.B. Schwartz and R. Lipson, 2023, *America's Hidden Economic Engines: How Community Colleges Can Drive Prosperity*, Harvard Education Press; H.J. Holzer, R. Lipson, and G. Wright, 2023, "Community Colleges and Workforce Development: Are They Achieving Their Potential?" American Enterprise Institute.

can be effective in increasing degree completion and substantially increasing earnings, although strapped budgets have limited the expansion of such effective supplemental programs at many community colleges.[33]

Partnerships between community colleges and industry may also play a role in allowing a wider range of students and workers to gain AI-related skills and take advantage of AI educational tools. For example, Amazon Web Services (AWS) has established a "machine learning university" with a new free program to help community colleges and universities teach database as well as AI and machine learning concepts.[34] It is providing an educator-enablement bootcamp along with curriculum and course delivery support. AWS is also partnering with the California community college system, the largest in the world, to identify the barriers to student completion of their educational goals. The colleges, in turn, are redesigning their programs and providing personalized advice to students to address these barriers and increase completion rates.

It has proven to be quite difficult to predict the specific skills and training needed for emerging employment opportunities beyond the very short run. A substantial share of employment ends up in new job titles and detailed occupations that did not even exist a decade or two before and often require new expertise.[35] Thus, one needs to be humble in forecasting the likely impacts of continued advances in AI on jobs and workforce training needs. But it seems likely that AI will be augmenting job activities and required expertise over a typical worker's career, reinforcing the need for an effective lifelong learning system for the workforce. Critical thinking, general adaptability, social and communication skills, and capacity for future learning are likely to remain valued worker attributes, and developing these capacities in K–12 and post-secondary schooling and ongoing adult education and training opportunities will remain crucial in the AI era. Training in more effective prompt engineering to take advantage of LLMs is likely to become essential in a broad range of occupations as well.

Progress in algorithmic predictive tools should also be helpful in providing job seekers with improved, more personalized, and better targeted information on relevant job opportunities that match their qualifications and education and training options for appropriate opportunities offering upward mobility.[36] AI-powered tools are already starting to affect recruiting processes—the paths by which students find the jobs for which

---

[33] C. Miller and M.J. Weiss, 2021, *Increasing Community College Graduation Rates: A Synthesis of Findings on the ASAP Model from Six Colleges Across Two States*, MDRC; C. Hill, C. Sommo, and K. Warner, 2023, *From Degrees to Dollars: Six-Year Findings from the ASAP Ohio Demonstration*, MDRC.

[34] The website for this "machine learning university" is https://aws.amazon.com/machine-learning/mlu, accessed June 29, 2024.

[35] D. Autor, C.M. Chin, A. Salomons, and B. Seegmiller, 2022, "New Frontiers: The Origins and Content of New Work, 1940–2018," NBER Working Paper No. 30389, August.

[36] A. Bartik and B. Stuart, 2022, "Search and Matching in Modern Labor Markets: A Landscape Report," WorkRise report, Urban Institute, https://www.workrisenetwork.org/publications/search-and-matching-modern-labor-markets-landscape-report.

they are qualified. AI tools potentially can help employers identify qualified candidates, can match job requirements to candidate qualifications, and may be able to help predict which candidates are most likely to succeed in a particular position. AI chatboxes can help job candidates with questions about job requirements and can connect them to recruiters. But systematic biases in such algorithmic prediction tools remain a concern. LinkedIn plans to roll out a new generative AI platform to help both recruiters and job seekers and has worked to try to reduce the biases in its existing AI platforms. Hired, part of the Adecco Group, offers an AI-enhanced platform to match technology and sales talent with job opportunities in major global companies.[37] AI-based approaches may also be able to assist with self-employment and entrepreneurial training.

FUTURE OPPORTUNITIES AND RESEARCH NEEDS

The rise of AI and student access to LLMs, such as ChatGPT, is already disrupting education at the K–12 and post-secondary levels, presenting risks of increased cheating and undermining the efficacy of traditional homework assignments and many approaches to student assessment (such as take-home exams). But AI also has the potential to greatly improve education by making it more personalized (to enhance teaching at the right level), engaging, and accessible to both traditional and nontraditional students. Much research is needed to develop new AI-based CALs and virtual tutors, to assess their impacts on learning, and to understand how to use AI more effectively to complement human teachers and enhance classroom peer interactions. And investments in more universal access to broadband and appropriate digital devices and teacher training to take advantage of AI-based educational tools will be essential to increase access to high-quality education for the less advantaged and not to further expand educational disparities by socioeconomic status. Beyond primary, secondary, and continuing education, research is also needed to understand how AI-based tools can help specifically with just-in-time job retraining.

The impacts of AI on the labor market remain highly uncertain. Nevertheless, AI is likely to impact the demand for different occupations and types of expertise greatly, as sketched in Chapter 4. Changes in the curricula of professional education programs to help new professionals work with AI-based tools will be essential. And increased access to evidence-based adult education and retraining programs will be needed to help workers avoid costly displacement and take advantage of new labor market opportunities.

---

[37] J. Kelly, 2023, "How AI-Powered Tech Can Help Recruiters and Hiring Managers Find Candidates Quicker and More Efficiently," *Forbes*, March 15, https://www.forbes.com/sites/jackkelly/2023/03/15/how-ai-powered-tech-can-help-recruiters-and-hiring-managers-find-candidates-quicker-and-more-efficiently/?sh=22f155ba3a3f.

6

Measurement

This chapter summarizes what needs to be observed about the impact of artificial intelligence (AI) on the workforce and economy, and it considers how successful such measurements are at present and what new data should be collected and made available for access. It describes the measurement and data access needs of key stakeholders (businesses, workers, policy makers, and the research community). The discussion explores data collected by the statistical agencies, administrative data housed in many government agencies, and new private-sector data sources from the increased digitization of economic activity.

Relative to the 2017 National Academies of Sciences, Engineering, and Medicine report[1] that emphasized that in many respects those looking at data were "flying blind" about the impact of AI and automation on the economy, this report describes the enormous progress that has been made in the availability of data tracking the development and use of advanced technologies and their impact on firms and workers. The cornucopia of data provides rich new perspectives and opportunities. A primary challenge now is how to provide access in a manner that enables integration of the increasingly rich data sources. Still, important knowledge gaps remain that are described in this chapter as well.

Compared to 2017, it is now possible to answer (or at least analyze) a range of questions and issues to a much greater extent. Statistical agency survey data collection by the U.S. Census Bureau through the new Annual Business Survey (ABS), discussed in

---

[1] National Academies of Sciences, Engineering, and Medicine, 2017, *Information Technology and the U.S. Workforce: Where Are We and Where Do We Go from Here?* The National Academies Press, https://doi.org/10.17226/24649.

detail below, now provides periodic measures of adoption and use of AI and advanced technologies at the firm level. The modules in the ABS vary over time, including information on the motivation for adoption of these technologies as well as barriers and obstacles to adoption. The ABS is a large firm-level survey that can be and has been integrated with a wide range of other business-level and worker-level data housed at the Census Bureau. This integration enables exploring the relationship between adoption of advanced technologies and key firm- and worker-level outcomes such as productivity, job creation, job destruction, and earnings. In a related manner, the integration with other business- and worker-level sources enables investigating the connection between changes in technology and the changing structure of the economy on measures such as market concentration, markups, and earnings inequality.

Private-sector digitized data sources provide novel perspectives on the changing nature of work by, for example, analyzing the skills and task requirements of job openings (scraped from the web). With machine learning methods, the requirements for skills and tasks involving AI and other advanced technologies can be identified. Other private data sources (e.g., ADP and LinkedIn) provide further insights into the changing nature of work.

Administrative data sources provide yet another rich source of information. For example, patent data from the U.S. Patent and Trademark Office now have been integrated into the longitudinal matched employer–employee data (i.e., Longitudinal Employer–Household Dynamics) at the Census Bureau. This data integration permits the tracking of inventors at the person and firm levels. The quality of patents for advanced technologies can be measured by the degree of citation for patents. Transformational versus incremental patents can be identified depending on whether primarily self-citations (within inventor/firm) or citations across inventors and firms exist. Clustering of inventors can be measured at specific firms and locations. The impact of patents on a wide range of outcomes at the firm, worker, and industry levels can be explored.

Substantial knowledge gaps and challenges remain for economics measurement and analysis of the impact of changing technology on the workforce. First, data access and integration of disparate sources are core challenges. Second, there are critical knowledge gaps in several areas. One is to measure the complementary intangible capital investments that inherently accompany adoption of new technologies. Historically, changes in the organization of firms adopting new technologies have been on many dimensions. The telegraph facilitated geographic dispersion of enterprises. The electric motor provided opportunities for factory designers to have greater flexibility in the placement of equipment. More recently, scanner data provided retailers and manufacturers with real-time tracking of sales, enabling changes in inventory management and distribution networks. Electronic data interchange, computer aided design, Internet-based procurement systems, and other interorganizational information systems have made it easier, faster, and cheaper to interact with suppliers—thereby changing incentives for vertical integration as well as for use of globalized suppliers.

Research has shown that successful adopters of new technologies who make such changes in their organizational structure also change their worker mix and workplace practices, how workers interact with each other and equipment, and their hiring and training of workers.[2,3,4] Finding the right mix of changes requires experimentation. Some firms inevitably will be more successful than others, so such experimentation typically yields restructuring and an accompanying shakeout process. Incumbents that have been successful under earlier technologies can find it challenging to change the firm and workplace culture to be successful with the new technologies.[5]

Measuring such intangible capital directly is inherently challenging and often is done indirectly (e.g., by constructing measures of the changes in the mix of capital and workers; the location of businesses; and the networks and relationships between businesses, between businesses and workers, and between businesses and customers). For the wave of technologies coming online now such as AI, it is unclear what organizational changes and other structural changes will emerge and in turn how best to track and measure these complementary intangible capital investments.[6]

Another knowledge gap reflects limited measurement of the task view of production and work. Traditional measurement of business and worker activity has focused on profits, employment (physical), capital investment, productivity, earnings, and skills by occupation and education. Productivity is measured as the output per unit of composite input (e.g., physical capital and labor). It has been increasingly recognized that quality adjustment of outputs and inputs is needed to measure productivity accurately. Adjusting for quality is especially important during periods of innovation in products and processes.[7]

---

[2] E. Brynjolfsson and L.M. Hitt, 2000, "Beyond Computation: Information Technology, Organizational Transformation and Business Performance," *Journal of Economic Perspectives* 14(4):23–48.

[3] S.E. Black and L.M. Lynch, 2001, "How to Compete: The Impact of Workplace Practices and Information Technology on Productivity," *The Review of Economics and Statistics* 83(3):434–445.

[4] E. Brynjolfsson, D. Rock, and C. Syverson, 2021, "The Productivity J-Curve: How Intangibles Complement General Purpose Technologies," *American Economic Journal: Macroeconomics* 13(1):333–372.

[5] E. Brynjolfsson and L.M. Hitt, 2000, "Beyond Computation: Information Technology, Organizational Transformation and Business Performance," *Journal of Economic Perspectives* 14(4):23–48.

[6] Some early work in this area is T. Babina, A. Fedyk, A.X. He, and J. Hodson, 2023, "Firm Investments in Artificial Intelligence Technologies and Changes in Workforce Composition," NBER Working Paper No. 31325, June, National Bureau of Economic Research, https://doi.org/10.3386/w31325.

[7] See J. Fernald, 2015, "Productivity and Potential Output Before, During, and After the Great Recession," pp. 1–51 in *NBER Macroeconomics Annual 2014*, J.A. Parker and M. Woodford, eds., University of Chicago Press; D.M. Byrne, J.G. Fernald, and M.B. Reinsdorf, 2016, "Does the United States Have a Productivity Slowdown or a Measurement Problem?" *Brookings Papers on Economic Activity* (1):109–182, https://doi.org/10.1353/eca.2016.0014; and G. Ehrlich, J.C. Haltiwanger, R.S. Jarmin, et al., 2023, "Quality Adjustment at Scale: Hedonic vs. Exact Demand-Based Price Indices," NBER Working Paper No. 31309, June, National Bureau of Economic Research, https://doi.org/10.3386/w31309.

Recent research has emphasized that it is insightful to measure output and productivity by tracking the tasks accomplished by different inputs.[8] This insight builds on historical studies of tasks[9] and time and motion studies from Frederick Winslow Taylor[10] in the early 20th century. This perspective is especially important to understand how adoption of advanced technologies (such as AI) affects the nature of production and work. Advanced technology adoption may substitute for or complement tasks accomplished by specific types of capital and labor. Measurement of tasks is an area that needs substantial work. Much effort has gone into mapping tasks to occupations (e.g., O*NET), with many insights emerging.[11] However, the classification of occupations and the mapping to tasks is a slow-moving process, which is a limitation in times of rapidly changing technology.

A related ongoing challenge is for economics measurement to be sufficiently timely. The statistical agencies' measurement of advanced technology in novel surveys such as the ABS is a major improvement, but the data are not very timely. Private data sources have the potential to provide real-time (or near real-time) tracking of the economy. The discussion below provides some ideas about how to improve the timeliness of data for tracking the impact of changing technology on the workforce.

This chapter proceeds as follows. The second section reviews new data sources—first from the statistical agencies and administrative sources, then from private entities. It also discusses how these data sources can be integrated with existing data sources to provide context for the impact of the changing structure of technology. The third section focuses on knowledge gaps and challenges.

NEW DATA SOURCES

Statistical Agencies

A major new data source is the ABS, first conducted in 2018. It is a large firm-level survey of a representative list of firms in the U.S. private sector. The ABS is conducted by the U.S. Bureau of the Census with the National Center for Science and Engineering Statistics at

---

[8] D. Acemoglu and P. Restrepo, 2018, "The Race Between Man and Machine: Implications of Technology for Growth, Factor Shares, and Employment," *American Economic Review* 108(6):1488–1542.

[9] J. Atack, R.A. Margo, and P.W. Rhode, 2019, "'Automation' of Manufacturing in the Late Nineteenth Century: The Hand and Machine Labor Study," *Journal of Economic Perspectives* 33(2):51–70.

[10] R. Kanigel, 2005, *The One Best Way: Frederick Winslow Taylor and the Enigma of Efficiency*, MIT Press.

[11] D. Acemoglu and D. Autor, 2011, "Skills, Tasks and Technologies: Implications for Employment and Earnings," pp. 1043–1171 in *Handbook of Labor Economics*, Vol. 4, O. Ashenfelter and D. Card, eds., Elsevier. See also National Center for O*NET Development, n.d., "O*NET OnLine," https://www.onetonline.org, accessed June 29, 2024; and D. Dorsey and S. Oppler, 2021, "An Occupational Taxonomic Approach to Assessing AI Capabilities," in *AI and the Future of Skills, Volume 1: Capabilities and Assessments*, OECD Publishing, Paris, https://doi.org/10.1787/2c1d8961-en.

the National Science Foundation. In its first year, the ABS had a sample of 850,000 firms. From then on, the survey has had a sample of about 300,000 firms. The antecedents of the ABS are the Survey of Business Owners, Annual Survey of Entrepreneurs, and the innovation section of the Business R&D and Innovation Survey and the Business R&D and Innovation Survey–Microbusiness.

Critically, the ABS includes rotating modules on advanced technology use. These modules are designed in collaboration with leading experts in the field (e.g., the 2018 survey with a research team led by Erik Brynjolfsson and the 2019 survey with a research team led by Daron Acemoglu). Figure 6-1 shows the range of questions asked in the ABS. Given that it is a firm-level survey conducted by the Census Bureau, it can be and has been integrated with the full range of business administrative and survey data at the Census Bureau. This includes integration with the Longitudinal Business Database (LBD), which provides comprehensive information on firm-level jobs created by firm start-ups, firm expansion, firm contraction and firm exit, firm-level productivity, and earnings. Characteristics of firms include detailed industry, location, firm size, and firm age. The comprehensive nature of the LBD enables further integration with the Economic Censuses and ABSs in individual sectors. Examples include the Annual Survey of Manufactures (ASM), which permits measuring TFP at the micro level and has modules on robotics, and the Annual Capital Expenditures Survey (ACES), which provides details on capital expenditures. ACES includes details on expenditures on capital investments in advanced technologies.

Outcomes for workers as well as firms can be integrated with the ABS, ACES, and ASM data on firms' adoption of and expenditures on advanced technologies. For example, these data on firms' technology use can be integrated with the longitudinal matched employer–employee data that permit tracking of worker outcomes such as hires; separations; earnings; and worker characteristics such as worker age, gender, education, and occupation (from U.S. Census Bureau household surveys).

Rich new facts have already emerged from these new sources. For example, the ABS 2019 (reference year 2018) provides much information about the extent of adoption as well as the motivation for adoption of technologies such as AI and robotics.[12]

Adoption of AI in the 2016–2018 period is relatively rare, with only about 3.2 percent of firms using AI in production (see Figure 6-2). This small fraction is somewhat misleading because larger firms were more likely to adopt, with 12.6 percent of workers employed at adopting firms. Adoption and exposure are substantially larger in the information sector, with a firm-level adoption rate of 8 percent and 30 percent of workers employed at adopting firms.

---

[12] D. Acemoglu, G.W. Anderson, D.N. Beede, et al., 2022, "Automation and the Workforce: A Firm-Level View from the 2019 Annual Business Survey," NBER Working Paper No. 30659, November, National Bureau of Economic Research, https://doi.org/10.3386/w30659.

E.3 Production Technology for Goods and Services

During the three years 2016 to 2018, to what extent did this business use the following technologies in production processes for goods or services?

Artificial Intelligence

- ☐ Did not use
- ☐ Tested, but did not use in production or service
- ☐ Low use
- ☐ Moderate use
- ☐ High use
- ☐ Don't know

Cloud-Based Computing Systems and Applications

- ☐ Did not use
- ☐ Tested, but did not use in production or service
- ☐ Low use
- ☐ Moderate use
- ☐ High use
- ☐ Don't know

Specialized Software

- ☐ Did not use
- ☐ Tested, but did not use in production or service
- ☐ Low use
- ☐ Moderate use
- ☐ High use
- ☐ Don't know

Robotics

- ☐ Did not use
- ☐ Tested, but did not use in production or service
- ☐ Low use
- ☐ Moderate use
- ☐ High use
- ☐ Don't know

Specialized Equipment

- ☐ Did not use
- ☐ Tested, but did not use in production or service
- ☐ Low use
- ☐ Moderate use
- ☐ High use
- ☐ Don't know

E.4 Motivation for Artificial Intelligence Technology Adoption and Utilization – Processes and Methods

During the three years 2016 to 2018, why did this business adopt or use **Artificial Intelligence**?

Select all that apply.

- ☐ To automate tasks performed by labor
- ☐ To upgrade outdated processes or methods
- ☐ To improve quality or reliability of processes or methods
- ☐ To expand the range of goods or services
- ☐ To adopt standards and accreditation
- ☐ Some other reason

E.5 Impact of Artificial Intelligence Technology on Workforce – Processes and Methods

During the three years 2016 to 2018, what were the effects of adopting or using **Artificial Intelligence** on the following?

A. The **number of workers** employed by this business

- ☐ Increased
- ☐ Decreased
- ☐ Did not change

B. The **skill level of workers** employed by this business

- ☐ Increased overall
- ☐ Decreased overall
- ☐ Did not change overall

C. The **scientific, technological, engineering, and mathematical skills of workers** employed by this business

- ☐ Increased overall
- ☐ Decreased overall
- ☐ Did not change overall
- ☐ Not applicable, we did not employ workers with scientific, technological, engineering and mathematical skills

E.6 Impact of Artificial Intelligence Technolog on Worker Types – Processes and Methods

Indicate what effect **Artificial Intelligence** had on the following types of workers employed by this business during the three years 2016 to 2018.

A. The number of **production workers**

- ☐ Increased
- ☐ Decreased
- ☐ Did not change
- ☐ Not applicable, we did not employ production workers

B. The number of **nonproduction workers**

- ☐ Increased
- ☐ Decreased
- ☐ Did not change
- ☐ Not applicable, we did not employ nonproduction workers

C. The number of **supervisory workers**

- ☐ Increased
- ☐ Decreased
- ☐ Did not change
- ☐ Not applicable, we did not employ supervisory workers

D. The number of **nonsupervisory workers**

- ☐ Increased
- ☐ Decreased
- ☐ Did not change
- ☐ Not applicable, we did not employ nonsupervisory workers

FIGURE 6-1 Example of questions about artificial intelligence, automation, and advanced technology use on Annual Business Survey 2019 (reference year 2018).
SOURCE: Extracted from U.S. Bureau of the Census, 2019, "2019 Annual Business Survey Questionnaire," https://www2.census.gov/programs-surveys/abs/information/abs_2019.pdf.

More mature advanced technologies exhibit higher adoption and worker exposure rates, especially in some sectors. Cloud computing has a firm adoption rate of 34 percent, and 62 percent of workers are at firms where cloud computing has been adopted. In the information sector, the firm adoption rate is more than 60 percent, and the worker exposure rate is about 80 percent. Robotics is mostly concentrated in manufacturing, with a firm adoption rate of 9 percent and a worker exposure rate of 45 percent.

Firms cite automation as a key driver for the adoption of AI and robotics, and to a smaller degree for the adoption of dedicated equipment and specialized software. About 30 percent of U.S. workers are employed at firms that use advanced technologies for automation. Moreover, firms often state that this adoption is to substitute for tasks previously conducted by workers. Firms that have adopted advanced technologies for automation have higher labor productivity, lower labor share, and higher wages than businesses of similar size and age in the same specific industry sector. Self-assessments by firms "point to an increase in the relative demand for skill but limited or ambiguous

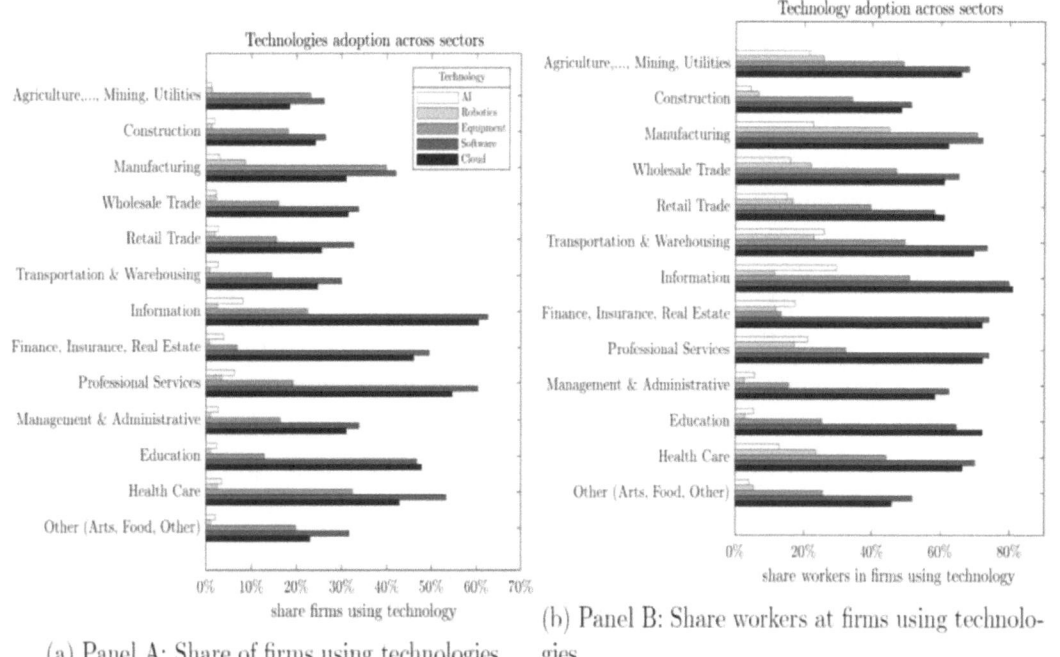

FIGURE 6-2 Adoption of artificial intelligence (AI), robotics, and other advanced technologies for the 2016–2018 period by industry: share of firms and share of workers exposed.
SOURCE: Figure 1 in D. Acemoglu, G.W. Anderson, D.N. Beede, et al., 2022, "Automation and the Workforce: A Firm-Level View from the 2019 Annual Business Survey," NBER Working Paper No. 30659, November, National Bureau of Economic Research, https://doi.org/10.3386/w30659; forthcoming in 2025 in *Technology, Productivity, and Economic Growth, Studies in Income and Wealth*, Vol. 83, S. Basu, L. Eldridge, J. Haltiwanger, and E. Strassner, eds., University of Chicago Press, https://doi.org/10.3386/w30659.

effect on their employment level."[13] Interestingly, automation is not the primary reason firms indicate for adopting AI. Rather, the primary reason is to improve quality and processes. This includes a significant share of firms with motivation to improve quality, add new goods, and improve processes without automation.[14]

This type of large-scale representative information on AI and other advanced information technology use is novel and extremely valuable. However, the ABS, ACES, and ASM data are not very timely. Alternative existing or new sources that enable timelier tracking of the development and use of AI and advanced technologies are discussed below.

---

[13] D. Acemoglu, G.W. Anderson, D.N. Beede, et al., 2022, "Automation and the Workforce: A Firm-Level View from the 2019 Annual Business Survey," NBER Working Paper No. 30659, November, National Bureau of Economic Research, https://doi.org/10.3386/w30659.
[14] Ibid, Figure 4.

New Digitized Data from the Private Sector

The digitization of economic activity has become widespread, offering novel tracking of economic activity. Firms increasingly are using companies such as ADP to handle their processing of payroll. This has led to the development of a rich alternative data source that tracks employment dynamics in the United States. ADP releases a national private-sector employment report (in partnership with the Stanford Digital Economy Lab) based on weekly ADP payroll data covering more than a half a million companies with more than 25 million employees on the Wednesday before the highly visible payroll report by the U.S. Bureau of Labor Statistics (BLS). While the latter is the standard, the underlying microdata from ADP offer great promise as they enable a real-time, matched employer–employee data infrastructure tracking employment, payroll, industry, location, and occupation. In contrast, the Current Employment Statistics (Establishment Survey) (CES) is a large-scale survey of establishments (about 300,000 per month), with limited information on employment, payroll, and hours and accompanying information on industry and location.

Other high-frequency and timely sources for tracking the workforce include Lightcast (formerly Burning Glass), which offers a comprehensive web-based scraping of job postings in the United States. The information collected provides novel insights in essentially real time into the skills and tasks needed. An advantage of these data relative to the occupation and task data from the statistical agencies is that they are much more flexible in capturing changes in the mix of skills and tasks as new technologies are being developed and adopted.

A potential limitation of these sources is their representativeness. Although ADP and Lightcast cover a large number of businesses and openings, a strength of the statistical agencies is that they have core benchmark sources that enable their statistics to be tied to the population of businesses and households.

Despite this limitation, private-sector data can complement the representativeness of public data sources. For example, Cajner and colleagues assess the quality of ADP data compared to the CES and the Quarterly Census of Employment and Wages (QCEW) produced by the BLS.[15] The QCEW provides a near-complete tally of businesses and employment in the United States, but it is released with an approximate 6-month lag, reducing its effectiveness as a policy tool. The researchers find that the ADP sample provides a better representation relative to the QCEW for smaller firms than the CES.

A similar example of complementarity is shown in the job postings data collected by Lightcast, which aggregates data from 51,000 job boards and company websites at a

---

[15] T. Cajner, L.D. Crane, R. Decker, A. Hamins-Puertolas, C.J. Kurz, and T. Radler, 2018, "Using Payroll Processor Microdata to Measure Aggregate Labor Market Activity," FEDS Working Paper No. 2018-5, http://dx.doi.org/10.17016/FEDS.2018.005.

daily frequency.[16] Its methodology builds on and expands the O*NET taxonomy to better leverage two key features of its postings data: granularity and high frequency. The full Lightcast product is updated every 2 weeks. In the rapid world of AI generation, innovation, and adoption, high-frequency taxonomies are equipped to keep pace.

The downside of private-sector taxonomy is the lack of standardization across other private- and public-sector sources of occupational skill attributes. Social media sources of self-reported skills on websites such as Indeed, LinkedIn, and ZipRecruiter can provide both skill demand by companies and skill supply by workers.

For example, from user-generated data, LinkedIn has offered through its partnership program data covering 100,000 users in 148 countries, providing information on 39,000 skills spanning more than 374,000 aliases (i.e., different ways to refer to the same skill).[17] This feature allows for the observability of skill creation and destruction in near real time on national and global scales.

As promising as new sources of data are, the lack of standardization across private and public data sources could be an impediment to broad-based analysis unless these sources are integrated into a consistent framework. The potential of blended data is that rich new data from government and private sources can be integrated at various levels of aggregation (industry, location, occupation, and in some cases micro level).

Blended data have become essential features of the national statistical infrastructure in general,[18] but the rapid evolution of AI technologies adds the complexity of combining slow-moving and largely survey-based public sources with customer-driven company transaction–based inputs that produce quickly evolving and idiosyncratic private taxonomies. AI technologies may be useful in developing new methods for blending.

A related but distinct limitation discussed in more detail below is data access. While some access has been provided to researchers on a case-by-case basis and new data products have been produced, the private-sector data sources are proprietary and sharing and integration of these novel sources with federal and state agency survey and administrative data is challenging.

As an additional note, AI can be used to improve the information available to firms, workers, and others in making decisions. For example, WorkRise, hosted by the Urban Institute, is an innovative research and action network on jobs, workers, and mobility.[19]

---

[16] The website for Lightcast is https://lightcast.io/about/data, accessed June 29, 2024.

[17] S. Macskássy, Y. Pan, J. Yan, Y. Li, D. Zhou, and S. Lin, 2022, "Building LinkedIn's Skills Graph to Power a Skills-First World," *LinkedIn Engineering Blog*, November 30, https://www.linkedin.com/blog/engineering/skills-graph/building-linkedin-s-skills-graph-to-power-a-skills-first-world.

[18] National Academies of Sciences, Engineering, and Medicine, 2023, *Toward a 21st Century National Data Infrastructure: Mobilizing Information for the Common Good*, The National Academies Press, https://doi.org/10.17226/26688.

[19] The website for WorkRise is https://www.workrisenetwork.org/working-knowledge/topics/job-search-and-matching, accessed June 29, 2024.

The objective is to use online platforms assisted by AI to improve the matching of firms seeking workers with workers seeking jobs.

KNOWLEDGE GAPS AND CHALLENGES

Although great progress has been made, many knowledge gaps and challenges remain. An important knowledge gap relates to tracking the tasks and processes for which AI is being used. AI use varies both between firms and within firms across employees. Quantifying both the between-firm and within-firm heterogeneity is important. Firm-level surveys such as the ABS and the Business Trends and Outlook Survey (BTOS) are asking questions about the tasks for which AI is being used and the intensity of use, but this remains an ongoing knowledge gap and challenge.

Another important knowledge gap relates to measuring and tracking the investments in complementary intangible assets that have been shown to be critically important in the adoption of new technologies—especially new general-purpose technologies. These intangible assets are inherently difficult to measure, especially because they include changes in the organizational structure of firms. Measuring organizational changes is difficult, especially because the successful organizational changes that will accompany the latest innovations (i.e., AI) are uncertain. It was only in retrospect that it became clear what organizational changes accompanied successful adoption of information technology in the 1980s and 1990s.

To understand productivity and economic growth, it is important to measure and model intangible capital. The most comprehensive definition of intangible capital comes from Corrado and colleagues.[20] Their characterization is summarized by Haltiwanger as follows:

> Intangible capital investment includes any inputs into future rather than current period production. In practice, the measurement of intangible capital has focused on key but limited components of such inputs: R&D, training, and brand capital.[21]

Measurement of organizational capital investments is less straightforward. The U.S. statistical agencies have helped contribute to measuring such activity, but there is ample scope for further measurement efforts. For example, young businesses, especially

---

[20] C. Corrado, C. Hulten, and D. Sichel, 2009, "Intangible Capital and U.S. Economic Growth," *Review of Income and Wealth* 55(3):661–685.

[21] J. Haltiwanger, 2023, "Reflections on FESAC (Federal Economic Statistical Advisory Committee) 'Ongoing Topics,'" Federal Economic Statistics Advisory Committee, June 9, https://apps.bea.gov/fesac/meetings/2023-06-09/reflections-on-ongoing-topics-for-fesac-6-9-23.pdf.

innovation-intensive industries, are inherently engaged in intangible capital investment in that they are developing products and processes for the future. Such investments are not well captured in current economic measurement. For organizational changes accompanying AI and automation, both the concepts and the measurement of accompanying intangible capital investment need attention.

The evidence on adoption of AI[22] highlights heterogeneity in patterns by sector and across firms within sectors. Agrawal and colleagues highlight that such heterogeneous patterns are inherently part of the adoption dynamics of new technologies including GPTs.[23] As they note, the benefits and costs of adopting GPTs are distinct across specific applications and will vary across sectors and firms within sectors. A measurement challenge is to quantify the nature of such heterogeneity in adoption patterns along with information on the idiosyncratic benefits and costs of adoption. The implications of AI adoption for productivity and its impact on the workforce depend not only on the average rate of adoption but also on the heterogeneous nature of adoption.

Another core, but not new, challenge is that the measurement of productivity and real output growth from advanced technology is limited by methodology and source data. The statistical agencies measure productivity using survey and measurement methods largely developed in the mid-20th century. These methods are better suited to measuring productivity and growth in the goods-producing sectors such as manufacturing, although they have limitations even for U.S. manufacturing given the challenges U.S. statistical agencies have in integrating their business data.[24] But for services (and much of the technology advancements in the 21st century developed and used in service sectors), these limitations are even more severe. An added complication is that the survey-centric approach of the 20th century is becoming less tenable given falling response rates on household and business surveys.

As already noted, data integration is a challenge not only between the statistical agencies but also with administrative and private-sector sources. Overcoming this challenge is of great importance because bringing together the needed information and overcoming the timeliness challenge of the statistical agencies (compared to private-sector sources of real-time data) are critical. Statistical agency sources are representative

---

[22] D. Acemoglu, G.W. Anderson, D.N. Beede, et al., 2022, "Automation and the Workforce: A Firm-Level View from the 2019 Annual Business Survey," NBER Working Paper No. 30659, November, National Bureau of Economic Research, https://doi.org/10.3386/w30659.

[23] A.K. Agrawal, J.S. Gans, and A. Goldfarb, 2023, "Similarities and Differences in the Adoption of General Purpose Technologies," NBER Working Paper No. 30976.

[24] Although the Bureau of Economic Analysis, BLS, and the Census Bureau are covered by common privacy and confidentiality protections under the Confidential Information Protection and Statistical Efficiency Act, which was passed to facilitate the sharing of their business data, the legislation that would enable the sharing of the federal tax information that underlies the Census Business Register (used for all Census business surveys) has yet to be passed. An implication of this restriction is that BLS and the Census Bureau have different business registers that are used for their respective business surveys. Research has shown that there are substantial discrepancies in the measurement of economic activity by location and industry.

but slow while private-sector sources have open questions about representativeness. An important issue is providing incentives for private-sector firms to share their data. Using secure remote computing is one option. Another is to enable private-sector firms to learn more about themselves and their data through such data integration.

ADDRESSING KNOWLEDGE GAPS

Several steps could be taken to help overcome these knowledge gaps and challenges. Enabling the legislation for the statistical agencies to share their business data (see footnote 24) would be a big step and would also facilitate integration of data from external (e.g., private sector) data sources. Even if the statistical agencies can share their business data, much work needs to be done to reconcile the data because the agencies have developed independent business data infrastructures. Data integration has particular value for tracking the impacts of advanced technologies such as AI on the workforce. Substantial insights could be gained by integrating business surveys at the Census Bureau that track technology and business outcomes with the business surveys at BLS that track earnings, employment, hours, and occupation. Integration of firm-level surveys with employee-level information about the tasks and processes for which AI is intensively being used is important. An open question is whether such information can be collected with sufficient probing questions about tasks and processes in firm-level surveys. Employee-level data from surveys or other sources are likely needed, and in turn that information would be integrated with firm-level data sources.

In addition, beyond integration and reconciliation of the data across the agencies, access to such data is still limited. The Federal Statistical Research Data Centers provide access to multiple agencies' proprietary data for approved projects, but typically data from multiple agencies cannot be integrated in a research project. Advanced technology has the promise of facilitating the integration of data from disparate sources as well as access to such data. For instance, machine learning can be used for integrating data from disparate sources. Furthermore, multiparty secure computing could be used to permit data users to tap into data sources from multiple providers while preserving privacy and confidentiality.[25]

Periodic modules on AI, automation, and tasks could be used to fill knowledge gaps on both household and business surveys in a timelier manner. The COVID-19 pandemic showed that the BLS and Census Bureau could put timely household and business surveys in the field (e.g., the Census Bureau's Business and Household Pulse

---

[25] Related to these objectives is the agenda of the Evidence-Based Policymaking Commission Act of 2016, P.L. 114-140.

surveys and the BLS Business Response Survey) and pivot questions to the rapidly changing conditions. Building on that approach, it would be useful to have periodic modules on AI and automation use in timely surveys such as the new BTOS conducted by the Census Bureau. The BTOS survey is conducted every 2 weeks, with sampled respondents rotating so that an individual business responds to questions every 12 weeks. It is a large survey, with 200,000 businesses surveyed in each 2-week round. Data are released biweekly on an almost real-time basis. A promising step in that direction is that the Census Bureau added questions on both current and future AI use to the fall 2023 survey.[26]

Timelier data are feasible from administrative sources as well. Enhancement of the new Business Formation Statistics (BFS) from the Census Bureau could be very beneficial. The BFS tracks the universe of applications for new businesses in an almost real-time manner. For example, the monthly BFS is released within 2 weeks of the end of each reference month. The BFS already provides novel data on the location and industry for business formation. Young businesses play a critical role in innovation and experimentation of new technologies.[27] The BFS statistics show a surge in new business formation since 2020 persisting through April 2023. Some of this reflects the changing nature of work and lifestyles during and after the COVID-19 pandemic. However, there has also been a surge in the nonmanufacturing high-tech industries such as the information sector and the professional, scientific, and technical sector.[28] Write-in information on the applications could be used to track businesses entering to develop specific new technologies (e.g., AI).

The core administrative data on payroll and unemployment insurance (UI) taxes that underlie the tracking of U.S. business activity have the potential to be timelier. Currently, BLS and the Census Bureau use these data to build their business registers and to produce key high value–added data products such as QCEW, County Business Patterns (CBP), the BLS Business Employment Dynamics (BED), and the Census Bureau Business Dynamics Statistics (BDS). However, the data are not timely. Tracking business dynamics is complicated and takes time to do correctly. However, administrative data are available on an almost real-time basis from quarterly payroll and UI tax reports filed

---

[26] See https://www.census.gov/hfp/btos/downloads/BTOS%20Content%20V2%20Supplement%2011.29.2023_Watermarked.pdf, accessed June 29, 2024.

[27] See, for example, R. Decker, J. Haltiwanger, R. Jarmin, and J. Miranda, 2014, "The Role of Entrepreneurship in US Job Creation and Economic Dynamism," Journal of Economic Perspectives 28(3):3–24, https://doi.org/10.1257/jep.28.3.3; L. Foster, C. Grim, and N.J. Zolas, 2016, "A Portrait of Firms That Invest in R&D," U.S. Census Bureau Center for Economic Studies Paper No. CES-WP-16-41, http://dx.doi.org/10.2139/ssrn.2845982; and D. Acemoglu, U. Akcigit, H. Alp, N. Bloom, and W. Kerr, 2018, "Innovation, Reallocation, and Growth," American Economic Review 108(11):3450–3491, https://doi.org/10.1257/aer.20130470.

[28] AI businesses are likely to be classified in one of these two sectors. For discussions of the surge in business formation in the past few years, see R. Decker and J. Haltiwanger, 2023, "Surging Business Formation in the Pandemic: Causes and Consequences?" Brookings Papers on Economic Activity, Fall:249–302, https://www.brookings.edu/wp-content/uploads/2023/09/Decker-Haltiwanger_16820-BPEA-FA23_WEB.pdf.

by employers.[29] Although this information is not a substitute for the benchmark statistics underlying CBP, BDS, QCEW, and BED, it could be a useful and timely complement. Moreover, modeling the relationship between the gold standard benchmark statistics and the real-time flow, potentially along with other sources (see below), appears to be a promising approach.[30,31]

Timelier processing of administrative data that permits tracking of alternative work arrangements, independent contractors, freelance work, and the gig economy is needed. AI has the potential to change the incentives for alternative work arrangements substantially for both firms and workers. The Census Bureau's nonemployer statistics and the Internal Revenue Service/Statistics of Income–related data are rich sources for this activity (both the microdata available for restricted-use approved projects and published statistics). However, the data are not timely (e.g., the public nonemployer statistics from the census for 2020 were just being published in summer 2023). The Current Population Survey tracks self-employment activity, but research shows a widening gap between self-employment activity in the administrative data relative to the survey data.[32] This reflects not only that self-employment is often supplemental activity but also that survey respondents are confused (e.g., they report that they are wage and salary workers when in fact they are independent contractors). The Contingent Worker Supplement conducted by the BLS in 2017 encountered challenges in eliciting responses about these alternative work arrangements, given this type of confusion.[33]

In sum, there is an increased rich and diverse data set available from both statistical agencies and the private sector that provides the opportunity for tracking the impact of AI on the economy and the workforce in a timely manner. Given the potential for the rapid changes AI may induce in the economy, developing these opportunities is of critical importance. Overcoming data access and data integration issues across the wide range of available sources will be key to enable the tracking of changes in AI use and in turn

---

[29] "The UI data flow from state UI agencies to BLS to build the QCEW (along with multiple BLS business surveys) and the payroll tax data flow from IRS to Census to build the Census Business Register (along with multiple Census business surveys). To build the high quality QCEW and CBP (and other) public domain data products takes time. However, given that there is a quarterly flow of data there is the potential for developing preliminary statistics on a timelier basis." See J. Haltiwanger, 2023, "Reflections on FESAC (Federal Economic Statistical Advisory Committee) 'Ongoing Topics,'" Federal Economic Statistics Advisory Committee, June 9, https://apps.bea.gov/fesac/meetings/2023-06-09/reflections-on-ongoing-topics-for-fesac-6-9-23.pdf.

[30] J. Haltiwanger, 2023, "Reflections on FESAC (Federal Economic Statistical Advisory Committee) 'Ongoing Topics,'" Federal Economic Statistics Advisory Committee, June 9, https://apps.bea.gov/fesac/meetings/2023-06-09/reflections-on-ongoing-topics-for-fesac-6-9-23.pdf.

[31] The JEDx (Jobs and Employment Data Exchange, see https://www.uschamberfoundation.org/JEDx) project for improving and enhancing the UI wage and employer records has many related ideas for making further progress using UI tax data.

[32] K. Abraham, J. Haltiwanger, K. Sandusky, and J. Spletzer, 2021, "Measuring the Gig Economy: Current Knowledge and Open Issues," in *NBER/CRIW Conference Volume on Measuring and Accounting for Innovation in the 21st Century*, National Bureau of Economic Research, pp. 257–298.

[33] U.S. Bureau of Labor Statistics, 2018, "Electronically Mediated Work: New Questions in the Contingent Worker Supplement," Monthly Labor Review, September, https://www.bls.gov/opub/mlr/2018/article/electronically-mediated-work-new-questions-in-the-contingent-worker-supplement.htm.

the impact on businesses, workers, and households on a timely basis. An aspirational objective might be, for example, to enable a timely and frequent task report analogous in spirit to the monthly jobs report that receives wide attention. One could imagine the task report providing guidance to businesses, households, and policy makers about the changing nature of tasks being performed by capital and labor as AI and other new technologies transform the economy.

7

Conclusion

The preceding chapters considered how artificial intelligence (AI) and related technologies might impact the workforce from a variety of perspectives, examining the state of AI technology and where it might be headed; its potential impact on productivity; how it might impact the demand and supply for different types of labor expertise; the need for and role of AI in education and workforce retraining; and the need and opportunities for collecting data to measure the changing state of the workforce, demand for different types of expertise, and availability of training opportunities for workers.

This chapter first presents the main findings arising from the analysis in the preceding chapters and then presents the study committee's conclusions about what levers are available to government leaders to influence the impact of AI on the workforce.

FINDINGS

This section presents the primary findings of this study. These findings, and support for them, are discussed in greater detail in earlier chapters.

> Finding 1: AI is a general-purpose technology[1] that has recently undergone significant rapid progress. Still, there is a great deal of uncertainty about its future course, suggesting that wide error bands and a range of contingencies should be considered.

---

[1] General-purpose technologies like the steam engine and electricity have widespread applications and were thus key drivers of economic growth. As discussed in more detail below, AI is advancing exceptionally rapidly, reflecting several key technical breakthroughs.

Generative AI systems released just over the past year—such as GPT-4, Gemini, and related foundation models—exhibit major new AI capabilities. These include the ability to hold meaningful conversations about diverse topics in dozens of languages, automatically summarize the key points discussed in large text documents, perform a variety of problem-solving tasks, write computer programs, write poetry, generate realistic images to match text specifications, interpret and reason about images, pass the high school Advanced Placement (AP) math exam, and pass the Law School Admission Test at the 88th percentile, which is a higher level than average among humans who take and pass this exam. Still, there is a great deal of uncertainty about AI's future course, suggesting that wide error bands and a range of contingencies should be considered.

> Finding 2: AI systems today remain imperfect in multiple ways. For example, large language models (LLMs) can "hallucinate" incorrect answers to questions, exhibit biased behavior, and fail to reason correctly to reach conclusions from given facts.

Note that passing a competency test is far from sufficient for having the human capabilities necessary to do a job. Note also that current generative AI systems are subject to error, to manipulation to produce false results, and even to hallucination. They also exhibit biased behavior and fail to reason correctly to reach conclusions from given facts. These systems are constantly being adjusted and improved to address these shortcomings and to erect guardrails to prevent them. Although such efforts have reduced these shortcomings, they have not been eliminated and are likely to persist to some degree for some time to come.

> Finding 3: Significant further advances in AI technology are highly likely, but experts do not agree on the exact details and timing of likely advances.

A variety of factors have created the environment for the recent acceleration in AI progress, including the increasing volume of online data to train AI systems, improvements to computer hardware and its computational speed, and improvements in AI algorithms. Over recent years, improvements in these three areas have led to remarkably consistent improvements in performance for AI foundation models. Because further increases in all three components in the next few years can be expected, including perhaps orders of magnitude improvement in computational power, it is likely that AI performance will also increase substantially. In response to this rapid AI progress, increasing investments in AI research and development and a burst of new start-up companies in this area create additional avenues for advances. Already, some of the directions in which the field may progress have emerged, including the appearance of multimodal models that go beyond text to accommodate images, video, sound, and speech; initial experiments to build more personally customized models by giving them access to one's e-mail; and incorporation of more traditional software such as calculators, search engines, and route planners into generative AI models to increase their capabilities. Furthermore, creative exploration and development of systems and infrastructure around base models, including software development environments and control methodologies, demonstrate impressive leaps in competency. For example, programming environments now enable the construction of collaborative communities of agents, each placing an LLM in a different role, which enables new forms of complex, extended problem-solving sessions. In parallel with such generative models that operate in the knowledge space of the nonphysical world, progress continues as well in robotics, although at a somewhat slower pace. However, there is a possibility that as generative models become more multimodal, they may lead to rapid advances in robotics as well.

> Finding 4: The substantial and ongoing improvements in AI's capabilities, combined with its broad applicability to a large fraction of the cognitive tasks in the economy and its ability to spur complementary innovations, offer the promise of significant improvements in productivity.

Considering all the factors on which productivity effects depend, there is considerable uncertainty regarding the specific size and timing of the increase in productivity resulting from AI, although some estimates suggest as much as a doubling of the rate of growth in productivity from about 1.4 percent per year in the recent past to 3 percent or more in the coming decade. There are important differences in the exposure of different sectors and occupations to AI, so its aggregate productivity effects will depend on how it affects the productivity of different sectors, different occupations, and different firms, and there is likely to be significant heterogeneity across all categories. There are also significant differences in the exposure of different kinds of worker tasks to generative AI. Generative AI can both substitute for labor and complement labor in these tasks. It can also generate new tasks and new activities for labor. All three of these effects can boost labor productivity over time, but the lags, the barriers, and the costs can be significant. Rapid AI deployment could cause considerable disruption in the labor market if workers must move quickly between tasks and occupations. This disruption could weaken AI's productivity effects if the necessary labor reallocation does not occur rapidly and if displaced workers are not deployed into new tasks with productivity levels at least as high as those in their previous tasks.

Finding 5: As was the case with earlier general-purpose technologies, achieving the full benefits of AI will likely require complementary investments in new skills and new organizational processes and structures.

New goods, services, and business models will emerge, and occupations will be significantly reorganized, across firms and industries. Typically, the productivity effects of new technologies can take many years to be realized, but there is reason to believe that the productivity gains of AI may be significantly faster. This reflects the fact that AI systems can often be delivered and implemented on the existing digital infrastructure and information systems built over the past decades. Furthermore, end users do not necessarily need to learn specialized interfacing skills to start using the technology—they can instruct LLMs with English or other natural languages. While further complementary investments can create additional benefits, significant productivity gains have already been documented quite rapidly in some applications, such as customer service and software development. That said, the trajectory of aggregate productivity growth is poorly understood and hence difficult to forecast.

Finding 6: The labor market consequences of widespread AI deployment will depend both on the rate at which AI's capabilities evolve and on demographic, social, institutional, and political forces that are not technologically determined.

These realities make forecasting labor market implications challenging. However, in attempting to foresee the impact of AI on employment, it is important to recognize that the United States, along with most industrialized countries, will face pronounced labor scarcity over the coming years owing to aging populations, low birth rates, a steeply rising ratio of retirees to workers, and, probably, restricted immigration. Depending on the magnitude of its impact, AI might simply reduce the negative consequences of this labor scarcity. While the net impact on overall employment levels is difficult to forecast, over the next decade AI can be expected to affect substantially the type of work many people do, the skills and expertise required for that work, and the market value of those capabilities. These effects will not simply follow the template of conventional computer-based technologies, which tend to impact routine, codifiable tasks, such as calculation, information storage, information search, and precise repetition of cognitive and physical tasks. In contrast to these routine capabilities, today's AI can sometimes apply to tasks requiring flexibility, ongoing learning, and a certain element of improvisation—tasks that have largely been beyond the reach of machine capabilities until recent advances in AI. Accordingly, AI tools will likely have the largest near-term consequences for knowledge work and cognitive tasks. A small subset of occupations that could be most affected include paralegals, customer service agents, software developers, commercial writers, editors, translators, and many managers. This creates a significant risk of worker displacement and skills devaluation. If, hypothetically, AI were to surpass human capabilities rapidly in key tasks required for software development, legal document creation, translation, crafting of business reports and presentations, engineering design, and even drug discovery, this could potentially reduce the earnings capacities of typically highly paid workers who do these tasks for a living—akin to how digital printing displaced skilled typesetters or how electronic telephone switching ultimately extinguished the once-vast telephone operator occupation.

> Finding 7: AI can be used to improve worker outcomes or to displace workers. Too often an exclusive focus on worker displacement neglects two other potentially positive labor market consequences of AI—new forms of work that demand valuable new expertise and AI systems that work jointly with workers to enable them to use their expertise more effectively to accomplish a broader variety of valuable tasks, perhaps with less formal training.

First, AI may usher in new varieties of job tasks (i.e., new work) that demand valuable new expertise. Historically, the contribution of new work has been quantitatively important. As noted previously, research finds that more than 60 percent of the job specialties in which U.S. workers were employed in 2018 did not yet exist in 1940. Research also finds, however, that although technological change displaced workers and created new employment opportunities at about the same rate during the period following World War II through the 1970s, since the 1980s it displaced workers faster than it created new opportunities. A key open question is whether under future AI-driven technological change, the displacement of labor will continue to outpace the creation of new employment opportunities. Second, although AI may displace some forms of expertise, it may complement others, enabling workers to use their expertise more effectively to accomplish a broader variety of valuable tasks, perhaps with less formal training. AI is already lowering barriers to computer software development by serving as a "copilot" for novice (and experienced) programmers to produce code more efficiently, with fewer errors and with potentially less mastery of technical details that can now be handled by AI directly. Looking forward, AI may enable medical professionals such as nurses and nurse practitioners to handle a larger range of diagnostic and treatment tasks with less oversight from doctors. Similarly, workers performing skilled tasks in the trades—plumbing, electrical work, construction, and aircraft maintenance and repair— may be augmented by the guidance and guardrails provided by AI assistants. Although AI-powered robots will not be able to tackle most of these physically dexterous, flexibility-demanding tasks anytime soon, AI will plausibly enable workers performing these tasks to deploy their expertise more effectively across a larger range of challenges.[2]

> Finding 8: History suggests that even if AI yields significantly higher worker productivity, the productivity gains might fall unevenly across the workforce and might not be reflected in broad-based wage growth.

In competitive market conditions, wage growth should reflect productivity growth, but during the past 20–30 years, real wages have grown more slowly than labor productivity in the United States and the other advanced economies. This was true during both the mid-1990s through 2005 period of strong productivity growth as well as the period of slow productivity growth through 2019–2020. In addition, the use of AI to monitor and surveil worker performance to achieve additional labor productivity may erode or enhance job quality, worker satisfaction, and worker commitment.

> Finding 9: AI will have significant implications for education at all levels, from primary education, through college, through continuing education of the workforce. It will drive the demand for education in response to shifting job requirements, and the supply of education as AI provides opportunities to deliver education in new ways. It may also shift what is taught to the next generation to prepare them to take full advantage of future AI tools and advances.

Changes in jobs and the expertise they require will increase the demand for continuing education and training. At the same time, AI may lead to a reassessment of what should be taught in primary and secondary schools. If AI makes it easier to access diverse factual knowledge, students might benefit from more emphasis on learning the reasoning skills needed to combine factual knowledge to make final decisions and on assessing the believability of seemingly inconsistent facts. Although computer programming is a widely taught skill today, AI coding tools such as GitHub Copilot are already changing the nature of programming. Some code can now be written purely in natural language rather than a programming language; hence, teaching the skill of coding is likely to take

---

[2] A further possibility is that AI capabilities will help to shift the structure of comparative advantage among nations. AI could, for example, enable the Global North to reduce its dependence on the Global South for labor-intensive service tasks, such as customer support, software development, and back-office operations. Alternatively, AI may increase the ease of outsourcing such tasks to the Global South while boosting the quality of services delivered. Simultaneously, it may enable many more low-income countries to compete in these tasks as machine translation erodes long-standing language barriers. Alternatively, by providing inexpensive access to expertise in medicine, engineering, science, and software development, AI tools may enable some low-income countries to tackle challenges indigenously that would previously have required importing foreign expertise. Because the range of possibilities is vast and multivalent, the committee does not venture an expert opinion on the question of AI and international comparative advantage.

a different form in the future. In addition to reshaping the demand for education, AI is likely to help in the supply of better education. Already there are multiple AI-enhanced online education platforms in use by millions of K–12 students as well as adult continuing education students. Several of these systems use earlier AI methods to customize instruction to individual students and use machine learning to discover which teaching tactics work best for different students. Furthermore, the burst of recent new progress in LLMs has led to a corresponding burst of exploration into new, more powerful conversational approaches to online education that customize even more adeptly to the needs of individual students. Although these new approaches are yet to be proven in practice, there are reasons to be optimistic about the prospects for AI to improve the delivery of education through personal customization.

> Finding 10: Better measurement of how and when AI advancements affect the workforce is needed. To help workers adapt to a changing world, improving the ability to observe and communicate these changes—such as the impact of LLMs on knowledge work and robotics on physical work—as they occur is crucial.

For years, government agencies such as the U.S. Bureau of Labor Statistics have collected and published data on topics including unemployment rates and numbers of new jobs, and in recent years the types of data available have increased. Nevertheless, these sources are far from providing the kind of real-time picture of the nature and pace of the adoption of AI in the workplace, the changing supply of and demand for different workforce skills, the wages being paid for each skill, continuing education opportunities available to acquire these skills, and where these opportunities are geographically, which would truly support workers seeking to improve their careers. Importantly, much of these data exist already, although they are in the hands of corporations such as LinkedIn, Indeed, Workday, and ADP. Government agencies would have difficulty collecting the volume and quality of real-time workforce data currently held by such corporations. However, new approaches to public–private data partnerships that allow the government to publish to the workforce valuable summaries of these data could make a great difference in the ability of the workforce to adapt to the unpredictable times that lie ahead. As AI expands further, there should be continued tracking of the nature of job displacement, jobs creation, and job transformation, and the implications for employment, education, career development, and the national economy.

> Finding 11: Responses to concerns that AI poses potentially serious risks in areas such as fairness, bias, privacy, safety, national security, and civil discourse will modulate the rate and extent of impact on the workforce. It will take deep

technical knowledge and may require new institutional forms for governments to stay abreast of and address these issues, given the rapidly changing technology.

These concerns have already led to initial government regulations around AI development and use, and additional future governance initiatives appear likely. Such initiatives to govern the use of AI will also modulate the rate and extent of AI adoption, and its impact on the economy and the workforce.

OPPORTUNITIES TO INFLUENCE HOW ARTIFICIAL INTELLIGENCE WILL IMPACT THE WORKFORCE

As AI technology advances and is broadly adopted by industry, there are numerous opportunities for businesses, nonprofit institutions, worker organizations, colleges and universities, civil society institutions, and government to influence the direction of this development. The impact of AI on the workforce is not preordained but will instead be influenced by what different institutions throughout society choose to do to guide AI's development and use. The following discussion breaks down these opportunities into the following types:

- Opportunities to influence the rates and direction of the development of AI;
- Opportunities to speed and share the productivity benefits of AI;
- Opportunities to influence the balance among worker augmentation, new work creation, and labor-displacing automation;
- Opportunities to understand the implications of AI for education and assist workers with retraining and continuing education;
- Opportunities for more exact and timely tracking of AI's impacts on the workforce and the economy; and
- Opportunities to consider more radical potential effects of AI on the workforce.

Opportunities to Influence the Rates and Direction of the Development of Artificial Intelligence

As discussed in Chapter 1, several factors have contributed to the accelerated pace of AI progress in recent years, including (1) the growing volume of available online text, video, and other kinds of data; (2) advances in the computational power of computing hardware; (3) advances in AI algorithms; and (4) the growing dollar investments in new research and development of AI by government and nongovernment organizations. At the same time, there are forces at work that may limit the rate of AI progress, including

(1) increasing secrecy around the exact AI methods used to produce state-of-the-art systems as companies compete for market share; (2) the possibility that large data sets needed to train advanced AI systems might not be widely available because they are held by private organizations that do not want to or cannot share them; (3) the possibility that U.S. research universities that have historically driven AI research and produced the AI experts hired by industry might not be able to afford the expense of developing and experimenting with frontier AI systems; and (4) societal concerns about the risks from AI including risks to safety, fairness, bias, surveillance, and privacy that could influence acceptance and adoption of AI in practice.

Given these considerations, opportunities for government leaders to influence the direction, robustness, and speed of AI development include the following:

- Support basic research in AI.
- Support research into standards and guardrails that could promote adoption of AI in business environments.
- Provide incentives, standards, and/or regulations to encourage sharing and transparency regarding the data used to train advanced AI models, enabling a level playing field where new companies can enter the market and contribute to progress while preserving privacy.
- Support AI research toward specific applications deemed to be of high societal priority, such as education and training, but where market forces appear to be insufficient to drive progress, although the benefits to society may be great.
- Fund initiatives such as the National AI Research Resource and the Microelectronics Commons that can provide hubs for computational resources and talent needed to keep U.S. universities vital players in the development of frontier AI methods and advances in AI safety, as well as evolve new research models.

Opportunities to Speed and Share the Productivity Benefits of Artificial Intelligence

Faster productivity growth would not only raise living standards but also make it easier to address a variety of national challenges including the budget deficit, poverty, health care, the environment, and national security. Rapid improvements in the technical capabilities of AI open the door to higher productivity growth, but they do not automatically translate into productivity gains. Typically, complementary investments are needed to translate technological advances into productivity gains, and there are a variety of bottlenecks and barriers that need to be addressed. Understanding the nature of these complements and barriers should be a key goal of policy makers. There are several opportunities for policy makers:

- Address the uncertainty about the most effective applications of AI. Government can help provide, fund, and disseminate data and statistics on what works and what does not. In part, this can be done by better documenting AI adoption across American firms and the variation in their performance through expanded investment in efforts by national statistical agencies and in public–private partnerships to collect and share information about the effects of AI on productivity in the economy. These data and statistics should help to provide policy makers with the knowledge to assess the benefits and risks accurately and motivate the speed of adoption, implementation, and productivity gains.
- Support research into the effectiveness of policies that could enable labor mobility between occupations, firms, and geographical regions, and help workers take advantage of new job opportunities. Potential policies include retraining programs to help workers develop the new skills that will be needed and portable benefits and sensible occupational licensing rules that would make it easier for workers to move from job to job.
- Support research into areas that contribute to regulatory uncertainty—including product liability, copyright, privacy, and bias—and that complicate efforts of decision makers to assess benefits and risks, speed adoption and implementation, and drive productivity gains.
- Support research to identify and assess the potential for AI technologies to create new harms either inadvertently or through abuse and help policy makers understand and consider the associated trade-offs and work with the private sector to develop sensible guardrails.
- Support research to understand the implications for market concentration in AI, such as winner-take-most dynamics, and options for ensuring that consumer product markets are competitive while still enabling the benefits of scale and scope.
- Increase efforts to identify which specific occupational tasks are affected by AI, as well as which old and new skills and expertise will therefore be in greater or less demand.
- Support AI research that speeds scientific discovery, which is a key contributor to productivity growth.

Opportunities to Influence the Balance Among Worker Augmentation, New Work Creation, and Labor-Displacing Automation

The degree to which AI will *assist* current workers to perform their work with higher quality, versus substitute for workers and *automate* their tasks, will depend upon a complex set of economic and technical factors. However, the mixture of automation, augmentation, and new task creation that takes shape in the years ahead will not be determined merely by the technologies themselves but by the incentives and institutions in which they are created and deployed. Some nations already use AI to surveil their populations heavily, squelch viewpoints that depart from official narratives, and identify (and subsequently punish) dissidents—and they are rapidly exporting these capabilities to like-minded autocracies. In other settings, the same underlying AI technologies are used to advance medical drug discovery (including the development of COVID-19 vaccines), enable real-time translation of spoken languages, and provide free online tutoring in frontier educational subjects. The potential effects of AI on the work of the future depend critically on what objectives individuals, corporations, educational institutions, worker representatives, and governments pursue and what investments they make.

A crucial contention of the current report is that by providing relevant information, guidance, and digital guardrails, AI can enable workers who possess expert judgment to perform a broader range of expert tasks—in effect, allowing less-expert workers to perform more expert tasks. These beneficiaries of AI augmentation need not be exclusively or even primarily workers with college and post-college degrees. They can and should include the vast number of workers whose jobs require judgment, problem solving, and decision making, such as modern craft workers, teachers, health technicians at all levels, designers, contractors, software developers, customer support workers, skilled repair persons, and workers of innumerable jobs that demand clear written communications.

This beneficial deployment of AI to augment labor, complement expertise, and create new forms of valuable work is a possibility but is *not* an inevitable outcome. Achieving these ends requires intentional design that seeks to complement and expand the applicability of expertise rather than primarily displacing it. Policies that could be applied to further these objectives include the following:

- Support research on human-complementary AI—research into the design of AI systems that augment, rather than replace, human workers, resulting in human–AI teams that produce higher-quality outputs than either could alone.[3]

---

[3] Much as the Defense Advanced Research Projects Agency made investments and held competitions to spur the development of dexterous robots and self-driving cars, the federal government could invest and foster competition in pairing AI tools with human expertise. See D. Acemoglu, D. Autor, and S. Johnson, 2023, "How AI Can Become Pro-Worker," Center for Economic Policy Research Policy Insight 123, October 4, https://cepr.org/voxeu/columns/how-ai-can-become-pro-worker.

- Support research into best practices for fostering inclusive AI adoption within firms and organizations.
- Support research into how the relative costs of capital and labor affect business decisions about AI adoption for automation and for augmentation.
- Support research to explore how to provide individuals ways to control and be compensated for the use of their creative works, their likenesses, and their other personal attributes.
- Build AI expertise within the federal government to support effective investment, oversight, and regulation across all mission areas including transportation, labor, health care, education, environmental protection, public safety, and national security.
- Provide technology certification through which appropriate investments are incentivized by offering advice on the quality of human-complementary technology and whether it is good enough for use in publicly funded sectors such as education and health care.[4]

Opportunities to Understand the Implications of Artificial Intelligence for Education and Assist Workers with Retraining and Continuing Education

Although the exact direction and timing of future AI advances and their adoption are difficult to predict, it is much easier to predict that AI adoption will result in changing the nature of many jobs, yielding a shift in the demand for various types of current expertise, and creating demands for new kinds of expertise not previously considered. These changes in labor demand will increase the need for retraining programs for many workers as they navigate the changing jobs landscape. Opportunities to assist workers in their efforts to adapt to these changes include the following:

- Support research on effective continuing education approaches, especially short-term programs that teach specific skills in high and growing demand. Community colleges and sectoral programs can be important in delivering such programs.
- Support research into the nature, types, and delivery methods for continuing education and training programs to foster workforce flexibility.
- Support research on how AI, augmented reality, and other technologies can be used to improve education.
- Support research into how standards and certification for training programs can help community colleges and other educational institutions more

---

[4] D. Acemoglu, D. Autor, and S. Johnson, 2023, "How AI Can Become Pro-Worker," Center for Economic Policy Research Policy Insight 123, October 4, https://cepr.org/voxeu/columns/how-ai-can-become-pro-worker.

effectively signal graduates' skills to employers and improve the match of new graduates to in-demand job opportunities.

- Support appropriate organizations to develop, maintain, and disseminate a "career roadmap" that would enable workers to understand the shifting demand for different types of skills and workers (and improve matching) as well as the continuing education opportunities available to them to acquire high-demand skills that will advance their career.
- Support research into new education objectives for all levels of education, including K–12, in order to provide the current and next generation with the knowledge and skills needed to take full advantage of future AI capabilities.

Opportunities for More Exact and Timely Tracking of Artificial Intelligence's Impacts on the Workforce and the Economy

Given the great uncertainty about exactly which AI technologies will become available when, as well as uncertainties around factors that will influence their adoption, together with the likelihood that AI will have a broad and profound impact on the workforce, it is essential to improve capabilities to observe and track in near real time the impacts AI is having on the economy, especially on the supply and demand for different types of worker expertise.

During the COVID-19 pandemic, the United States experienced significant supply chain challenges in areas ranging from masks to semiconductors, and efforts to gain greater real-time situational awareness capitalized on emerging private-sector data sources and methodologies that used machine learning. This effort underscored the challenge of integrating public- and private-sector data, particularly firm-level data that provide vital insights but include strategically sensitive information. During the Great Depression, a similar recognition of the need for greater situational awareness of the state of the economy sparked a comprehensive effort to advance new methodologies and build an infrastructure for the collection of employment data (and the development of new areas of academic research[5]).

Collecting and transparently disseminating this information to the workforce is one of the best ways to support workers in making their own career and continuing education decisions during a time of rapid change. This is a task over which government leaders can have significant control, including the following:

---

[5] For example, D. Card, 2011, "Origins of the Unemployment Rate: The Lasting Legacy of Measurement without Theory," *American Economic Review* 101(3):552–557, https://doi.org/10.1257/aer.101.3.552.

- Improve and expand existing data collection efforts by government agencies, including high-frequency, real-time tracking of the use of AI by businesses and workers and the impact on the workforce.
- Create new public–private data partnerships in which privately held data about skills supply and demand, and wages currently paid for these positions as well as continuing education opportunities and their link to getting a better job are collected, with summaries made available in real time to members of the workforce to support their efforts to improve their livelihoods.
- Explore the development of an independent, not-for-profit, government-chartered entity to create the infrastructure, protocols, and expertise needed to support public–private data sharing and integrated analysis. The goal would be both to support the above goal of keeping the workforce well informed about risks and opportunities and to provide greater situational awareness of the general state of the economy by building an infrastructure for data collection and development of new methodologies for assessing the contributions of goods and services, especially digital goods and services that are poorly accounted for in the current national accounts.
- Measure and mitigate disparate impacts of new technologies on under-represented groups or communities as well as the global impact of differences in AI adoption between high-income and low-income countries.
- Measure and characterize the heterogeneity in patterns of AI adoption across economic sectors, across firms within sectors, and across geographical regions, along with their heterogeneous impacts on productivity and the workforce.

Opportunities to Consider More Radical Potential Effects of Artificial Intelligence on the Workforce

Recent capabilities of AI, especially those relating to LLMs and their multimodal counterparts, have advanced faster than many experts expected. Accordingly, it is possible that more radical improvements will emerge in the coming decade as funding increases, the models get larger, hardware improves, more data are used, and research continues. The effects on the workforce could be commensurately greater than anything seen so far. Consideration of these possibilities suggests several actions, including the following:

- Dramatically expand the research needed to inform policies and strategies that can assess the social and economic implications of emerging AI technologies. Build the instructional capabilities and scale training and educational programs accordingly.

- Undertake scenario planning to consider more extreme cases, even if they currently appear unlikely, such as AI's being able to do a large majority of cognitive, emotional, and/or physical tasks currently done by the workforce, and the implications for wages, employment, and income distribution.
- Develop a comprehensive and timely dashboard of key economic and social indicators that reflect potential changes in the economy that might be expected if AI becomes substantially more pervasive and powerful, including the extent of AI use in the workforce, capital–labor substitution in various tasks, resources devoted to training and deploying AI models, and productivity gains in particular tasks and activities as well as in the aggregate.
- Undertake modeling and simulation exercises to consider the potential effects on employment, capital allocation, government budgets, household incomes, and other metrics of sharply more capable models.
- Explore policy options and pilot programs that could be appropriate to implement or scale up if AI becomes radically more capable.

THE ROAD AHEAD

In the 7 years since the previous National Academies' report on automation and the workforce,[6] and even in the time since this committee began work on this study, AI capabilities have improved tremendously. Moreover, it is reasonable to expect even greater advances in the years to come. Improved intelligence is key to solving many of the nation's thorniest problems and unlocking greater prosperity and well-being. As a result, AI, the technology of intelligence, ranks among the most general of all general-purpose technologies.

Although technical progress and business transformation will continue, it is impossible to predict exactly the nature of the coming changes and all their effects on the economy and society. Accordingly, it makes sense to build in the ability for rapid data gathering and analysis to track these changes, and to build as flexible an approach as possible for reacting to the changes observed. Fighter pilots are most likely to be successful when they have a fast and accurate OODA loop—the ability to observe, orient, decide, and act—and the same applies for individuals, organizations, and even societies. In practice, this means increased capacity for research not only in AI but also in social science so AI's implications can be understood better.

---

[6] National Academies of Sciences, Engineering, and Medicine, 2017, *Information Technology and the U.S. Workforce: Where Are We and Where Do We Go from Here?* The National Academies Press, https://doi.org/10.17226/24649.

Rather than trying to predict any specific future path, it is important to have the flexibility to sense and respond rapidly to opportunities and challenges and be prepared for a variety of scenarios and possibilities.

Most importantly, individual people, businesses, nonprofits, colleges and universities, institutions of civil society, and governments each have agency about the type of society to which they belong. AI is a tool that is meant to be directed by humans. As it becomes more powerful, it will afford greater ability to shape the world in accordance with society's values and goals. All elements of society can and should think carefully about what ends they seek to achieve with this tool.

Appendixes

A

Statement of Task

In response to Section 5105 of the 2021 National Defense Authorization Act, an ad hoc committee of the National Academies of Sciences, Engineering, and Medicine will study the "current and future impact of artificial intelligence on the workforce of the United States across sectors." The study will build on and update the 2017 National Academies' study *Information Technology and the U.S. Workforce: Where Are We and Where Do We Go from Here?* and consider other recent studies, results from related research programs such as the National Science Foundation's Future of Work at the Human-Technology Frontier, and other research insights. The committee's report will review current knowledge about the workforce implications of artificial intelligence and related technologies (including for economic productivity and growth, job stability, equity, and income inequality), identify key open questions, and describe salient research opportunities and data needs. It will not provide recommendations.

B

Presentations to the Committee

JULY 6, 2022

    Jack Clark, Anthropic AI
    Eric Schmidt, Schmidt Futures
    Andrew Ng, Coursera

AUGUST 11, 2022

    Sebastian Thrun, Stanford University
    Charles Isbell, Georgia Institute of Technology/University of Wisconsin–Madison
    Jamexqs Manyika, Google
    Nikolas Zolas, U.S. Census Bureau

SEPTEMBER 12, 2022

    Daron Acemoglu, Massachusetts Institute of Technology
    Van Ton-Quinlivan, Futuro Health

DECEMBER 7, 2022

Fei-Fei Li, Stanford University
Fred Oswald, Rice University

Appendix B

C

Committee Member Biographical Information

ERIK BRYNJOLFSSON, *Co-Chair*, is the Jerry Yang and Akiko Yamazaki Professor and senior fellow at the Stanford Institute for Human-Centered Artificial Intelligence (AI), and the director of the Stanford Digital Economy Lab. Dr. Brynjolfsson is the Ralph Landau Senior Fellow at the Stanford Institute for Economic Policy Research and holds appointments at the Stanford Graduate School of Business and the Stanford Department of Economics, and at the National Bureau of Economic Research (NBER) as a research associate. One of the most cited authors on the economics of information, Dr. Brynjolfsson was among the first researchers to measure productivity contributions of information technology (IT) and the complementary role of organizational capital and other intangibles. He has also done research on digital commerce, the Long Tail, bundling and pricing models, intangible assets, and the effects of IT on business strategy, productivity, and performance. In 2020, he was awarded an honorary doctorate from the University of Turku for his research on the effects of IT and AI on innovation, productivity, and future work. Dr. Brynjolfsson speaks globally and is the author of seven books, including, with co-author Andrew McAfee, best-seller *The Second Machine Age: Work, Progress, and Prosperity in a Time of Brilliant Technologies* and *Machine, Platform, Crowd: Harnessing Our Digital Future*, as well as more than 100 academic articles and 5 patents. He holds bachelor's and master's degrees from Harvard University in applied mathematics and decision sciences and a PhD from the Massachusetts Institute of Technology (MIT) in managerial economics.

TOM M. MITCHELL, *Co-Chair*, is the E. Fredkin University Professor at Carnegie Mellon University (CMU), where he founded the world's first Machine Learning (ML) Department. Dr. Mitchell's research lies in ML, AI, and cognitive neuroscience. His current research includes developing ML approaches to natural language understanding by computers, as well as brain imaging studies of natural language understanding by humans. Dr. Mitchell is a member of the National Academy of Engineering (NAE) and the American Association of Arts and Sciences and is the past president of the Association for the Advancement of Artificial Intelligence (AAAI). In 2015, he was awarded an honorary doctor of laws degree from Dalhousie University for his contributions to ML and cognitive neuroscience, and in 2017 he received the 10-Year Outstanding Research Contributions Award from the Brain Informatics Conference for his research studying language processing in the human brain. Dr. Mitchell received his PhD in electrical engineering and computer science from Stanford University.

DAVID H. AUTOR is the Ford Professor in the MIT Department of Economics, vice president of the American Economic Association, and the co-director of the NBER Labor Studies Program and the J-PAL Work of the Future experimental initiative. His scholarship explores the labor market impacts of technological change and globalization on job polarization, skill demands, earnings levels and inequality, and electoral outcomes. Dr. Autor has received numerous awards for both his scholarship—the National Science Foundation (NSF) CAREER Award, an Alfred P. Sloan Foundation Fellowship, the Sherwin Rosen Prize for outstanding contributions to the field of labor economics, the Andrew Carnegie Fellowship in 2019, and the Society for Progress Medal in 2021—and for his teaching, including the MIT MacVicar Faculty Fellowship. In 2020, Dr. Autor received the Heinz 25th Special Recognition Award from the Heinz Family Foundation for his work "transforming our understanding of how globalization and technological change are impacting jobs and earning prospects for American workers." In a 2019 article, *The Economist* magazine labeled Dr. Autor as "the academic voice of the American worker." Dr. Autor received his PhD in public policy from the John F. Kennedy School of Government at Harvard University.

JOHN C. HALTIWANGER is a distinguished university professor in the Department of Economics at the University of Maryland. Dr. Haltiwanger is also the first recipient of the Dudley and Louisa Dillard Professorship in 2013. After serving on the faculty of the University of California, Los Angeles, and Johns Hopkins University, he joined the faculty at the University of Maryland in 1987. In the late 1990s, he served as the chief economist of the U.S. Census Bureau. He is a research associate of NBER and a fellow of the Society of Labor Economics and the Econometric Society. Dr. Haltiwanger has played a major role in developing and studying U.S. longitudinal firm-level data. Using these data, he has developed new statistical measures and analyzed the determinants of firm-level job creation, job destruction, and economic performance. The statistical and measurement methods he has helped develop to measure and study firm dynamics have been increasingly used by many statistical agencies around the world. His research has been recognized in his being awarded the Julius Shiskin Award for economic statistics in 2013, the Roger Herriott Award for innovation in federal statistics in 2014, the Global Entrepreneurship Research Award in 2020, and the Society of Labor Economics Award for Contributions to Data and Measurement in 2021. He has published more than 100 academic articles and numerous books, including *Job Creation and Destruction* (with Steven Davis and Scott Schuh, MIT Press). Dr. Haltiwanger received his PhD in economics from Johns Hopkins University in 1981.

ERIC HORVITZ is Microsoft's chief scientific officer. Dr. Horvitz has pursued research on principles and applications of ML and inference, including projects on diagnosis, prediction, and decision making in health and bioscience, transportation, aerospace, and computing systems. His current research foci include methods for leveraging the complementarity of human and machine reasoning and for enhancing the robustness of AI systems in the open world. He is a member of the NAE. He received the AAAI/Association for Computing Machinery (ACM) Allen Newell Award, the Feigenbaum Prize, and the ACM International Conference on Multimodal Interaction Sustained Accomplishment Award for contributions to AI. He was elected to the CHI Academy for research on human–AI interaction. He serves on the President's Council of Advisors on Science and Technology and the scientific advisory board of the Allen Institute for AI. Dr. Horvitz previously served on the Computer Science and Telecommunications Board of the National Academies of Sciences, Engineering, and Medicine. He has served as the president of AAAI, on the Board of Regents of the National Library of Medicine, on NSF's Directorate for Computer and Information Science and Engineering Advisory Board, on the Defense Advanced Research Projects Agency's Information Sciences and Technology advisory group, and on the National Security Commission on AI. He was a member of the National Academies' Committee on Information Technology, Automation, and the U.S. Workforce, and was a co-author of the 2017 National Academies' report authored by that committee. Dr. Horvitz received his PhD and MD in medical information science from Stanford University.

LAWRENCE F. KATZ is the Elisabeth Allison Professor of Economics at Harvard University, a research associate of NBER, and the co-scientific director of J-PAL North America. Dr. Katz's research focuses on issues in labor economics and the economics of social problems. He is the author (with Claudia Goldin) of *The Race Between Education and Technology* (Harvard University Press, 2008), a history of U.S. economic inequality and the roles of technological change and the pace of educational advance in affecting the wage structure. Dr. Katz has been the editor of the *Quarterly Journal of Economics* since 1991 and served as the chief economist of the U.S. Department of Labor in 1993 and 1994. He is the past president of the Society of Labor Economists and has been elected a fellow of the National Academy of Sciences, the American Academy of Arts and Sciences, the Econometric Society, and the Society of Labor Economists. He currently serves on the board of MDRC. Dr. Katz graduated from the University of California, Berkeley, in 1981 and earned his PhD in economics from MIT in 1985.

NELA RICHARDSON is the senior vice president and chief economist at ADP. In this capacity, Dr. Richardson is also the co-head of the ADP Research Institute and leads economic research for ADP. Previously, she was principal and investment strategist at Edward Jones, a financial services firm. In that role, she analyzed and interpreted economic trends and financial market conditions and recommended investment strategies. She is also the former chief economist at Redfin Corp, where she led a team of data scientists, economists, and writers to track trends in the housing market. Dr. Richardson regularly provides insight on the economy, real estate trends, and capital markets to policy makers, consumers, and media. She earned a doctorate in economics from the University of Maryland, College Park, with concentrations in financial economics, international finance, and economic development. She is also a graduate of the University of Pennsylvania and Indiana University, Bloomington. Dr. Richardson is a member of the Bureau of Economic Analysis Advisory Committee and the Conference of Business Economists, and sits on the Chamber of Commerce and National Association of Business Economists foundation boards. Dr. Richardson received her PhD in economics from the University of Maryland, College Park.

MICHAEL R. STRAIN is the director of economic policy studies and the Arthur F. Burns Scholar in Political Economy at the American Enterprise Institute. His research focuses on labor economics, public finance, and social policy. Dr. Strain is the author of *The American Dream Is Not Dead*, which studies longer-term economic outcomes for workers and households, and is the editor or co-editor of four volumes on economics and public policy. His research articles have been published in academic and policy journals. He is a research fellow with the Institute for the Study of Labor in Bonn, a research affiliate with the Institute for Research on Poverty at the University of Wisconsin–Madison, and a member of the Aspen Economic Strategy Group. He is an elected member of the National Academy of Social Insurance. He also writes frequently for popular audiences, and his essays and op-eds have been published by the *New York Times*, the *Wall Street Journal*, the *Financial Times*, and the *Washington Post*, among others. A frequent guest on radio and television, Dr. Strain is regularly interviewed by broadcast news networks. He has testified before Congress and speaks often to a variety of audiences. He holds a PhD in economics from Cornell University.

LAURA D. TYSON is a distinguished professor of the Graduate School at the Haas School of Business, University of California, Berkeley. Dr. Tyson is the co-chair of California Governor Gavin Newsom's Council of Economic Advisors. She serves on the board of directors of Lexmark International and Stem, Inc. In 2019, she was the Richard C. Holbrooke Fellow for the American Academy in Berlin. During her fellowship, she researched the effects of intelligent tools on employment, inequality, and livelihoods in Germany. Her research in this area is part of a broader interdisciplinary project that she co-founded at the University of California, Berkeley, on the effects of automation on labor markets in the advanced industrial countries. She has received support for her work in this area from the Kauffman Foundation and the Germany Federal Ministry of Labor and Social Affairs. Dr. Tyson has given numerous presentations and is the author of several academic papers, reports, and book chapters about the effects of automation in labor markets in the advanced industrial economies. She has served as a senior external advisor at the McKinsey Global Institute for many of its reports, including *The Future of Work After COVID-19*. From 2020 to 2021, she served on French President Emmanuel Macron's Commission d'experts sur les grands défis économiques. Previously she was a member of the National Academies' Board of Science, Technology, and Economic Policy and a member of its Innovation Policy Forum. Dr. Tyson has a summa cum laude undergraduate degree from Smith College and a PhD in economics from MIT.

MANUELA VELOSO is the head of J.P. Morgan Chase AI Research and the Herbert A. Simon University Professor Emerita at CMU, where she was previously on the faculty in the School of Computer Science and later the head of the Machine Learning Department. Dr. Veloso conducts research in AI, with a focus in robotics and recently in AI in finance. At CMU, she founded and directs the CORAL research laboratory for the study of autonomous agents that collaborate, observe, reason, act, and learn. Dr. Veloso and her students research a variety of autonomous robots, including mobile service robots and soccer robots. She is a past president AAAI and the co-founder and a past president of the RoboCup Federation. Dr. Veloso is a fellow of AAAI, the American Association for the Advancement of Science, ACM, and IEEE. She was elected in 2022 to the NAE "for her contributions to artificial intelligence and its applications to robotics and the financial services industry." Dr. Veloso received her PhD in computer science from CMU.